A *Passion* For Purpose

Building Cities for Our Children

"We loved our time in Kansas City and the decision to come was in large part due to the vision laid out by Mayor James and his team. His leadership is manifested in modern Kansas City– a town filled with culture, great food, and revitalization. We experienced his passion first-hand while in that beautiful city, and there is no one better to share their strength and leadership than Mayor James."

– The Fab 5: Bobby Berk, Karamo Brown, Tan France, Antoni Porowski, Jonathan Van Ness

"President Harry Truman said that "Progress occurs when courageous, skillful leaders seize the opportunity to change things for the better." Decades hence, Sly James powerfully delivered on that opportunity in Truman's hometown, and far beyond.
Sly James is a change maker. Time and again he has demonstrated the courage to fight for progress – to the game-changing benefit of the City and the country he loves. He is a rare mix of strategic energy, pure grit, authenticity, and boundless passion.
Sly is the real deal; a great read lies ahead."

– Roshann Parris, Crisis Communications executive; White House Lead International Advance/Presidents Clinton and Obama

"Kansas City, Missouri is safer, greener, more inclusive, and more innovative thanks to the bold leadership of Mayor Sylvester "Sly" James. His authenticity and commitment to improving the lives of all the residents of his hometown made it a pleasure for us to work together to help him achieve his ambitious goals. I am glad we now have the chance to learn more about this superstar, one-of-a-kind Mayor through his new book."

– George Fertitta, CEO of Bloomberg Associates, an international philanthropic municipal consulting firm

"Over the past 20 years, I've worked with thousands of politicians. I was lucky that most were dedicated public servants. Yet, it's easy for me to say that Sly is unlike anyone else. His tenure was always guided by what's right for the city. He brought people together but wasn't afraid to take a stand. He's loyal, a mentor to many, but also gives people the tough talk when they need it. But I think what really sets him apart is his experience living in many different worlds – black and white, poor and rich, and powerless and in power. That unique perspective gives him the view that many elected never have. It's what makes him most effective. He says what he thinks and does what he says. It's an honor to call him Mayor, boss, and, most important, friend. This book brings all of those life lessons to life in a manner as dynamic as the man himself."

    – **Larry Jacob,** VP of Public Affairs for The Kauffman
        Foundation.

"Mayor James' vision, tenacity and infectious optimism have left a lasting and profoundly positive impact on Kansas City. Mayor James has been a tireless champion of women's equality and empowerment, and we were proud to work with him on initiatives to close the leadership gap and empower women across the region."

    – **Wendy Doyle,** President & CEO, Women's Foundation

"Sly James is a leader amongst leaders. His vision to treasure the authenticity of his hometown, while simultaneously transforming it into a 21st century smart city, has made him the envy of his colleagues across the globe. I'm incredibly happy that he is sharing his story."

    – **Mayor Steve Benjamin,** Mayor of Columbia, SC,
        President of the US Conference of Mayors

"The Sly James that I know is an honorable man. In fact, in the short time I've known him, he has become one of my heroes. Here is a man who is using all his knowledge and experience gained during his rich and varied life, to serve the city he came from, the city he loves. What became evident to me in talking with him, Sly James will serve Kansas City in whatever capacity he is in, whether as mayor, or as citizen. A pastor I knew once asked of his congregation not just to give, but to give from substance. Following his Marine Corps dictum of "never leave one behind", Sly James' insistence on early childhood education is a transfer of that motto to civilian life. Sly James will leave no one behind. He gives from substance. Here is his story."

    – **Yo-Yo Ma,** acclaimed cellist and composer

"I have watched the work of Sly James since he became Kansas City's Mayor in 2011. I admire the things he's accomplished in the city that I have chosen for my home. I admire that Sly looks at our city and focuses on our children. He worked tirelessly to start his Turn the Page program and to open Kansas City's Urban Youth Baseball Academy. He understands the importance of getting our young people educated and engaged with good mentoring at an early age. We worked together to help open the Academy, and Sly was a great teammate on that endeavor. I really admire that Sly sees the importance of collaboration with other entities in order to accomplish something big. He's been a great mayor and we will all miss his strong leadership. "

    – **George Brett,** Kansas City Royals, Baseball Hall of Fame
       Inductee 1999

"There is only one Sly James, be it mayor, Marine, or just one solid and compassionate man. "A Passion for Purpose" is a manifesto on how to live a full and meaningful life and a primer for all seeking to make their community a better place – as a citizen or public servant. Sing it, Sly!"

    – **Greg Fischer,** Mayor, Louisville, Kentucky

A *Passion* For Purpose

Building Cities for Our Children

Sly James

with Sean Wheelock
Foreword by Kit Bond

Requests for permission should be addressed to: Ascend Books, LLC, Attn: Rights and Permissions Department, 7221 West 79th Street, Suite 206, Overland Park, KS 66204

10 9 8 7 6 5 4 3 2 1

ISBN: print book 978-1-7323447-3-0

ISBN: e-book 978-1-7323447-4-7

Library of Congress Control Number: 2019937957

Publisher: Bob Snodgrass
Editor: Mark Fitzpatrick
Publication Coordinator: Molly Gore
Sales and Marketing: Lenny Cohen
Dust Jacket and Book Design: Rob Peters

The goal of Ascend Books is to publish quality works. With that goal in mind, we are proud to offer this book to our readers. Please notify the publisher of any erroneous credits or omissions, and corrections will be made to subsequent editions/future printings. Please note, however, that the story, experiences, and the words are those of the authors alone.

www.ascendbooks.com

Contents

Dedication

This book is dedicated to all those good souls who stand by me, overlook my failings, and push me when I need it most. Without their love and support, I never would have become who I am.

Invocation Prayer
by Father Thomas B. Curran

Leadership requires a vision, a plan, and the ability to inspire and accompany the ones you lead. Today we gather to give thanks for the generosity of service exhibited by Mayor Sly James. We also gather to ask for God's continued blessings upon Sly and our community, so that our efforts may truly reflect those of the ruler of all humanity.

Our Mayor calls these efforts the 4-Es: Education, Employment, Efficiency, and Enforcement. For each of these petitions please respond, **Empower us, O God.**

May we turn the page in our schools and in all of our educational efforts from exclusion to inclusivity, from the have-nots to the all-haves, from the being marginalized to the being valued. We pray:
Empower us, O God.

May our community move closer to efficiency, as it reflects a city that treats and serves all of its citizens with respect and dignity. We pray: **Empower us, O God.**

May we continue to create jobs and a workforce, and generate economic development that is focused upon the promotion of human dignity and the pursuit of the common good. We pray:
Empower us, O God.

May our enforcement of laws be done in fairness and in pursuit of justice that is demonstrated in a right relationship with God, with others and with our environment. We pray:

Empower us, O God.

Empower us, O God, and our mayor with the 4-Es, and shepherd us into that fifth E – Eternal joy in your presence. Amen.

Father Thomas B. Curran, S.J.
President
Rockhurst University

Foreword
by United States
Senator Kit Bond

They say politics makes strange bedfellows. And my relationship with Sly James is proof; we make quite an "odd couple."

While Sly is known for his style and "magic bowtie," I am more reminiscent of Mexico, Missourah-chic. We both chose to study law, which exposed us to the usual biting comments from wise guys. (My favorite bad lawyer joke for your enjoyment—"Walking through a graveyard a guy saw a headstone that read, 'Here lies a lawyer and an honest man.' The jokester asked, 'How could they get two guys in one grave?' ") But despite our law backgrounds Sly and I charted very different paths to public service. And, unlike Sly, I never came close to winning an election with 87 percent of the vote!

Not only are we two guys with totally different upbringings, we are about as far apart on the political spectrum as you can get. In fact, I am already anticipating a fervent campaign to revoke my Republican Party membership for penning this piece.

Despite our undeniable differences, what we do have in common is far more important than party identification or any other label—our passion for pragmatic public service and putting people over politics.

In the following pages you will journey with Sly, growing up in segregated Kansas City through his rock band days to his service as a Marine during the Vietnam era, to his election as Mayor of Kansas City. The key to Sly's success—from his school days to the ballot box—is his ability to communicate and motivate.

Mark Twain famously said, "There are basically two types of people. People who accomplish things, and people who claim to have accomplished things. The first group is less crowded." Unfortunately, in an age of 24-hour news and social media, too many of our leaders are accomplishing little beyond securing the title of the loudest or most provocative voice of the day. Screaming on cable news and talk radio or trolling on Twitter might create headlines and garner new followers, but it rarely creates consensus that leads to real change.

Sly is the rare leader who has kept his candor, but communicates his message clearly with good humor, care, and optimism. Even if you disagree with his policies, you cannot help but like him! Even more importantly, Sly connects with the public through messages that motivate, build consensus, and move his agenda forward—whether it's targeting reading proficiency in third graders, revitalizing forgotten neighborhoods, or making Kansas City a model for family leave.

As Sly will make clear in the coming pages, no political party holds him hostage. His refusal to be captive to the Democratic Party explains not only why this old Republican is writing this foreword, but also why Sly has achieved so much as mayor. While the words "bipartisan" and "compromise" have become dirty words, my 40 years of political and policy battles taught me that our best work—in our cities, in our states, and as a nation—is accomplished when we work together. This mayor's commitment to innovative solutions and partnership with stakeholders of all political stripes, in both the private and public sectors, has paid off—from developing the economy-stimulating streetcar to putting Kansas City on the map as the "Smartest City in America."

And when Kansas City made an all-out effort to win the 2016 Republican National Convention, Sly was all in, chairing regular weekly committee meetings and traveling to Washington, D.C., where he put on a great show for the RNC Committee—even dancing as he sang, "We're going to Kansas City, Kansas City here we come." Even though K.C. didn't win, it was no fault of Sly's. While there will always be issues where people of good conscience cannot come together, Sly has never let what *cannot* be done interfere with what *can* be done.

As the father of a Marine (Ooo-rah!), I have seen in Sly that inherent work ethic and determination all Marines seem to possess. For more than 200 years, "Send in the Marines" has been a rallying cry when our nation needs to get a hard job done swiftly. And whether answering the call while in uniform or in public office, Sly is known for working tirelessly until the job is done. As mayor, Sly indefatigably held town hall meetings, chaired committee hearings, organized rallies, created campaigns, and employed the media to advance his agenda on behalf of the City. And like a good Marine, Sly didn't duck even the thorniest issues and most intractable problems—from tackling long-held racial divides and inequality to combating violent crime. In this next chapter of his service, readers will see that Sly is just as determined to chart a new course for the Democratic Party.

At the very core of Sly's drive and work ethic is a soft heart—I'm sorry Sly, the secret's out! Sly cares about people—and he puts people over politics. Just ask those who have worked for and with him, or the countless Kansas Citians whose lives he has helped improve, or the families he has mourned with at murder scenes. Most fervently, Sly has a soft heart for the kids of Kansas City. It was over this shared concern for Missouri's children, and the impact of literacy later in life, that Sly and I first connected. As Governor of Missouri and later a United States Senator, helping ensure kids enter school ready to learn was a cornerstone of my career, and I count the early childhood education program known as *Parents as Teachers* as one of my greatest accomplishments. Seeing a serious need at the local level, Sly created the *Turn the Page* program; you can still find the mayor reading to third graders weekly! As a result of Sly's vision and commitment, Kansas City is now a national model, inspiring communities across the country to prioritize childhood reading.

Sly's successful early childhood education initiative reveals more than just a soft heart for kids, however. As a mayor, Sly is anything but shy when it comes to extolling the virtues of politics and policy on the civic level. He knows firsthand that the best ideas do not originate from think tanks or politicians in Washington, D.C.; rather, they come from the people in our communities. Policymakers' most trusted advisors should be our local leaders, pastors, neighborhood associations, chambers of commerce, health-care providers, and small business owners, who are living, working, and serving in our communities. From our cities and states, local and community leaders can identify not only the challenges, but also the solutions.

As you read this book, it is my hope you truly get to know my friend Sly James. He is a big, strong Marine, with a boisterous voice and a clear vision, but underneath it all is a soft heart that cares for others.

Christopher S. "Kit" Bond
U.S. Senator
Governor of Missouri

Introduction
by Kansas City Royals
GM Dayton Moore

As **general** manager of the Kansas City Royals, and throughout my entire career in baseball, I've come to understand that the clubhouse is a true representation of society. You have a mixture of players coming from different races, ethnicities, economic backgrounds, religions, communities, and educational levels. And yet, everyone has to be brought together so that a true team is created. Otherwise, it's just a collection of individuals, making success an impossibility.

As mayor of Kansas City, Sly James was the quintessential leader who brought everyone together, and helped form a great community. He understands that leaders are strong only because of the strengths of others, that people are different by design, and that those differences must be recognized and understood. From my perspective, this is his formula for uniting people, and for simply getting everyone to work together for a purpose beyond themselves.

Throughout Mayor James' eight years in office, no single person made Kansas City stronger and more hopeful. But his genuine compassion and love for people was most vividly displayed during one of our community's saddest moments.

During the 2015 American League playoffs, two Kansas City firefighters, Larry Leggio and John Mesh, tragically lost their lives while serving our community. This really hit me hard personally, as it did our entire organization. The deaths of these two heroes brought everything into perspective for all of us.

The memorial service took place while we were in Toronto to play the Blue Jays, and our team was saddened not to be able to attend and show our support to the families. I made a concerted effort the morning after the service to view and read any and all coverage that I could find online. From my hotel room I was able to watch Sly give the eulogy. He sang *Amazing Grace*, and I was overcome with tears and emotion. I could feel his passion for our city, and his sincere empathy for what the firefighters' loved ones were dealing with. Our hearts grieved for their families, and Mayor James brought things into perspective with his moving tribute.

I knew in that moment that Sly wasn't just the mayor of our proud city–this man was an inspirational leader.

Throughout my career I've been blessed to meet and interact with some truly special leaders across the United States and internationally, be they in baseball, business, the clergy, or members of the military. Mayor James' leadership style, and who he is as a person, puts him honorably on par with the best of the best. He unites people unlike anyone I've ever encountered. Sly isn't concerned with a person's political affiliation or faith. He simply wants to know the individual as a fellow human being.

Mayor James has the unique ability to genuinely listen to others. He seeks to learn what they think, and he is interested in hearing their opinions. Because of this, people feel appreciated when they interact with Sly. And they are happier for the experience.

But it doesn't stop there, as Mayor James is an unbelievable doer. Some people talk, but then there is no action behind what they say. Not Sly. He listens, and then he makes a decision. And regardless of what side of the debate you're on, there's always respect, as you know that he has truly considered the issue from all angles.

I first began working with Mayor James when we were in the very early stages of launching our Kansas City MLB Urban Youth

Academy. Quite frankly, we didn't even know if it could ever move from a vision to full-fledged reality.

But when we presented the idea to Mayor James, he immediately made us feel that it was something that he, and the entire community, would get behind and bring to fruition. Sly and his staff worked tirelessly with us on strategy and on introducing us to key people. Because of him it gained momentum very quickly. During the final month of the 2015 regular season, Sly attended a Royals game and asked to meet with me one-on-one.

Coming off of the heartbreaking disappointment of losing to San Francisco in Game 7 of the 2014 World Series, my focus was now almost entirely on returning to the playoffs, then the World Series, and then ultimately bringing home a championship. (Which of course we did!)

But on this night, while he understood I had a lot going on, Sly let me know we were at a pivotal time in the evolution of this remarkable project– the Urban Youth Academy. We simply could not let up now. After asking me to sit down, Mayor James looked me squarely in the eyes and said, "If we're going to make this happen, we have to start moving things forward." There were other details that still needed to be settled, but I completely understood his call for action. And I appreciated his direct, no-nonsense approach as a part of his leadership style.

What I took away from Sly's dedication to this project is his sincere love for the future of our city and our country. He believes in his DNA that providing hope, opportunity, and direction for children is what it's really all about. Many of us share this in spirit, but Mayor James actually lives it.

On numerous occasions I've seen him give his time to young people. Sly makes an immediate connection, as he wants to know their stories and he wants to know if he can help them in any way. There are always words of encouragement, and of hope.

In my own role as general manager of the Kansas City Royals, I've modeled my leadership style on Sly's: leadership begins and ends with putting others first. This man has served as an inspiration, and he's helped mold me to be more effective in my own job.

Mayor Sly James always goes out of his way to spend time with people, to listen to them, and to know their stories. We should all aspire to act this way.

Sly is one of those people whom you want everyone you care about to meet. When you're around him, you feel good; you feel better. No matter who you are or what you're experiencing, you'll have a more enjoyable day when you get the chance to interact with Mayor James.

He is my friend, and he is truly amazing.

Dayton Moore
Senior Vice President/General Manager
Kansas City Royals

Prologue

I always knew that my old man wasn't to be tested. On anything. Ever.

Our family outing to the Kansas City Chiefs game at Municipal Stadium had been planned for weeks. And we were all going: my father, my stepmother, my younger brothers, and I. I loved football; we all did, and I really wanted to go. This was my father's plan for the family, and we were all looking forward to it. End of discussion.

But my bandmate Chris had called earlier that Sunday morning to let me know that our agent had actually landed us an audition–to open for Jefferson Airplane before their upcoming concert at Memorial Hall. And the audition was set for later that afternoon, at the same time as the football game. So I took a deep breath, and then told my father that I couldn't go with them to see the Chiefs play. This was too big of an opportunity for me to miss. And besides, the guys in the band were depending on me. I was the lead singer, and without me there would be no audition.

Sylvester James Sr. predictably didn't want to hear any of this. "Nope, you're going to the game."

And with that, my father turned his back and walked away.

A short time later, with nothing more said between us, we were all heading outside to the car for the drive to the game. I intentionally and covertly lagged just behind my brothers, at the rear of our group of five.

"I'll be right out. I just forgot something," I announced to the family.

"Hurry up, and lock the door behind you," was my father's terse reply.

I walked purposefully to the small bedroom that I shared with my brothers. I grabbed my school books, a sweatshirt, and whatever else I could carry, and went straight out the back door. I then climbed over the backyard wall, and with that I was gone.

Even at 16 years old, I knew that this was it. There was no going back with my father. You just didn't do that with him or to him. Had I tried to return home, I knew that first he would whoop my ass, and then make me quit the band. And whatever limited trust that I had built up with him and my stepmother would be gone, as though it had never existed.

And I wasn't going to allow any of those things to happen.

So instead I went to the audition that afternoon, and we booked the gig. And the next day, on a Monday morning, I went straight to the bank and withdrew from my savings account all that I had earned from a wide variety of low-paying adolescent jobs. My stepmother was the co-signer on the account, and I knew that if I didn't empty it she would. As soon as I arrived at my school, Bishop Hogan High, I paid my tuition in full for the next two semesters.

Chris' parents let me crash at their house for a few days, before I started the circuit of staying at the homes of other band members and school friends.

By the next year I was making enough money with the band that I was able to afford rent for a small house and live alone for the first time in my life. Not once did my father ever try to contact me, nor did I try to contact him. For my father it was, "If you want to be gone, then be gone. So now show me what you've got."

But I know now, and I think that deep down I knew then, that he knew where I was. And he knew what I was doing with my life: school, the band, my friends, and the rest. I realize now that what I did really hurt him, but I didn't fully understand this at the time.

The thing that bothered me the most about leaving home was the feeling that I had abandoned my younger brothers. But it was a choice that I made, and a choice that I stand by to this day. The term collateral damage sounds heartless, but what happened to them with this situation was just that—collateral damage.

In life, when decisions are made there are always unintended consequences. I just didn't fully appreciate this then, even though on some level I was aware.

The next time I saw my father was five years later, when I was set to be transferred overseas after enlisting in the Marine Corps during the Vietnam War. Nothing was spoken then, or ever, about the day that I left. Nor had I ever expected anything different.

My father and I are a lot alike. He was headstrong and he had no qualms about being different. And he was very, very ambitious—ambitious for himself, and for his family. He never accepted the limitations that society and the era placed on his life. But my father was working without some of the knowledge and opportunity that, thanks to him, benefitted me. Perhaps his limited options made him act in ways that then and now appear harsh, but even in those moments we knew he was simply pushing us to be better, to overcome.

On that Sunday afternoon my father was exactly who he was, and the only person who he really could be. Never before had I stood up to him. Not even close. But I somehow saw my two choices in a remarkably clear-eyed fashion, and I knew then that whatever I decided would put me on a new path. I could now be one type of person or the other: independent or subservient. It was up to me, and truly me, alone.

As I said, my father and I are very much alike.

Chapter
1

The Beginning

My earliest memories are of living at 1118 Armstrong in Kansas City, Kansas. I don't know how long we lived there, and I don't know how we got there. It's kind of like I just woke up there one day.

The house was owned by Alice Lewis. I never learned how she knew my father, but he must have trusted her, at least a little bit, to give her custody of my brother LaFrance and me. Not that it was legal custody. Rather, this was a practical custody, in that Alice was supposed to look after my younger brother and me while of course collecting a monthly fee. She didn't act like a mother or grandmother, but more like a loving aunt.

But I never sensed that this was a business arrangement. Had Alice been my actual aunt things would have felt, and likely played out, exactly the same. It was Alice, her husband, her two daughters Clemmy and Maxine, LaFrance, and me, all in that tiny house—in this pseudo-blended family.

While I wouldn't call this period of my childhood idyllic, it was certainly pleasant, though just a tiny bit confusing. My father, who I thought was a professional boxer at the time, among other things, would stop by for occasional and irregular visits. Nothing was ever predetermined or planned, at least not as I knew. He

25

would just randomly show up, spend some time with LaFrance and me, and then leave for parts unknown until the next time. It was as though he had some type of visitation arrangement, but just never really stuck to the schedule. And I never knew where he lived, or where my biological mother lived for that matter. Or who either of them lived with, if anyone. They would just arrive and then disappear, with the difference being that my father's interactions were vastly more frequent.

I don't recall ever being troubled about this relationship. It simply was what it was. I never longed for my father, or my mother for that matter. At all times I felt like an adult, because I knew that LaFrance was my responsibility. And I realize now that this not only helped me adjust to my unique situation, it helped me find my place in it.

I only recall seeing my natural mother twice, and neither time was very pleasant. She was distant and cold, and on the two occasions that I recall seeing her she seemed extremely disinterested. One of those visits–the one most vivid to me–took place at a bowling alley. I recall that LaFrance and I were told to go play with other kids whom we didn't know.

This really seemed to be a recurring theme for me at the time–be it with my mother, my father, or whichever adults were present. Kids left the grownups alone, and went off to play. Don't get too loud and don't start acting crazy. Just go play with those other kids.

While not a surrogate mom, Alice was someone for whom I really cared. She, her husband, and their two daughters were genuinely good and kind people. Alice was very religious, and she adhered to a strong code of discipline–which was pretty much universal in the black community at that time. But she always had a warmth to which I truly responded and respected. And anyway, I had my younger brother always by my side–and that gave me an actual member of my family in my daily life.

The Lewis Family house was in a working-class, all-black neighborhood. If I use the term "ghetto" it is in a loving sense.

The house sat atop a little hill that seemed huge to me at the time, just a block east of Minnesota Avenue and across the street from a baseball park, where we would watch games. There was a long flight of steps leading up to the house from the street, sans safety railing of course. It was a wood-framed house with a wood porch. The tiny kitchen was in the back and led to a small backyard that held chickens.

My brother and I would ride our bikes down the long hill to the bottom of Armstrong and across Minnesota—all unsupervised of course. This was a time of catching crawdads in Big Eleven Lake during the summers, and sledding down those impossibly steep hills in our neighborhood in the winters. In the summer we'd get big cardboard boxes from the furniture and appliance store on Minnesota. We'd then break them open and use them as sleds to slide down the grassy slope of the park.

It was school, and church, and movies, and running the streets. Kids were left to be kids and to pretty much do their own thing.

I settled into my routine of being my brother's keeper and finding happiness with my place in the Lewis home. Eventually, it came to be my home, which is a true credit to Alice. Looking back, I don't really think that it was ever about the money for her. Clearly she had to accept something for taking in LaFrance and me—if nothing else than to cover the daily expenses of raising two young boys. But she treated us like her own family. It's a mystery as to how she came to know my father, and how she came to take us in. He must have sensed the good in her and knew that his boys would be all right under her care.

When I was nine years old, completely unexpectedly, my father arrived at the Lewis house and told LaFrance and me to pack our things. As with all of his previous visits, I had no idea that he was coming. But this time it wasn't for a trip to a restaurant or a shoe store. He was with a woman whom he introduced as his wife. She looked young and pretty—definitely younger than my father. No one had bothered to tell me that he was getting married, or that this woman—Melva—even existed. And no one certainly had told LaFrance or me that today was moving day.

You know how in the movie, there is that joyous moment when the absent parent comes back for the previously abandoned kid? Well, this was the polar opposite. I was devastated. And so too was my brother. This was our home, our place in the world, and we didn't want to leave. Everything we knew in life was here: our friends, our church, our school, our neighborhood, our fun. If I had ever lived anywhere other than with Alice and her family in this house, I had no memory of it.

To me this felt as though we were being snatched up, almost by a stranger, to be taken to a strange place to now live with other strangers. Not only was there my father's bride Melva, but there was her son, who was younger than both LaFrance and I were, named LaVance. Now I know that this is a bit odd that I already have a brother named LaFrance, and now I'm getting a stepbrother named LaVance. Pure coincidence on the names. LaVance was not my father's biological son. I never learned who his natural father was, and I never bothered to ask. As with so many things at that time I didn't even think to pose the question, because I had learned from experience that no one would have given me the answer.

As an aside I'm happy to acknowledge that we do have some very unusual and often entertaining names in the black community. True then, and true now.

So in 1960 my world was officially upended. LaFrance and I said goodbye to Alice, her husband, Clemmy, and Maxine—our surrogate family—and moved out of 1118 Armstrong in Kansas City, Kansas, across the state line to a brand new life.

We arrived at 4425 Montgall Avenue in Kansas City, Missouri, in another, but completely foreign to me, all-black, working-class neighborhood. Until that point in time my universe had consisted largely of the few blocks surrounding the Lewis family home. And now I had to start anew. Although the move was only a few miles, it might as well have been across the country.

The house had about 950 square feet and one bathroom. There were two bedrooms, the smaller of which I also was to share with LaFrance and this stranger LaVance, who was now my brother, and my responsibility.

My father always, and I mean always, valued education. Now that we were with him, he decided that public school would no longer do as it had when we lived with Alice and her family. He and Melva felt that the best option for us was in a Catholic school, so they decided that we three boys were going to become Catholics, which at that time was required to attend Catholic schools. I don't think that this conversion extended to him or to Melva, but it certainly did to LaFrance, LaVance, and me. We started attending catechism classes at Blessed Sacrament Church, located on 39th Street within walking distance of our new house. This allowed us to enroll at Immaculate Heart of Mary School on Swope Parkway, also an easy walk from our home.

I immediately took to this new school, I think, because I always loved school and because I've always been very adaptable. Now, LaFrance was not just my brother, he was my boy. But even then I knew that we were very, very different people. If I got into trouble at school, it was from being a smart-ass or a class clown. Meanwhile, LaFrance would get into more serious trouble, mainly due to what are now called anger issues. Plus, he was never a good student, which certainly added to the volatility. I think that his main motivation to show up every day was sports. He was always a gifted athlete, whereas I unfortunately am not. From the time we were very young he could do anything athletically. But that only got him so far, as he was constantly reprimanded at school—which of course led to being constantly reprimanded at home.

There are constant news stories now about black athletes and entertainers who are accused of beating their kids, with all of the requisite claims of child abuse and criminal behavior. But this is the way that we were raised. This was the way my parents were raised. This was a way of life in the black neighborhoods. It was a way of life for every single black family. Kids were whipped, plain and simple. It's a cultural difference that now pisses off a lot of non-black people who simply don't get it. This corporal punishment goes back to slavery and how black people were disciplined. They learned that whippings kept them in line, so it would therefore keep their kids in line. There were no books available on the philosophies of parenting and behavior correction. This is how they were taught, and what they learned. I never believed we were abused. I understood that the punishment was to teach us to stay out of trouble, especially with the law and the police, which was a constant fear.

This all filtered down through the generations—using physical punishment as a consequence to bad behavior. And when slavery was finally gone in this country, this attitude remained for black people. It didn't simply go away because of the Emancipation. It was already ingrained in black culture. Now a parent could go too far, and other family members or neighbors might say something. But nobody, absolutely nobody, was going to tell you to stop whipping your kid. Nobody who lived in my neighborhood, at least.

My father worked nonstop and was rarely home when we were there. He was a chef at the Black Angus restaurant, and simultaneously was trying to launch his own janitorial business. So he'd get off work, and then go straight to an office building that he'd clean through the night.

My stepmother Melva was always working as well, and just like my father was similarly absent during our after-school hours. She was a key punch operator, doing seasonal work for the IRS and whatever clerical jobs she could find. On top of this she started taking college classes, which in retrospect seems right, as she was of college age.

The fact that Melva was so young and so new to us made her a target of resentment for LaFrance and me. Unfair as it was, in our young minds we blamed her for being snatched from the Lewis household. Our resentment of her, however, did not extend to

LaVance. Almost immediately he stopped being our stepbrother and became our brother. He followed me around like a puppy, and he became inseparable from LaFrance, who was of course closer to him in age.

And just as I did with LaFrance in the Lewis' home, I became LaVance's unofficial guardian in our new house—while still holding this role for LaFrance. With the Lewises there was at least a family structure, as Alice, her husband, and her two daughters were in the home with us—Alice of course serving as the strong and caring matriarch.

We were kids but we knew the rules of the house. Do your chores. Do your homework. At all cost, avoid having the nuns call home to report bad behavior. Never lie! Failure to adhere to the rules would lead to a long-term grounding at the least, and a whipping if egregious. I was in charge when my parents weren't at home. If I let things get out of hand when they were gone, I would be punished along with the offender. Thus I was very motivated to keep those situations to a minimum.

What I never thought about then, but which occurs to me now, is that my father never treated LaVance any different from how he treated LaFrance and me. There was no resentment of LaVance, even though he was another man's child. Nor was there any favoritism, since he was his new wife's young son. He treated us all equally, which I fully accepted, and in retrospect truly admire.

The dynamic in the house settled into two opposing teams: us vs them. And the "us" of course were the three kids. We always looked out for each other, and there was a genuine love among us boys.

It took me to become a father myself to realize that my father and my stepmother did the best they could for us with the knowledge, resources, and information that they had. Like it or not, to some extent we are all products of our environments and of our times.

There is a concept called presentism, which is the process of looking at situations from the past and making judgments on them based on the standards and morals of today. But how it seems now, and how I lived it then, are two very different things.

My father and stepmother worked their butts off to provide us not only with a home but with a private school education. And this was for all three of us. Every other kid in our neighborhood was attending public school, where it would have been the easy place for my parents to send us. But they understood that a high-level education was a gift that they could give to us, and we would then have the ability to change our lives and circumstances for the better. Deep down I appreciated that then. Now I openly appreciate and fully respect those sacrifices.

Chapter
2

Why Local Government
Works Best

Local government is the most functional level of government in this country. Period. There are numerous reasons for this. Local government must produce and provide services every day, while the state and federal governments are usually bound up in hyper-partisan ideological arguments. Local government is often nonpartisan, and local leaders are almost always more approachable than the distant, partisan politicians in the state capitals or Washington, D.C.

Another reason for the high level of functionality of local governments is that mayors collaborate. We all have the same problems, and we all face the same obstacles. And this is true if you're the mayor of Kansas City, or New York, or Anchorage, or Palm Springs.

So because of this commonality we share information, we ask each other for advice without regard to party affiliation or ideology, and we happily provide answers. On the state and federal levels, policy proposals and solutions lie in party ideology rather than a pragmatic approach based on facts and data.

The U.S. Conference of Mayors is bipartisan. It's made up of Democrats and Republicans, liberals, centrists, and conservatives. And yet those differences take a back seat to pragmatism and service delivery.

Our jobs as mayors are actually quite simple—to bring the people of the city together in order to get things done. That's it. There is no other agenda, because there can't be one. If we are dividing people, then we are losing.

And we rely on facts and data to guide us, rather than on ideology and polling. And we do this because it is the best, most practical, and smartest way to make decisions. So we rely on objective rather than subjective criteria.

Now, in order for this approach to work, people must first agree on the basic facts and data. We have to acknowledge that the things in question are true. And then, after acknowledging that they are indeed true, we have to figure out how to analyze these things, and determine what solutions will come from the analysis.

From there it becomes all about problem-solving and determining what is the best course of action to take. So, this then requires us to focus on reality rather than ideology, and pragmatism rather than expediency. And this requires people to commit to long-term approaches that are wholly necessary in order to accomplish big things.

As a mayor you can't say that you're going to build a streetcar for your city, but that if it doesn't happen in the next year, well, then forget it. It's all about long-term rather than short-term thinking. We build cities for our children and our children's children.

You also have to be able to sort through things dispassionately and admit that certain plans aren't working, then find new approaches and solutions. And it's working in conjunction with your city council, city manager, and administrative staff—all as a team for the greater good of the citizens.

On the federal and state levels there is too often collaboration only within one's own political party. And then of course the two parties don't work together—they can never seem to cross the bridge which divides them on the issues. And because of this, things just don't get done. Nothing is ever really accomplished. Long-term issues and challenges are seldom addressed with long-term sustainable solutions.

A troubling byproduct of this inertia at the federal and state levels is that the entrepreneurial spirit is dampened, which leads to even more inactivity and lack of problem-solving.

In essence, local government focuses primarily on service delivery rather than philosophical issues. And when you are mayor, you are directly accountable to your citizenry. There's nowhere to hide. The mayor's office at City Hall is just a short drive away. As mayor, people could easily find my house–they could come and knock on my door. And sometimes they did. Political ideology is one thing. Not having your street cleared of snow is something else entirely.

As mayor I lived with the people whom I served. I was as much a part of their community as they are of mine, which is to say one big community which comprises our city. And this is a universal truth for all mayors. People see me not just at speeches and events, but also at restaurants, in the supermarket, at the movie theater. Mayors are accessible in a way unthinkable to governors and our elected officials in Washington, D.C.

And this accessibility flows directly into accountability. If people have a problem they'll tell me to my face. Usually in a polite and respectful way, but not always. How often do you think that a state or federally elected official encounters this situation? The answer of course is not very often at all. Even with members of the U.S. House of Representatives this level of daily personal interaction with constituents simply does not exist. They have residences and offices in their districts, but make no mistake, these politicians for the most part live and work in Washington, D.C. Marching in a Fourth of July parade or attending a major sporting event is absolutely not the same as living daily in the community that you serve.

Many governors, senators, and representatives, and of course the president, are going to say and do what they feel they have to do in order to be reelected. This is their primary concern. It's important to understand that while mayors are accountable to the people of their city, state and federal politicians are accountable first and foremost to their party. If they go too far off message, then the party money for their re-election campaign suddenly disappears.

In my lifetime, I have never seen our country more politically divided than it is today. During the Vietnam War it was certainly contentious, but not like today. Everybody is at everybody's throats. The Democrats and the Republicans simply won't work together, to the absolute detriment of the people they represent. And yet in local government this dynamic does not exist. This is of course not to say that everything is harmonious, and people of course do want to be reelected, but there is no concept of toeing the party line. The concept of the mayor is instead to get things done. And if things are not getting done, then figure out a solution; otherwise you're probably going to get yelled at while shopping with your family at Target.

I'm a firm believer that the political parties in this country no longer adequately address people's needs. And when people's needs aren't being addressed, the people feel ignored, which leads to them acting out. What we are seeing is frustration and anger, and justly so, because the people are being ignored by both state and federal government.

And they're not just being ignored, they're being taken for granted. The Democrats do this with black people, just as Republicans do this with white people. Plus we are now seeing both parties vilifying the other, which moves things that much further away from meaningful and productive political discourse.

It's interesting to listen to the pronouns that people use. If it's "I" and "me", then we are going to have a problem. If it's "we" and "us", then we've got something to work with. Right now, it's all about "I" and "me" in American politics.

Mayors are political pragmatists, which is a label that I'll proudly wear. I'm all about getting things done rather than having ideological arguments about the issues. Because all of those arguments, and all of that negativity saps a person of energy and strength. Ideological debates generally solve absolutely nothing. Seldom do we see either side significantly change their core political point of view. Methodically, intelligently, and dispassionately working on solutions is the only way to go for me.

Leaders have to make decisions to get things done. And I can't make a decision until I account for the other side. If this is going to hurt people, then how do we remedy the situation? Or, if it's going to help people, then how do we make certain that everyone is helped, not just a select few? Often this means then that you are going to have to modify your position, some way or somehow. I saw my job as mayor very simply: provide the best services for as many people as possible every single day. And to this end, provide the best outcomes and options for as many people as possible to help them resolve problems that they are facing.

And to reiterate, this is not political theory; it's political pragmatism. During my term as mayor we had an issue on the Plaza. For those of you not familiar with my city, the Plaza (or formally known as the Country Club Plaza) is an area located just south of midtown that contains high-end restaurants, bars, shops, and hotels. It's a place where locals and tourists happily come together and is one of the most vibrant districts in all of Kansas City.

Large groups of black kids started gathering en masse, especially on Friday and Saturday nights. Now had this been white kids, things probably would have played out differently. But it was black kids, mainly of middle school and high school age, who would congregate without spending money, much to the dismay of numerous Plaza businesses. There was an uproar on social media and in the local press that quickly gained momentum.

I was pressured to enact a curfew as a solution to this growing problem. But my immediate reaction was against a curfew of any kind. I decided to enlist the aid of a few local ministers and walk with them on the Plaza during a weekend night. Once we were there, I saw kids as young as 10 completely unaccompanied by a parent or adult. Why anyone would leave a 10-year-old alone on the Plaza, or anywhere, is beyond me. The ministers and I spoke with a lot of kids, many of whom were just hanging out and behaving themselves. But many others were being loud and disruptive, and doing stupid things like running in front of moving cars.

After a couple of hours, we heard from the police that there was going to be a knife fight in the park bordering the Plaza's eastern edge. As we quickly headed in that direction, we saw behind us a massive wall of kids moving en masse toward the park. As they were about one-half block away from me and my security detail, three gunshots were fired, and everyone scattered in a scene of sheer pandemonium. My security detail literally threw me into the bushes next to The Cheesecake Factory, while the kids ran in all directions. Clearly, something had to be done. This wasn't a time for debate, it was a time for problem-solving.

The next day I called Philadelphia Mayor Michael Nutter, who I knew had experienced a similar situation in his city. I didn't care about his political party or political leanings; rather, I only cared about his advice. Mayor Nutter was tremendous. He alerted me to issues which I would almost certainly encounter with the ACLU and the black community if a curfew was instituted. And he told me about his experience with creating alternate venues for these kids to attend, as the vast majority of them just wanted a safe place to hang out.

After our discussion I decided that we did in fact need a curfew, but with a caveat. So I went to my city council and laid out my position: a curfew is necessary, but we can't tell kids where they can't go unless we offer them a place where they can go instead. As a first step, we then invited in numerous kids and asked them what they wanted. What came back was that what they really sought was a place to spend time with their friends on weekend nights. It became clear that 95 percent of them were good kids, and the five percent who were causing the problems on the Plaza were causing the entire group to be labeled as unruly.

These kids had very limited options for a safe place to socialize, and meeting up on the Plaza was a direct outgrowth of this reality. The racial history of the city had left the black community generally, and these kids specifically, without the same array of social amenities available to their white counterparts. We asked them what they would do if they had their own place. They answered that they wanted a place where they could dance, listen to music, talk, play games, see their friends, meet new people, and generally just act like normal teenagers. It was all completely reasonable, and of course completely understandable.

From this we created Club KC for high school kids. This filled a number of neighborhood community centers on weekend nights. Food vendors and professional DJs were brought in, as were police officers to provide security. The kids had to register to gain entrance, which allowed us to quickly eliminate the five percent who had really instigated the issues in the first place. We also established activities for middle school kids, as well as programs focused on basketball, soccer, volleyball, and the arts.

These were kids, not criminals, and they were the people of the city that I served as mayor. And guess what? This worked. In the first year we served more than 10,000 kids who otherwise would have been God knows where, doing God knows what.

This program costs $500,000 annually, and it's been money extremely well spent. Most of the troubling issues on the Plaza were eliminated, and these kids now have a safe and fun place to hang out. It's something that makes me extremely proud.

And this serves as a vivid example of a situation on which I evolved. I had originally been dead set against a curfew, but it became clear to me that I couldn't take an ideological stance. This wasn't just about unhappy merchants in a wealthy shopping district; this was about public safety. The three gunshots I heard that night on the Plaza, and the kids who were shot, made that all too clear.

I evolved because practicality, the facts, and the data showed me that I needed to evolve. A curfew was instituted, but in conjunction with a new social program that not only changed lives but very likely saved lives.

We knew that as the City we absolutely needed to do something. So we found a way to get it done. Local government in action.

Chapter 3

A New Life in Kansas City, Missouri

Growing up in the Lewis home in Kansas City, Kansas, I can't recall ever having actually met any white people. Alice's house was in an all-black neighborhood, which of course meant that our local grade school was all-black (students, teachers, and staff), the shops, restaurants and businesses around us were all-black, and all of the people who we saw on a daily basis were black. If a random white person was ever spotted in the area, which was seldom, we knew to scatter, as there was likely some sort of problem.

And when my father brought LaFrance and me to live with him (along with Melva and LaVance) in Kansas City, Missouri, that was in a completely black area as well. But the difference, which was my first experience with desegregation—in other words my first experience with white people—came during our conversion to Catholicism and our attendance at Immaculate Heart of Mary Elementary School.

To reiterate, I had always loved school, and I especially loved Immaculate Heart. There were definitely other black kids at this Catholic school, but we were a small minority. In that era there was a suspicion that black people had about white people.

My father loved to take us on family road trips, especially to see his family in Louisiana. I always looked forward to seeing my grandmother, Uncle Wally, and a wide array of cousins, aunties, and distant relatives. But these trips took planning, and not in the conventional sense. As black motorists heading cross country and into the South, one had to know in advance where to stay, where to eat, where to get gas, where to use the bathroom. And you had to know when to be there, because if you arrived after sunset, things might not go smoothly.

My stepmother Melva, who very quickly became to LaFrance and me our mother and no longer a "step," had a precise way of speaking that was sometimes mistaken for a white woman's voice, and she would make hotel and motel reservations for us on the phone. But on numerous occasions, when our all-black family arrived for check-in, the reservations would suddenly disappear. Physical threats would be made if you happened to stop at the wrong gas station to fill up. The toilets, sinks, and water fountains were always disgusting in the "Colored Only" restrooms. I think that they were intentionally left in an unsanitary state, simply to make them less inviting, so as to keep black people away. Ironic of course, since they were created for black people's use in the first place. Thus, "Colored Only" facilities weren't even welcoming to "colored" people.

Like a lot of black people at the time who were inclined to travel, my father owned a copy of *The Negro Motorist Green Book*, which listed safe places for black people to do normal human being things, like eat, sleep, use the bathroom, buy goods, and get gas. Known now to a new generation because of the Academy Award winning film that bears its name, *The Green Book* was something very real and very necessary for black travelers and vacationers in this era.

White people often only view segregation from their perspective, and really, why would they view it any differently? But there was of course the black perspective, my perspective, where white folks were the mysterious and sometimes hostile figures, living just out of reach.

From my earliest childhood I was instructed on how to deal with white people, as I think virtually all black kids of that era were as well. This came from Alice Lewis, my father, teachers, older kids, adults around the neighborhood. It was like a lesson on proper behavior in race mixing. Things such as how to speak to a white person if they ask you a question. How to look or not look at white people. How close to stand near them in public. How to approach them in conversation. Yes sir, no ma'am. Watch out for the white man!

I really believe that the biggest curse we have in society is the lack of understanding among the races. Then, and now. So many of the problems we have in our country emanate from white people failing to understand what it is really like to live as a non-white person. It was different for me as a kid in an all-black neighborhood, and it's still different for me as the former mayor of Kansas City. Being black in the United States is just different from being white in the United States. And I know that not everyone wants to hear this, but it is of course the truth.

Despite my minority status at Immaculate Heart and the affiliated church (as we were now Catholic), I had a great time. We all got along really well, black kids and white kids. But it was still weird. The Beatles were Number One in my school, but certainly not in my neighborhood. I was suddenly infused with two cultures, and now I was not only seeing white people but actually making white friends for the first time in my young life.

It helped that I was really good at school, and that I'm a natural smart-ass. Plus I've always been uninhibited, and I didn't really know my limits on what I could and couldn't get away with. Come to think of it, I still don't.

Sister Mary Lucy was my favorite teacher, and the nun we all thought was the prettiest. Her perceived physical beauty was based solely on her face, as everything else, apart from her hands, was of course covered by her black habit. But we could certainly imagine. The nuns at our school were from the order of the Sisters of Charity of Leavenworth, BVM–the "BVM" for Blessed Virgin Mary–which we secretly changed to "Black Veiled Monsters." But not Sister Mary Lucy. She was cool.

Our annual school play had gone extremely well, and she wanted to give our class a reward. We collectively clamored for ice cream, and Sister Mary Lucy told us that she'd bring it to school tomorrow. I reminded her that there was a grocery store less than two blocks away and that she could walk down there now, buy the ice cream, and have it back to us in a matter of minutes.

She correctly retorted that there was no way that she could leave a classroom full of kids unattended while she departed school grounds to go buy ice cream. I then countered with what I thought was a brilliant idea. I knew that Sister Mary Lucy had a tape recorder in her desk, and I suggested that she turn it on, and record us while she was gone. This way, she could monitor our behavior when she returned. And besides, knowing that we were being recorded would ensure our excellent conduct.

Shockingly, Sister Mary Lucy agreed, and after starting the recorder she promptly headed out for the grocery store to buy our ice cream.

Within about 20 seconds three close friends and I started yelling, making funny noises, and telling jokes. In short order, the entire class joined in. It was chaos. We were so loud that a nun teaching in a nearby classroom came in to see what was going on. We covered for Sister Mary Lucy, by saying that she had stepped out to use the restroom. And we apologized profusely for our loudness, and promised to quiet down, which of course we didn't.

Upon her return, with bags of bags of ice cream containers in hand, Sister Mary Lucy found her class in a vocal frenzy, and one student now absent.

That student was of course me. She asked the other kids where I was, and then started calling my name, more and more frantically.

Finally, I popped out of the class room's storage closet, and yelled "Ta da!"

Well, Sister Mary Lucy the cool nun suddenly wasn't so cool. She immediately sent me, and my three friends who were identified as my fellow ring leaders, straight home. Grab your things, bypass the principal's office, and exit Immaculate Heart immediately. She didn't play.

Now we were screwed, but I of course had a plan. If we confronted our respective parents together as a group, then their anger and outrage would be lessened with the four of us present. We'd hit all four of our homes, one by one, keeping solidarity.

First stop–Eddie's house. His mom was furious and told him to go straight to his room. And then there were three. Next stop–Jay's house, and exactly the same result. So our group was reduced to half its size, but two is still better than one when it comes to dealing with a parent's ferocity. And of course at Joe's house he was told to stay inside, and I was sent on my way alone, to my house to face my father.

Because of his night and overnight two-job work schedule, my father was home sleeping during school days. I contemplated walking around until school was dismissed for the day, and then coming in the house as though nothing had happened. But I of course knew that my school would eventually, probably sooner rather than later, let my father and mother know that I had been booted and why.

So, with my brilliant plan now completely shattered, I slowly entered the front door, hoping my father was still asleep. He of course demanded to know why I was home so early, leaving me with no choice but to tell him all about the ice cream, the tape recorder, and my grand entrance from the storage closet.

You know how earlier I was discussing discipline in black families between parents and children? Well, let's just say that I don't remember the next few days. Head trauma will do that to a kid.

In all seriousness, my father's reaction and subsequent punishment vividly illustrated just how high of a premium he

A PASSION FOR PURPOSE

put on his sons' education. All three of his sons. He and my mother were busting their asses to send all of us to an expensive Catholic school.

Time, effort, and money—all for a quality education that he and Melva never had the opportunity to receive. And we weren't going to blow it.

This wasn't about us boys serving as the representatives of the black community in this predominately white school, and it wasn't about being ambassadors for our family. My parents didn't care about any of that.

What they cared about was education. And looking back, I'm truly appreciative that they did.

46

Chapter 4

Term Limits and Guns

As the mayor of Kansas City, Missouri, I was term-limited. Two four-year terms, and then I was gone. I was elected, won re-election, and then I left office, feeling as though my city was in a much better place than where I had found it.

In modern politics there is the issue of the campaign promise approach: winning the first time, and then winning every time thereafter to stay in. Winning is the only goal, rather than serving the people.

Politicians are now constantly shifting from one agenda to the next as quickly as possible, so as to hastily fulfill campaign promises. This leaves the long-term problems, and their solutions, on the table. And this eliminates consistency, as ideologies constantly shift based on the mood of the political parties and administrations.

Rather than have the people who actually hold the levers of government in a position to innovate and think, our system now puts them in a reactionary position. They do what they are told to do, rather than what needs to be done.

In local government it's very different. The programs created are sustainable. When we came up with a 20-year, $800-million general obligation bond for infrastructure, the blueprint was set. When we laid out our five-year city budget, the blueprint was set.

But this is not the case with partisan politics. When the governorship of a state, any state, switches from Republican to Democrat, or vice versa, everything comes to a halt. The bureaucrats in state government are forced to stop what they are doing and then shift to the other side. It doesn't matter if they were working on good programs, because those were the previous administration's programs. The agenda has changed with the party change. And then problems do not get solved.

And yet I don't like or agree with term limits. My autonomy to do the right thing as mayor, to solve problems and get things done, stemmed not from term limits but from a nonpartisan structure of government.

To me, term limits are the lazy way to deal with politics. The theory seems to be: we don't like politicians, so let's limit their time in office. And then let's put in a bunch of new people. This is somehow supposed to solve all of our problems. Well, this hasn't solved any problems on the state or federal levels. And this is because of partisan politics.

If a state representative is term-limited, then they start looking at a way to get into the Senate. If they are term-limited in the Senate, then they begin to eye a run for governor or president. Because of this these term-limited officials, who are supposed to have more freedom to act independently, instead stay mindful of keeping their political party, donors, and the special interest groups happy. As a result, the real power brokers are special interest groups and lobbiests.

These politicians continue to do things for the purpose of getting elected, which means avoiding controversy at all costs. This is not the way to solve problems faced by the people and by society. It is politics as a substitute for leadership, ideology as a substitute for action–plain and simple.

These politicians are terrified to step out sans cover from their party. If they are so bold, then they get snapped off immediately because they can't fight off all of the people who are opposed to their way of thinking, which veers from the party line. And make no mistake, that line is in large part drawn by special interest groups.

Take for instance the issue of guns. It's an issue that has become all about political ideology, and has absolutely nothing now to do with practicality. As mayor of Kansas City, I was subject to the gun laws of the state of Missouri. And those laws allow for people age 19 and older to own a gun without a permit or training. This is just asking for trouble. It's absolutely ridiculous that it takes more training, testing, and processing to drive a car legally in Missouri than it does to carry a gun. A huge part of training and licensing drivers is based on a car being a potentially lethal weapon. How is this any different from guns? And yet none of this exists for firearm ownership and use in Missouri.

Kansas City and St. Louis rank in the Top-10 nationwide for gun violence. And this falls directly back on Missouri's incredibly lax gun laws. The state lacks a system to determine who can and can't own and carry a gun. Simple and tragic, cause and effect.

When everybody has a gun, and an intense argument breaks out, the likelihood dramatically increases that guns will become involved. These are not premeditated crimes, but rather heat of passion crimes. And the person firing their gun, who is now fully aware that this is shoot or be shot, fires 10 bullets, spraying innocent bystanders in the process. It's what we are seeing on the streets daily across the country, completely unchecked.

My Chief-of-Staff Joni Wickham, was traveling in Europe and met an English family who was on vacation. During their conversation, Joni found out that the teenage daughter would soon be heading to Missouri to play college soccer on scholarship. When asked lightheartedly by Joni if she had any concerns about heading off to the U.S., such as the weather, or homesickness, the English teenager said that she was concerned about being shot and killed.

When people from outside of the U.S. are legitimately worried that a move to this country could very well end in their homicide by a firearm, then it's something that as a society we all need to address. It's something that as mayor, I felt compelled to address. And yet, I was completely restricted by the state gun laws of Missouri, which govern my city.

The United States Congress set forth policies that prevented both the Centers for Disease Control and the ATF from keeping a computerized list of gun violence and gun issues. That's crazy, and it's ideological. It has nothing to do with practicality. So, are we putting the absolute right to gun ownership above the absolute right to life, liberty, and the pursuit of happiness? These two are in direct conflict. Ultimately, we have to choose one.

I know that there are those Second Amendment absolutists who claim that gun ownership must be protected as a defense against government tyranny. The argument goes that a strong Second Amendment creates the opportunity for a noble citizen militia to overthrow an unjust and oppressive regime. This is fanciful thinking.

Yet this line of thinking appeals to a certain population: conspiracy theorists, homegrown terrorists, those people who absolutely hate all forms of government, especially the federal government.

And then there is the much larger group of people who feel that owning a gun will somehow protect them in a deadly situation. In a few instances it certainly can and has. But the harsh reality is that in a life-or-death situation, people who have never had to fire a gun at another person have no idea what this is really about. Police officers, who are of course highly and consistently trained with firearms, make mistakes all of the time when firing a weapon.

There is a gun rights fantasy scenario about a righteous law-abiding citizen shooting an evil home invader. First of all, how many homes actually get invaded? Secondly, what are the chances that you'll actually be there if your home does get invaded? Thirdly, if you are there how likely is it that you'll be able to get to your gun in time? And finally, if all of the above plays out, do you really think that you'll be able to hit your target?

Training or no training, it's difficult to hit a stationary target, harder still to hit a moving target, and extremely hard to hit a moving target while under extreme duress. Law enforcement officials and soldiers who have fired their weapons in stress-filled situations can absolutely attest to this reality.

I just don't buy into this philosophy of, "I'm entitled to have a gun, and therefore I should have a gun." And, "I'm going to have a gun, be it a pistol or an AK-47." This line of thinking is impractical, and it's just not well-reasoned. Yet public and political discourse is continuing to be fed by the marketing arm of the gun manufacturers in the United States, the NRA, through its campaign of utter paranoia.

To be clear, all that the NRA really does is promote the sale of guns. Right now the NRA is heavily promoting plastic guns, which are untraceable. Why do we need untraceable guns? Why do we need bump stocks? Why do we need assault rifles?

This is nothing more than adding to the problem, and completely neglecting the search for a solution to the gun violence that is overwhelming our country. It's furthering the problem, rather than solving it.

Add all of these guns into the mix of people who have a lack of education, are caught in a cycle of poverty, and have been overcome by feelings of hopelessness and despair. This of course creates an incredibly volatile environment—one which the police can't control.

You simply can't have 500,000 police officers for a city, and even if you did people are still going to get shot due to the proliferation of guns. In Kansas City we had a situation where police officers were standing 15 yards from a guy shooting into a crowd, and they couldn't stop him. At our crime lab there is cache of confiscated weapons that you wouldn't even see in most military units. This is not unique to Kansas City. It's in *every city* in the United States!

And yet there is nobody in state and federal government who is willing to address this situation, this crisis, in a truly meaningful and problem-solving way.

When I was mayor, I spoke to a group of teenagers who were doing internships with local entrepreneurs. I wanted to impress upon them how much their generation had the power to affect change. And I did this by telling them that they are the long-term buyers who marketers and advertisers eagerly seek. They are the primary target of commercial consumerism. And with that, they possess a tremendous amount of power and influence. They can do this not only by purchasing products, but by *not* purchasing products en masse. Guns for instance. If a product doesn't sell, it gets removed from the store shelves. And to go a step further, if a retail chain fears a boycott because they are selling a product such as guns, then they are going to stop selling that product. Money trumps everything, and this younger generation will very soon control the money.

And in partisan politics, money not only trumps everything, it rules everything. If you don't believe me, just ask the NRA.

Chapter 5

Bishop Hogan High School

I **instinctively knew** that being the oldest brother came with a high degree of responsibility. But while I took this role very seriously, I was far from the perfect child. Nothing big, mind you. Rather just everyday kid stuff that seems to drive all parents crazy—certainly things that drove my father and mother crazy.

For instance, I never liked grits, a staple of many black and southern households, including my own. I hated grits then, and to this day I still hate grits. But they were always served at our table. And by the time that I sat down to eat breakfast, they were usually cold and lumpy. Me being me, I knew that eating them again and again was simply not an option. So I came up with a solution. Our expandable metal kitchen table had pull out leaves, with a lip perfect for storing grits. I would surreptitiously move the grits from my plate to my left hand to under the table for safe keeping. Then, after school, before my father and mother came home from work, I'd remove the abandoned grits, wash them down the sink, and wipe away all of the incriminating evidence.

Eventually, due to overconfidence, I grew lax in my grit removal operation and piled up meal after meal of uneaten grits sitting precariously on this lip under the table. On the occasion of dinner guests coming to our house and the table needing to be extended, my father went to work on pulling out the leaves. They were stuck shut, literally. Finally, after he applied severe force, the table flew open, and a massive pile of unwanted and discarded grits fell to the floor. My father did not find the humor in this incident.

I always took grief from my friends for what I wore, as did my younger brothers. As black kids attending predominately white schools, we really needed two different sets of clothes. What was cool in our neighborhood didn't translate to school, and vice versa. Two cultures, with entirely different ways of dressing.

But my father and mother weren't interested in accommodating our early 1960s hippy fashion needs. They told us what to wear, and that was that. So, I came up with a solution. There was a rock wall located along the walk to school. In it was a small hollowed-out area that I discovered. Thus, in went the white people clothes, to be safely hidden away until we could retrieve them on school mornings after we left the house. My brothers and I would then take the alternate wardrobe with us to a nearby gas station, change in the bathroom, put our cool black people clothes in the wall, and then reverse the process on the way home after school.

Yes, we actually would have two different outfits every day. Life would have been much simpler had Immaculate Heart instituted school uniforms for boys. But, alas, no such luck.

Worse for us were the peonies that my mother would make us wear for special occasions. If you're not familiar with peonies, the best way that I can describe them is as "a big ass flower." She grew her peonies in our backyard, which perpetually attracted a swarm of bees. For some unknown reason, she'd pin a peony on the suit jackets of LaFrance, LaVance, and me, which would make us look completely idiotic. So there we'd be, going to Mass or a Mother's Day lunch or a birthday party, with a big bush on our shoulder, accompanied by dozens of bees. I'm telling you, wearing peonies wasn't a cool look.

A subtle rebellion for me, and one of the pleasures of my young life, was to sneak out of bed after everyone else had gone to sleep, and read.

Usually my father was working his janitorial gig overnights, so I didn't have to worry about waking him up. But I still had to be very quiet for fear of disturbing Melva. Almost every evening I would quietly walk up the attic steps, slowly sit down, turn on my flashlight, and then read. I especially loved Doc Savage, who began his heroic life in 1930s pulp magazines, and eventually moved to comic books and paperbacks. I was so into those Doc Savage books that I was transported, living his adventures with him.

But perhaps because of my father's influence, or maybe it was just because of who I am, school always came first for me. I had my close friends, both white and black, and I definitely had fun. But for me education was the priority. School wasn't a chore or an obligation; rather, it was the center of my life.

My Catholic school education progressed to Bishop Hogan High School, where I was the only black male student. While I certainly faced casual and passive racism, it was usually not overt in school. Certainly I would hear the occasional racial slur, but it was of the behind-my-back rather than the to-my-face variety. This was not the case everywhere, however. There were plenty of places we dared not visit, and plenty of people who were quick to remind us of the fact that we were black.

While racism was not a part of daily academic life, it occasionally became part of my athletic life. As a nearly all-white private Catholic high school, Bishop Hogan would regularly compete against similar schools, complete with the same lack of racial diversity. So not only was I the lone black kid on my team, I was the lone black kid on either side. There were never threats or incidents of physical violence, but there was certainly name-calling, and ugly name-calling at that. I'd hear the shouts, but tried not to pay any attention. My teammates, and my friends, would always stick up for me. So too did their parents, and my coaches as well. I was one of their own, and I was not to be disrespected in this way, nor in any way for that matter.

But being black at Bishop Hogan really wasn't an issue, at least not as I was concerned. And anyway, I was now well-versed in how to navigate this majority-white education system, having done it since age nine. School naturally came easy for me, the work part and the social part, so it was a really positive time in my life. I loved school. It was home base, and it was a place where adults gave me credit when deserved.

Consider as well that I was a completely non-threatening teenager. There was no menace about me, I was an athlete (albeit not a great one), I was friendly, and I got really good grades. And I fully understand now, and partially understood then, that because I was different this worked in my favor in some circumstances. I was given a lot of access and gained a lot of leverage that I would not have received if I were just another white student there.

For as long as I can remember, I've generally gotten along with everybody. And, while not in a ladies man way, I've had a natural comfort around females. Guys of course can be knuckleheads occasionally, especially at high school age, but girls are different. More compassion, more kindness, more willingness to be open-minded.

When a person is different, for whatever reason, they learn almost instinctively with whom they can and can't be cool. At Bishop Hogan I knew that there were a few students who were never going to accept me as their classmate, let alone their friend, because I was black. So I decided that they weren't worth the effort. But for everyone else I was open and available.

I was actually elected Junior Class President, and I also managed to edge my way into a band. Tom Cassidy, who was an extremely talented and imaginative musician, had originally formed the group, and named it The Amelia Earhart Memorial Flying Band. I became the lead singer, as well as the only black member. Race, however, was never an issue in our band.

We were even able to attract a fairly prominent local agent, Irv Goldman, who had an office at Wornall Plaza in Kansas City. I can confidently say that we were actually very good. Our full lineup consisted of Chris Immeleon on lead guitar, Chipp Tate on rhythm guitar, Jim Fox on base, Robert "Bucky" Kort on drums, and Tom on keyboards and guitar. He also served as our songwriter.

We played a lot of the protest music of the day, covering hits by popular performers such as Buffalo Springfield, Jimi Hendrix, and Jefferson Airplane. We'd mix in some Motown as well, with songs by artists like the Temptations and Smokey Robinson. And we'd even break out a few blues numbers on occasion. Our band started off playing small house parties and CYO (Catholic Youth Organization) mixers; then soon progressed to numerous Battles of the Bands competitions, local clubs such as Aquarius, and dances and proms at large high schools around Kansas City and throughout the state of Kansas. We became quite popular and fairly well known on the regional music scene.

Although we were good enough and productive enough to have Irv Goldman as our booking agent, we lacked a professional road manager. As a substitute, Tom's older brother Jim acted as our executive assistant and chauffeur.

On what seemed like a typical Saturday night gig, Irv had booked us to play a high school dance in the Kansas City suburb of Belton, Missouri, which still had the characteristics of a small town. Throughout the course of the gig, it became increasingly clear that not all of the attendees were happy that we had travelled to their school. Some of the guys made it quite clear that they didn't particularly like our music in general, and me in particular. Adding to this was the fact that many of the girls were paying particularly close attention to my fellow band members and me.

Eventually, both Jim and Chris decided that it would be a good idea to cut our set short and depart Belton as quickly as possible. After finishing the final song of our performance, we quickly began to break down our equipment and pack it back up in our van.

As we were carrying out the last of the amps and drum cases, we heard a few of the guys yelling about what they were going to do to us. Shortly afterward, we saw a mob of these high school toughs round the corner of the building and head straight toward us. Stoked by beer-fed bravado, they made it clear that we were going to get our asses kicked.

Perhaps they believed that because we were musicians we must also be pacifists. This was absolutely not the case. However, as we were outnumbered at least four to one, the prudent thing was clearly for us to get in our van and on the road as quickly as possible.

As we all piled in, the mob began to charge. Jim reacted by driving straight at the teenage thugs, which caused them to immediately scatter in all directions. A few of these idiots regrouped and made a second charge, only to be deterred by Chipp swinging a mic pole out the rear side window directly at their heads. With that, the mob's threats of physical violence were reduced to yelling and a few thrown rocks at our van. As we drove back to Kansas City, we all thanked Jim, who seemingly had added bodyguard to his growing list of duties for the band.

The ever-growing list of gigs coupled with high school life in general became the center of my teenage universe. As a result, I became less and less involved with my two brothers. It wasn't a conscious decision on my part, but it was reality just the same.

Although LaFrance and LaVance were step-brothers, they were virtually identical in terms of personality and disposition. Both were poor students, largely because of disinterest. LaFrance in particular seemed to be having a tough time of things at school, which of course led directly to added conflict at home. Because I still considered myself to be responsible for them, I always felt guilty when my brothers got into trouble. There was no doubt in my mind that I should have been able to prevent it, and then protect them from the inevitable consequences. The problem–I wasn't smart enough to know how.

One particular Christmas, after returning home from midnight Mass, we woke early to give our parents the types of presents that kids of our means could afford. The gifts from LaVance and me to them were certainly nothing special, but they were well received nonetheless. LaFrance, however, surprised us all by presenting our mother with a pair of silver candle holders. Rather than being happy, she immediately declared that they must have been stolen, and demanded to know where LaFrance got them. He claimed to have found the candle holders in a trash bin, but my mother was having none of it. She was absolutely furious.

The Christmas morning argument raged, as LaFrance continued to protest his innocence. In an ill-advised move, I began to defend my brother, which of course only made things worse. Quickly, I was close to becoming a co-conspirator in this candle holder caper.

Our family dynamic had evolved into my brothers screwing up, me acting as their ineffective advocate, and my parents then growing that much angrier and upset.

But outside of the home things were different. There was far less conflict, and far less worry. Looking back now, I was simply trying to live my young life in the same way I ran track for Bishop Hogan: lower my head, steel my gaze, and keep moving forward.

Chapter
6

The New KCI Part 1

Kansas City International Airport, known officially as MCI but called KCI by locals, was an issue long since before I was in office. Opened in 1972 and sporting a design of the future, it eventually became a relic to an era of air travel passed long ago. The fact is that KCI was never built for a post-9/11 world with all of the added security and screening. Truly though, KCI was already starting to become a dinosaur in the late 1980s, as the commercial air industry changed rapidly from just a decade and a half before.

During my first year as mayor, KCI's director at that time told the press, "We're going to get a new airport, whether you like it or not." This was a really unfortunate statement, as it basically threw down the gauntlet. The public's immediate reaction was negative and created a situation where we were fighting from behind at the very beginning.

But he was right. It was clear to anyone who really looked at KCI that a modern replacement was absolutely needed. But the way he expressed this sentiment immediately turned people off.

KCI was never designed for security. Even a few months after its grand opening, as hijackings and terrorist activity started to increase, this deficiency became glaringly obvious. It was the equivalent of a convertible designed with only warm, sunny weather in mind. Nobody had the foresight to see the storms looming, as security measures were increased after 9/11.

There's a total of just 78 feet from the front entrance doors (curbside) to the back wall (boarding gates), no matter where you are in the horseshoe-shaped terminals. Until a small upgrade was completed in 2004, there were no bathrooms or concessions inside security. None. What few bathroom and food/drink options that existed were all located in the narrow corridor between the front doors and the security screening checkpoints. And this was identical in all three of the terminal buildings.

When first conceived in 1966, KCI was dubbed "The Airport of the Future." In terms of its convenience and ease of access, it actually was cutting edge. But its revolutionary design became a liability, as terrorism and security became major issues. Though it was meant to change air travel in this country, KCI was never duplicated in a major or even midsized city airport.

So as I took office it was clear that getting Kansas City a new airport would be a priority for my administration. One of my first moves was to appoint a citizen's commission, on which I purposely included critics of the idea of dumping KCI. I wasn't going to allow anyone to say that I had stacked the deck in our favor. There was already a huge anti-new airport groundswell that seemed to be growing.

I also included people who lived in neighboring communities located on the Kansas side of the state line. The unique nature of Kansas City as a metropolitan area is that the population base is split between two states. Kansas City, Missouri accounts for just under a quarter of the metro's population of about 2.2 million. Johnson County, Kansas is home to numerous suburban cities that are part of the Greater Kansas City area, and has a total population of about 600,000. And then there is Kansas City, Kansas, also in the metro, which is located in Wyandotte County and has around 150,000 people. We are all Kansas Citians, no matter if you reside in Kansas or Missouri. Or at least that's what people say while traveling, when they're asked, "Where are you from?"

Beyond this, recognizing the regional nature of KCI and its potential replacement, I also appointed people who lived in smaller Missouri communities located outside of the metro.

This citizen's commission met regularly in an open and transparent public forum at City Hall. To co-chair the commission I appointed Dave Fowler, a managing partner at KPMG, and Bob Berkebile, an environmental architect at BNIM.

The three options open to the commission were to leave KCI as is, renovate it, or build a new airport. This commission was extremely diligent in speaking with multiple experts, touring other airports across the U.S., gauging public opinion, and studying cost-benefit analyses.

The very detailed and well-written report they ultimately produced recommended that a new single terminal airport be built at the site of Terminal A at the current KCI, to replace the three old horseshoe-shaped terminals. Immediately the public assumed that the taxpayers would be funding this massive project. Predictably, more outcry then followed. We heard a lot of *I never fly anywhere, so why should I pay for a new airport?!* And, *Why can't the rich airlines build this themselves?!*

The reality is that airports aren't built with tax dollars. All of the funding comes from money generated by the airport itself, such as passenger enplanement and landing fees (essentially ticket taxes), fuel tax, cargo handling, concessions, and parking, as well as the airlines that use the facility.

With or without a new airport, the enplanement and landing fees exist, and would continue to do so. This is for every single commercial airline ticket purchased in the country, regardless of where you are flying to or from. And all of the enplanement and landing fee revenue collected nationally is placed into a pool and distributed by the federal government. So, for example, when Indianapolis built its new airport, some of the funding came directly from enplanement and landing fees paid by Kansas Citians into and out of KCI.

Airports in the United States are federal government entities. They are governed by the Federal Aviation Administration (FAA), not the city, county, or state. All of the money generated by airport functions stays within the airport system for maintenance and operations. It's a closed loop.

And yet a large number of people were convinced that they would still be footing the bill through their taxes. To counteract this false belief I repeatedly used the Wheeler Downtown Airport as an example. This is Kansas City's largest non-commercial airport, used primarily for corporate and recreational flights, and occasionally for Air Force One. In 2006 there was a $20 million hangar complex built at Wheeler.

So I'd ask the naysayers, "How much in taxes are you paying for Wheeler Airport? Where on your tax bill is there a line item that lists this?"

I'd then inform them that they weren't paying now and never did pay previously for this project through their taxes. The money all came from the government and airport revenue.

Still, I'd get back the answer: *Well, it must be hidden in there somewhere. I just know that we're going to be paying for the new airport.*

There are always contrarians when it comes to new projects and ideas. I call them CAVE (Citizens Against Virtually Everything) people. When it came to the development of our streetcar, which I'll discuss later in the book, the contrarians could at least argue about our projections. With the new airport, they were arguing against fact. It was maddening. In many cases these were people who knew better, but simply wanted to spout fiction in order to further their own narratives and agendas.

We enlisted the support of the Kansas City Chamber of Commerce in what really became an educational campaign. What we discovered was that the vast majority of people knew that KCI was a relic of travel from long past, and that we clearly needed a new airport. Their opposition came not from progress, nor nostalgia, but the misconception of their financial responsibilities.

People had to be convinced that the new airport would in essence pay for itself. Taxpayers would pay the sum total of zero.

I spent many meetings during the day at City Hall, and many nights at formal and social gatherings, explaining this concept to citizens.

The polls started to shift in our favor, as the *You mean we actually get a new airport for free?* reality began to stick. But we then had to make everyone understand why there would still be a vote on this issue, even though the taxpayers were not going to be responsible for anything.

The reason was that this would be a revenue bond, and under Missouri state law every bond issue has to be placed on the ballot regardless of how the bonds are repaid. Still the opposition continued.

One City Councilwoman told me that she was against the new airport, because KCI was "convenient." I then told her that of course it was convenient for her, and the Kansas Citians who make up 30 percent who use the airport. She and they actually live in the Kansas City metropolitan area. For the other 70 percent, namely those who fly into KCI from out of town, it's not convenient at all. Sure it's great to be dropped off curbside, 78 feet from your gate and 45 minutes before departure. You've eaten, had a cup of coffee, and used the bathroom at home. I agree; it's great.

But for the 70 percent who aren't area residents, KCI is a nightmare. The food and drink vendors are scarce, and generally closed early in the morning and late at night when flights are still running. The bathrooms are small and scarce, especially near the gates inside the security checkpoints. The three-terminal design has no walkable access between the buildings. If you land in one terminal and have to transfer airlines to another, your only option is the Red Bus, which can be up to a 30-minute wait.

Due to the wave of airlines consolidating and going out of business since the 1990s, three terminals at KCI were no longer needed. Terminal A closed in January, 2014, and still there are unused gates and check-in counters at Terminals B and C. This is another antiquated holdover of KCI's 1970s concept and design, when space was needed for a slew of now defunct airlines such as TWA, Eastern, Continental, Pan Am, and Braniff.

And because the airport was designed in an era when you just *walked up and boarded the plane*, TSA precheck is often not an option, and there's no chance of ever installing CLEAR, the advanced security system which uses biometric scanning. This leaves us way behind the times with our airport in a city that prides itself on being technologically advanced.

And for those who said that they never flew and therefore reasoned that the airport didn't affect them, well, they were dead wrong. Anytime Kansas City bids on major sporting events, conferences, and conventions, KCI is always a concern.

When the Republican Party was considering our city to host the 2016 National Convention, we flew the heavy hitters into the Wheeler Downtown Airport, as the initial report on KCI from their advance team was so scathing.

A key person with the Republic National Committee told me, "Mayor, we love your city. But you have to do something with that airport."

The Republicans wound up choosing Cleveland instead.

We've lost numerous businesses and business deals because of KCI. The first thing a visitor flying into our city sees upon arrival is KCI, and it leaves a bad taste. Plus, the word "International" in Kansas City International Airport was almost a misnomer. There were limited flights to Mexico and Canada, and that was it. For a lot of multi-national corporations, this lack of direct flights overseas is basically a deal killer.

Personally I'd rather show visitors a modern door emblazoned with *Welcome to Kansas City,* rather than one that looks like it was built in 1972. Thankfully, the citizens saw it the same way. All of the misconceptions were cleared up and the message eventually came through. On November 7, 2017, 76 percent of the voters cast their ballots in favor of a new airport for our city.

The very next day, Icelandic Air called to inquire about opening up flights to Europe, via regular service between Kansas City and Reykjavik.

While I was pleasantly surprised by the huge support for the new KCI and the ecstatic support that immediately followed, it was clear my fight was really just beginning.

Chapter 7

Leaving Home

In addition to the importance of education my father instilled a genuine work ethic in me as well. And to be fair, my mother added to this. Both were extremely hard and tireless workers, without question.

From the moment that we moved from the Lewis family home in Kansas City, Kansas to what became our family home in Kansas City, Missouri, I worked. It started with a paper route, delivering *The Call*, Kansas City's major black newspaper at the time. From there I got a job at Wimpy's Hamburgers, taking out the trash, wiping down the grill, and washing dishes. That led to work alongside my father: busing tables at The Black Angus while he was doing his chef gig, and also serving as his assistant cleaning office buildings for his janitorial business.

While I didn't enjoy picking up plates of half-eaten food, or cleaning toilets, I cherished this time spent with my father. Because he was always out earning money, I never really got to see him at home. What I was now doing was hard work, but I was actually being paid to have father-son time. We would talk, really talk. The first time that we ever did so. And it was just the two of us, with no Melva, LaFrance, or LaVance to steal his attention. Then after work, we would go and have a meal together—a hamburger or pig ear sandwich—and talk some more.

My father was an absolute stickler for doing the job right. Make that perfect. His janitorial clients loved him because he was so incredibly dedicated and detail-oriented. And they loved him at the Black Angus as well. The Bishop of the Diocese of Kansas City-St. Joseph was a regular diner there and he would always shake my father's hand upon entrance—and slip him a $20 bill. He was just one of the city's powerful and important people who knew my dad and came in to eat his food. There were business leaders, athletes, entertainers, and other assorted local movers and shakers.

The Black Angus actually set up a glass booth in the restaurant so that my father would be fully on display, proudly and almost artistically preparing his steaks for the high-end clientele. He created his own recipe for fried green tomatoes, which was a huge hit at the restaurant. And he created a recipe for steak butter that actually changed his life.

The recipe was so well-received that he decided to enter it in a contest sponsored by Del Monte. He claimed first prize, and with it a check for $50,000—which would be the equivalent of about $400,000 in today's money.

When he won, my father's only extravagant purchase was a brand new Cadillac. He set about automobile shopping dressed in his worst, to see if he would be treated with dignity. It took quite a while, but when a dealership actually showed him respect, my father paid for the Caddy in cash, and drove it off the lot. But other than the car, nothing else changed in my father's daily life. He kept right on working both of his jobs. But for the first time he now had financial security, which is a game-changer for anyone.

When we had our massive blowup over the Chiefs game so that I could instead audition with my bandmates for the opening act of the Jefferson Airplane show, it was really the lesson of his financial prudence that made it possible. As headstrong and ballsy as I was, willing to be a homeless 16-year-old suddenly excommunicated from his own family, it was only an option made possible by money. And the money came from seven years of constantly working jobs, and then saving the meager pay in a bank account until it accumulated into a sizeable sum.

Independence in life is often only made possible through financial independence, and to this I was a full beneficiary. My mother had also continually preached fiscal responsibility, and would never allow us to spend more than 25 percent of our pay. While it seemed unfair, even cruel at times, I now fully respect her judgement on these matters. Kids with money don't generally think "save"–they think "spend". But my mother made sure that LaFrance, LaVance, and I were always saving our money. It's incredibly ironic that I was able to fully put these fiscal lessons to use when I had my first true act of defiance and left home for good.

As I look back, it's almost impossible to believe that I was willing to immediately transition from kid to adult with one decision. But it certainly wasn't a rash decision. As I wrote in the opening of this book, my old man was not to be crossed. And if you did cross him, well, there was no going back. I had a clear-eyed understanding of this, and made my choice accordingly.

Being gone from the house meant being out of my father's and mother's lives completely. Gone just like that was the job at the Black Angus, and gone as well was working with my father as his janitorial assistant. And gone too, of course, were our post-work dinners, and all of our one-on-one father-son time.

My father knew a lot of people around Kansas City, which meant that he was secretly keeping tabs on me. I knew this even then, which gave me some comfort. What did not though was my sudden extraction from the daily lives of LaFrance and LaVance. These were my brothers–my team in the ever-raging family war of kids vs parents. And I always felt as though they were my responsibility. After I moved out we'd sneak around to see each other, but it certainly wasn't the same. And since we attended different schools our contact became less and less frequent. They weren't allowed to see me, and I certainly wasn't allowed to come over and see them—or even meet up with them in a planned, non-clandestine visit.

My only regret about my decision to leave home, and I mean the only regret, was that I abandoned my brothers. It really bothered me then, and it did for years after. Clearly this was an unintended consequence, but it affected me just the same.

After my long stint of crashing with friends and even spending a few nights on the steps of the Nelson Atkins Museum, I rented a house by myself. From living in a tiny house with four other people and sharing a bedroom with two of them, I now lived alone for the first time in my life.

Completely unchecked (within the bounds of being a student in good standing at Bishop Hogan High School) I quickly morphed into a full-blown hippie. This involved growing my hair out, acquiring an updated and trendy wardrobe, and, predictably, using marijuana.

During my senior year, Sister Agnes Virginia called me into her office with what she thought was exciting news. She happily explained that the following day an admissions officer from Notre Dame University was coming, and he wanted to meet with me.

I asked, in my best smart-ass way, what for? *Why would I want to go to college there?* She patiently explained that Notre Dame was looking to "ethnically diversify", and that I was being considered for admittance.

What is this? *They need to get some Negroes?*

I told her no thanks, but she pleaded with me just to meet with the man. He was traveling all the way from Indiana, and this was a huge opportunity not to be missed. Reluctantly I agreed to meet with the admissions officer, not for myself, but because I wanted to appease Sister Agnes Virginia. This seemed to be a really big deal for her.

The next day at school, I patiently and politely heard the man's pitch. When he was finally finished, he earnestly asked me what I thought. I replied that I thought he only wanted me because I was black. And that was the end of my academic recruitment by the Fighting Irish.

I actually can now sympathize with this poor guy, who seemed decent enough. His job was to find black Catholics in the United States with the academic credentials to attend Notre Dame, and in the late 1960s there weren't that damn many of us out there!

But I wasn't going to be his Jackie Robinson. No thank you.

By the closing stages of my senior year I no longer really cared that much about school. And I had figured out that I didn't have to care that much about it, and yet I could still get great grades. Case in point: marijuana had led me to acid, and eventually to taking a biology test while tripping on acid–which I passed.

My band was booking paid gigs almost every Friday and Saturday night across Kansas City. And I would often play with other musicians in the park on Sunday, in impromptu jam sessions. I absolutely loved it all. And I loved the independence and freedom of living alone, even though I missed LaFrance and LaVance.

As the son of a father who always prized education, traditional education suddenly didn't really matter to me anymore. I started studying the doctrine of the Black Panthers, which I found incredibly intriguing. Antiwar protesting appealed to me as well. Even though I was a lifelong smart-ass, I had never once been a rebel. But rebellion was now on my mind. I was making money, I had friends, I found school incredibly easy, and I didn't feel the need to follow any set path.

I could only imagine what my father would have said had he learned that I told Notre Dame, "No." But he was no longer in my life. It was all me.

Chapter
8

The New KCI Part 2

Prior to the vote for the new airport I received a call from Ray Kowalik, CEO of Burns & McDonnell, the Kansas City-based engineering, architecture, and construction firm. He told me that he had an out-of-the-box idea for the airport, and wanted to meet. So we agreed to meet for lunch with Ray and his group.

With me at this lunch meeting were City Manager Troy Schulte, Finance Director Randy Landes, Councilwoman and Airport Committee Chair Jolie Justus, and my Chief of Staff Joni Wickham. Ray brought Mike Merriman, along with their attorneys and other staff. We were told that they had a possible plan to privately finance, design, and construct the entire airport project. Ray further explained that Burns & McDonnell had already spent a great deal of time and money on this bold plan, but didn't want to go any further without knowing if this proposal interested us. And he said that he had to speak to the major airlines about all of this as well.

I told him that I while we were intrigued, they'd have to present us with a lot more information regarding exactly how this would work. And I let Ray know that we wouldn't discuss this again until after the impending vote on the GO Bond for infrastructure.

Shortly after the successful GO Bond vote, Ray reached out and brought us up to date, and said that he wanted to continue our conversation. So we scheduled another meeting with Ray and his core team at Burns & McDonnell. They let us know that since we had last met they had refined their numbers, and felt more confident than ever that they could handle the entire new airport project through this private finance plan.

My staff, the City Manager, and I all agreed that this proposal had serious merit, and was potentially a great idea. Because of the private financing, it would now be clearer than ever that no tax money would be used, no existing taxes would increase, and no new taxes would be levied for the airport. The financing of the new KCI would never have used tax dollars, because airports are built from funds generated by airports. Citizens, however, were usually confused about this, and Ray and his team's plan could potentially end that confusion.

Additionally, we loved that Burns & McDonnell is a Kansas City company, and would be the sole source of funding, design, and construction. Before I was mayor, Kansas City's new downtown arena, Sprint Center, was built by a firm from Minneapolis. This caused outrage locally, and I didn't want to repeat that misstep of a previous administration at City Hall.

This seemed like a dream scenario. Burns & McDonnell is highly respected in our community, they're assuming all of the risk, and they're fully committed to using partners and labor from across the Kansas City metropolitan area. All that was left was to discuss this with the City Council to see if they liked the idea, and then if so, it seemed as though everything could move forward.

Our desperately needed replacement for the antiquated KCI finally seemed to be moving from wishful thinking to reality.

Nothing of course is this simple in politics. Upon being informed of the Burns & McDonnell plan, one of the City Council members called our local daily newspaper, the *Kansas City Star*, and told them that we had engaged in a "backroom deal" to build the new airport.

My first thought was, *Bullshit! If this is a backroom deal, then why did we tell the City Council?*

We got word from a member of the Chamber of Commerce that he'd received a call from the *Kansas City Star's* main political reporter, Dave Helling. In this call, Helling revealed that he was going to run a story exposing this supposedly nefarious contract unless someone went to the *Star's* offices to meet with him about this.

So, reluctantly, but absolutely needing to set the record straight, Troy and I met with Helling and the *Kansas City Star's* editorial board at the newspaper's offices.

Helling started in on me about everything that I had done wrong in our discussions with Burns & McDonnell. He was aggressive and accusatory, which quite frankly pissed me off. Finally, I stopped him and said calmly, "Dave, it sounds to me like you don't want a new airport."

"I do want a new airport!" he yelled, and then slammed his fist into the conference table around which we all sat. "I just want transparency!"

We then explained to Helling and the editorial board how the issue had arisen, and that representatives of Burns & McDonnell were in the process of a conducting a series of meetings with the City Council. But they'd never had the chance to finish this process, as after the very first such meeting a member of the Council had called the newspaper.

There was now a meeting in two days' time with the major airlines to inform them of how this would all work, and to see if they thought the plan had merit. If the airlines didn't have any interest in this unique scenario, then it would be a complete nonstarter. So, we asked that they please hold off on their story until after our meeting with the airline executives in 48 hours.

Dave's response was a firm and unequivocal *NO!* With this meeting having achieved nothing and having been contentious throughout, I was definitely fired up when we departed. As I headed to the elevator, Officer Casey Jones, a member of my security team, told me, "Mayor, Dave Helling just called you an asshole." Now my fuse was really lit. I then immediately began to retrace my steps, and found Helling standing with a few of his colleagues.

Walking right up to him, I announced, "So I'm an asshole, Dave?"

Completely mortified, Helling immediately denied that he'd said this.

"Yeah you did, but that's ok," I responded, "because you're an asshole too."

I then turned away and walked back toward the elevators, never hearing Helling say anther word.

In the next day's edition of the *Kansas City Star* an editorial ran under the headline "Another KCI debacle? This is why people don't trust government."

The meeting with the major airlines went extremely well, as they all expressed interest in the Burns & McDonnell plan, and told us that they'd like to explore the potential deal. But real damage had been done from the *Kansas City Star's* scathing editorial, as the City Council was now all fired up.

Suddenly we were inundated by Council members who said that they needed to be engaged in the entire process, every step of the way. The main problem with this rests in the policy developed over the years, which basically tries to limit elected officials meddling in the procurement of multimillion-dollar contracts. People have gone to prison for this type of thing.

But apparently the procurement rules didn't apply to this City Council, especially one councilman in particular. He was going to be the champion of transparency, and the one who saved the day. After less than one year in office, he declared that he didn't have faith that the city's legal department was competent to handle this project. As such, Lucas convinced enough of his colleagues that outside law firms needed to be retained. The City Council then approved a local firm, and another from New York with a billing rate of $600 per hour plus expenses. At our first meeting four of their attorneys traveled to Kansas City, and three of them never said a word, aside from introducing themselves. In fact, I never saw those three again. I still have no idea what any of them did, other than send us a massive bill.

The Kansas City firm we retained was deemed to be lacking in diversity, so then an area minority law firm was brought in as well. The total cost for the legal services of these three firms was more than $1.5 million.

Our own legal department would not only have been free, because they already work for the city, but they were fully capable of determining to what extent they needed the assistance of outside counsel on this project. They definitely didn't need any outside interference from a fledgling councilman. It's what they do all of the time.

This was a real and disrespectful kick in the ass. Our internal lawyers are the experts on municipal law; it's what they do. The people who were absolutely needed on the new airport deal were right there in our building, and yet they were basically told that they weren't competent to do their job.

Burns & McDonnell, along with three other firms, submitted proposals for the new airport. This trio was comprised of the Los Angeles-based AECOM, Edgemoor Infrastructure and Real Estate, which was headquartered in Bethesda, Maryland outside of Washington, D.C., and BlueScope Construction from here in Kansas City.

By this point the City Council was demanding to be fully involved in the entire procurement process, which involved attending every meeting and reading every proposal. Procurement rules were designed so that the city manager, the heads of the various city departments involved, and the chairpersons and one representative of the affected City Council committees (in this case the Transportation and Infrastructure Committee and the Airport Committee) would be the active participants in dealing with these proposals and contracts.

But when it came to the new airport, the procurement rules somehow didn't apply. The entire City Council wanted to have their seat at the table, literally and figuratively.

And of course, some City Council members started getting a little too close to a few of the bidders, and started to advocate for them a little too hard. This is exactly what should not happen, and exactly why you have procurement rules in the first place.

Funny enough, the opposite happened as well. Because if you attend one presentation, then you have to attend all of them; and because if you read one proposal, then you have to read all of them. Natural selection took hold. Some of these City Council members, who were so adamant that they must be involved in every step of the way with the new airport, were confronted with the reality that this involved a lot of work. Apparently the procurement rules did apply to them after all, as they no longer wanted to be involved in this aspect of the project. I had declared early on that I would not engage in the process at all, as I had full confidence in how this would all proceed.

The process of dealing with the array of bidders and their proposals was an experience unto itself. One would think that these firms, all of which are highly accomplished, would have their act together. But this often wasn't the case. One company's plan involved demolishing the existing KCI Airport Marriott and building the new terminal on that site. This had nothing to do with anything that had ever been discussed. They were immediately eliminated.

Burns & McDonnell, who raised the issue of private finance, decided to run their bid proposal like a political campaign. They actually held a pep rally in the Power & Light District, one of our city's main entertainment zones.

This looked too much like a victory celebration when they had not won anything. It would only serve to piss off the City Council members who were still actively involved in the process.

In the end, though, none of this mattered. Bond counsel reviewed their clarification work, and opined that something in there violated our general bond law. Our bond counsel told us that Burns & McDonnell had to be disqualified immediately, and they were.

Of the four companies who had responded to the RFP/Q (Request for Proposal and Qualifications), only AECOM and Edgemoor were now left. Ultimately, Edgemoor was awarded the contract to build Kansas City's new $1.5 billion state-of-the-art airport. Their bid includes Edgemoor's parent company, Clark Construction, and the independent Kansas City firm Clarkson Construction. The only nay votes came from those who had advocated for AECOM and Burns & McDonnell during the lengthy bid process.

But this didn't mean that the bulldozers and earth-moving equipment would be working immediately. Not even close.

The first hurdle to be cleared was an environmental assessment from the FAA. Apparently when KCI was originally built, there was concern that it had been done so on land which had been used as both Native American and slave burial grounds. Although this issue had previously been studied and resolved during both the original KCI construction and a subsequent runway expansion, an advocacy group still voiced their renewed concerns.

For the construction on the new airport, the proper steps were now taken to make certain that no graves would be disturbed. To conduct and complete this assessment, numerous Native American tribes and organizations had to be engaged and to ultimately sign off. Happily, KCI was never on burial grounds, so this was resolved. It just took a long time to reach that point.

Next up was the issue of baggage at the new airport. Make that a fight about the baggage system at the new airport. At KCI every airline operates their own baggage loading and unloading systems. But at the new airport, this will all be unified. The project's operational cost is projected at $20 million annually. The contentious question at hand was, *How much will every airline pay toward this $20 million?* The big airlines proposed payment percentages that the smaller airlines thought inequitable. Instead, the smaller airlines wanted to pay a reduced percentage based upon a formula they thought was reflective of their usage. So, for example, American Airlines operates more flights and has more passengers than Spirit Airlines, and thus handles more baggage.

I really didn't care who paid what; I just wanted it to be figured out so that we could keep everything moving forward. But the protracted negotiations eventually stalled out. So, I called a meeting with the airline representatives and asked them if they had come to an agreement. They informed us that they hadn't, and that they wanted the city's aviation department to decide who would pay what on the baggage system. I asked them if they were certain, and if they wouldn't instead rather pursue mediation or arbitration. When it came to the cost of the baggage system, the only thing on which the airlines were in total agreement was they wanted the aviation department to decide the payment obligations.

I again asked the airline execs if they were absolutely certain that they wanted us to make this decision, as I knew that we could be in store for a major blowback on this highly contentious issue. Again, they all assured me that all of them–every carrier, big and small–felt that this was the best approach.

As the meeting was wrapping up, I gave everyone one final chance to back out. I again offered that they work together to solve the baggage cost situation, and then tell us how they'd like to proceed. And if not, then arbitration and mediation were both readily available.

The response was a unified chorus of "*We want the city to make the call.*"

A few weeks later, after diligent work had been completed, the aviation department went back to the airlines with a cost-sharing proposal for the new terminal central baggage system.

The airlines immediately balked. They had problems with the plan, and wanted to further negotiate the issue. I couldn't even muster the strength to argue.

We were then informed by the airline executives that they didn't fully trust the numbers on the cost of construction for the new airport. They all felt that the projections were likely off.

I reminded them that an outside independent agency had already checked the numbers and issued a report stating everything was accurate. That didn't matter though, as the airlines now wanted a second outside independent agency to repeat this process.

Reluctantly I agreed, but with the caveat that if this second group said the numbers looked good, then the airlines would all be ready to move forward. The answer was *"Yes"* all around, and so the cost projections were run once again.

And once again, the numbers were deemed on point. This second agency reported that they were accurate within "2.9 percent," which is well within the acceptable margin of error.

Edgemoor was required to provide what's known as *the maximum guaranteed price.* This is a number which, if executed, places the developer at risk for the overage. Of course it's extremely difficult to give an accurate GMP (guaranteed maximum price) when the design and engineering work is not completely finished. Thus, the GMP builds a level of contingency, so as to hopefully avoid an overage. Being within 2.9 percent of the GMP this far out is as good as you're ever going to get. It was still higher than the comfort level of the airlines though. I did, however, understand their point of view, since the airlines are to a great extent responsible for contributing revenue to pay off the construction of the airport. Regardless, they now wanted $100 million cut from the total budget.

I did remind the airlines that the total budget had ballooned because they included items such as more gates, increased space for the tarmac, and room for future terminal expansion.

After more delay and negotiation, the seven largest airlines involved with the new airport finally agreed to the specifics of the $1.5 billion single terminal, rather than the original $1.6 billion. The momentum toward the new airport had become so strong that there was no way it was now going to be stopped.

The Airport Committee unanimously recommended and then the City Council approved the issuance of $90 million in bonds to get construction officially underway. On March 25, 2019, I attended the ground-breaking ceremony for the new single-terminal Kansas City International Airport. Joining me were numerous airline officials, business and community leaders, politicians, media members, and private citizens—a few hundred people in total.

Given the opportunity to speak, I said that Kansas City is no longer an understudy to anybody with this new airport. This state-of-the-art terminal would showcase to the world exactly the type of progressive and thriving city that we are.

And I said to the assembled crowd, "We used to be known as a city that would never miss an opportunity to miss an opportunity. That is no longer the case."

Many naysayers have since suggested that, and others have asked if, I want the new KCI named after me. My answer has never wavered. Getting my name on an airport was never my goal. I wanted a new KCI that generates more flights and revenue and that satisfies the needs of our business and leisure travelers. I wanted a proper front door for our great city. This airport was never about me; it was about all of us as a city, and as a community stretching across multiple counties and a state line. I'm extremely proud that while in office I was able to help deliver to Kansas City the airport that it truly deserves. What it's called has never mattered to me in the least.

Looking back, I have two major takeaways from the entire ordeal of working years to bring the new airport to reality.

The first is that not everything in government can be immediately transparent. To achieve that lofty goal we'd have to alert the media, the City Council, and the public every time someone first calls us with an idea. We were elected to vet ideas and present proposals to the public. Our job is not to do so with every thought presented to us in an embryonic stage.

We all felt that the initial private financing deal pitched by Burns & McDonnell could be a great thing for Kansas City. But in our very preliminary discussions we were accused of lacking transparency. And that is when the shit hit the fan. Just look at everything that followed.

Some things are better off not being seen, and not everybody has to see everything. Once you elect people to do a job, then you have to step back and trust them to do their job. Every single person doesn't have to weigh in on every single thought. If you want this type of system, then get ready for paralysis, because nothing is ever going to get accomplished.

We wanted to fully explore the inventive proposal from Burns & McDonnell, but that wasn't ultimately possible because we were accused of "backroom dealings" before we even had a chance. So we went the RFP/Q route, and in that phase Burns & McDonnell got themselves disqualified. There was then a huge outcry, because apparently the public had wanted to go with "the hometown team" all along.

I discussed all of this with the *Star's* Dave Helling over an arranged lunch, after that contentious meeting with my staff and his editorial board. But this get-together became uncomfortable, just as the one at the newspaper's offices.

"I feel like there's tension between us," Helling said to me.

"Yes there is," I responded, "because you made me out to be a dishonest and sneaky person. I don't care if you criticize what I do, or what I think, or the plan that I propose. But when you act as though I've done something under the table, then that's attacking my character and my name. I've worked my entire life to ensure that I always act ethically, and you tried to ruin this with one article that wasn't even true."

"I'm sorry that you feel this way," Helling replied. "But that's my job."

I didn't buy that then, and I don't buy it now. Even after we explained the circumstances of how everything had transpired, Helling continued with the same derogatory themes. And he not so subtly tried to take credit for what he called "an improved result." Start your own fire, put it out, and then declare yourself a hero. Clever.

My other main takeaway with the new airport is that while most people don't like the way things are, they really hate change. And within reluctance resides a high level of apathy.

There's this feeling that persists of *My house is good, so why should I care about anyone else's house.* As mayor, my job was to care about every single house in my city. We live in a community, not a collection of individuals.

Chapter
9

Marriage and the Marines

I wasn't sure if I was going to attend my Bishop Hogan High School graduation ceremony. It was 1969, and my attitude was that of the vast majority of my generation: "Who cares?" Now I don't mean "Who cares?" on the big issues of the day: Vietnam, civil rights, racial equality, sexual liberation. It was "Who cares?" about convention.

I just wanted my diploma, not to walk across the stage in a formal stodgy ceremony. But then I figured that I'd do it. For all of my recent embrace of hippie counterculturalism, I had always loved school, and I'd always been an excellent student, going back to my earliest days of kindergarten. School had reliably been another home for me and often my escape–when I lived with Alice Lewis and her family, when I lived with my father and mother, and now that I was living on my own. So I walked across the stage in cap and gown, and received my high school diploma alongside my friends and classmates. Unlike them, however, I was alone that night. There were no James family members in the audience to cheer my name. My father didn't go, which made sense since we weren't speaking and had no contact of any kind. So this meant of course that Melva wasn't there, nor were the two people whom I really wanted to see: LaFrance and LaVance.

Instead of then being taken out to a post-graduation ceremony dinner, or being the guest of honor at a party, or being feted in other some way by family, I went back home alone to the house that I rented at the corner of 40th and Warwick in the Midtown area of the city.

Looking back, I have no idea how I was able, financially or practically, to rent a house on my own while still a high school student. But of course I did, and I did it completely by myself.

My steady gigs with our band somehow provided the income that I needed to pay the rent, as well as all of my bills, plus leave a bit extra for fun. We continued to grow in popularity, so much so that we attracted the attention of somebody claiming to be from the estate of Amelia Earhart, or her foundation or some such thing. This person threatened us with legal action unless we changed the name immediately. Thus, The Amelia Earhart Memorial Flying Band was redubbed Manchester Trafficway.

I didn't have a car, and I didn't have a roommate. A car would have been useful, but a roommate was not something that I ever sought. After a lifetime of sharing bedrooms and bathrooms in cramped houses, I adored the freedom of movement and the quiet of an empty home. Besides, all of my friends and peers were high school students who of course were with their families. I was the only one who actually needed a place to live.

My post-high school life quickly evolved into one of playing music, hanging out with friends, and just running around and being a kid with no real responsibilities or long-term plans. It was during this time that I met Karen, the woman who would become my first wife.

Karen and I started living together and moved into a nicer house located in the Hyde Park district, just west of 39th Street. We rented the bottom floor and had the band over almost nightly. No one ever complained about our rehearsals and jam sessions, allowing our residence to become party central. This was a great time.

The lone negative was Karen's mom, who refused to come inside our home for the sole reason that her white daughter was with a black man. Whenever she came over to see Karen, which was often, she'd sit outside in her car and honk the horn. Then Karen would dutifully come outside, and off they'd go. Finally, I said *Bullshit, this isn't happening any longer!*

So begrudgingly, and because of my insistence, Karen stood up to her mom and told her that she'd have to come inside moving forward. And Karen's mom did, although with obvious reluctance. She was never warm to me, and barely cordial. After hearing her tell us that "blackbirds and redbirds don't mix," I knew all too clearly just what type of person I was dealing with. But at least she was no longer parked on the street in front of our house and blowing that damn horn.

Karen and I were married in October 1970, when I was 19 and she was heavily pregnant. Suddenly life wasn't so carefree. When our son Eric was born soon after our wedding, officiated by the father of my friend and bandmate Steve Hauser, I knew that I had to earn money above what my burgeoning music career would generate.

I got a job working for Avon, in their warehouse located off of Prospect Avenue. Every day I would load trailers and box up products destined to be dispersed across the country. And most every night I would play music. But the economic realities of three people, one of whom is a baby, are of course far different from that of a single guy. The backdrop of this was the Vietnam War, which felt to me like a looming storm.

I had a fairly high draft number and knew that it was only a matter of time before I was called. So, I began to look for a way to get out of military service, and avoid being part of the war that I detested.

Being a married man with a young son did not make me draft-exempt. And I didn't have anything that would make me ineligible for service, such as a health issue or physical ailment. The idea of being in the United States military didn't really bother me. It was the idea of being in the United States military on active duty in Vietnam that did.

Looking for alternatives and solutions to this problem that was weighing very heavy on my mind, I met with the Coast Guard. They weren't interested in me, however, so that was a non-starter. So, I then visited a Marine recruiter and told him flat out that I didn't want to be in-country in Vietnam. The answer, he told me, was to enlist for more than two years. This, he assured me, would make it extremely likely that I would be stationed elsewhere, away from the war zone.

I then asked him for how many years would I need to enlist. "Four years or six years," was his reply. I took four years, and signed my enlistment papers on the spot. When I told Karen of my decision later that day she was extremely upset, to say the least. I'd gone to the Marine Corps recruiting station without telling her, and so all of this was a complete surprise. She definitely knew that I was extremely worried about being drafted, and that this worry was taking over my life. And she knew that I was continually looking for alternatives. But my young bride had no idea that her husband would leave home that morning as a civilian, and return that afternoon as an enlistee in the United States Marine Corps. A year out of high school, I was now a husband, a father, and a Marine, headed to boot camp in San Diego.

The trip to Southern California from Kansas City was the first flight of my life. I'd never even seen an airplane up close, let alone actually flown on one. My welcome upon landing, like that of all of my fellow young recruits, was to be bum-rushed by the drill instructors, and ordered to stand on the yellow footprints in the Marine Corps receiving area at the airport. They were calling us every name that I'd ever heard, and a few that I hadn't, from a distance a few inches away from our respective faces. This scared the holy crap out of me, as it did everyone else.

We were then loaded onto buses and instructed to stay absolutely silent.

Don't talk, don't smoke, don't eat, don't drink, don't move. Upon arrival on base we were hustled off of the buses and into Quonset huts.

These were basic buildings with curved corrugated steel roofs. Inside was our new home: beds (racks in Marine speak, called bunks in the Army and Navy), footlockers, a bathroom, and well, not much else.

Completely intimidated and utterly disoriented, we were ordered to unpack, and to absolutely not smoke. Now this was an era when a lot of guys in this age group of late teens and early 20s were heavy cigarette smokers. So of course, some idiot decided to sneak a smoke anyway.

With that, the drill instructor came barging in, made a show of smelling the air, and screamed, "Alright bitches, saddle up!"

None of us knew how he could have smelled that lone cigarette from outside, and of course he hadn't. By this stage of his Marine Corps career, our drill instructor was well-versed on the realities of scared young boys, whisked from their hometowns across the country and into this godforsaken Quonset hut. It was wholly inevitable, and thus wholly predictable to our drill instructor, that at least one of us was going to defy this early and simple order, and light up anyway.

None us knew as well what "saddle up" meant, but we quickly found out. We were forcefully told to put on our shoes, as we hadn't even been issued our gear yet, and get out onto the adjacent asphalt road. Our drill instructor then led us on a merciless five-mile run. Guys were puking, faking injury, begging for help. Our drill instructor didn't want to hear any of this. It seemed as though he didn't care.

But what I quickly learned was that he was actually teaching us how to survive in combat. What if the enemy saw the flash of a lighter, smelled the tobacco smoke in the air, or found a cigarette butt on the ground? We could all be killed, because of one person's reckless and thoughtless actions.

The lesson of course was that if one person messes up, then everyone quite possibly would pay the price. In battle, that price very likely could be death. Here at boot camp, that price was a punishing run.

Our drill instructors, and all drill instructors, knew that they had to instill a self-policing attitude in their young recruits. It wasn't theory or doctrine; it was really a matter of life and death. Very soon after, when one person did something wrong, the drill instructors didn't have to say anything or do anything. We would take care of the matter ourselves. And make no mistake, it was generally not in a pleasant way.

But on this first night in the Marines, away from my wife, my baby son, my band, my friends, my city, none of this really mattered. All that I knew was that I was exhausted to the point of nausea, which was piled on top of my already overwhelmed senses. I had always been able to adapt my entire life. A new family, a new home, a new school, a new job–no problem. But this was something very, very different. Suddenly the prospect of being the token black guy at Notre Dame didn't seem that bad.

Chapter 10

Partisan Party Politics

As I'm sure you've been able to determine by now, I'm no fan of party politics. Let me go one step further: I hate party politics. They are ineffective, because they do not allow for sustainable solutions to chronic problems.

Instead, party politics are all about winning. A cycle has formed around this, in that the candidate running against the incumbent (regardless of who is the Democrat and who is the Republican), will always try to separate themselves from the incumbent. And the way that they do this is to trash whatever programs the incumbent has been involved in. Then of course the incumbent makes promises as to the changes that they will enact if reelected.

Take the situation of the Affordable Care Act (ACA). If you believe that it is more socially desirable and advantageous for as many people as possible to have access to health care, then your actions as a politician should be to make the ACA as good as it can possibly be. Clearly, the ACA was far from perfect. It was a flawed system, no doubt. Things did not function nearly as well or move as efficiently as planned.

So then it's imperative that our elected officials work to tweak it, change it, and ultimately make it better. The goal should be to give more people more access to health care at a lower cost. Yet as soon as the ACA was unveiled, it became an issue of political ideology. Because this was a plan of President Obama, the Republicans were immediately and reflexively opposed to it. And they made a vow to get rid of it, simply because it came from the opposing party's president.

The cost of not having health care is extremely high, not just for the individual when medical situations and emergencies arise, but also for society as a whole. This seems indisputable to me. Yet this became nothing more than a political issue: us vs them. Them vs us. The ACA became a Republican platform campaign for the 2016 elections, and it was a foundation of Donald Trump's presidential campaign. The Republicans wanted to get rid of the ACA, rather than work with the Democrats to make it better.

Instead of trying to find a sustainable solution to the chronic problem of lack of access to health care, the Republicans wanted to do away with the ACA altogether. And they did so with no alternative plan.

If you've made campaign promises, then the first thing that you're going to do when you get into office is attempt to fulfill those promises, whether they make sense or not. Then you can say to your voters, "Look, I kept all of my campaign promises."

Then during the next round of elections, the politicians go out on the campaign trail and tell the public, "See, I told you that I was going to do all of these things, and I did."

But almost nobody ever asks about the impact of all of this. Well, I ask those questions, and I'm now going to answer this particular one myself.

The impact of the whole debacle with the ACA is that fewer people had access to health care. And those who did found it much more difficult to navigate the market. So in the end, society wasn't served, but political ideology was. There was no genuine attempt to ask, "What can we do to solve this problem?"

Campaign promises are the bane of the people. They are the polar opposite of meeting society's needs. Campaign promises instead meet the needs of the politicians in their drive to be elected.

When you have a system such as this, then everybody is going to make all types of promises, they're all going to fight, and then retreat back to their respective corners of political ideology. And nothing is going to get accomplished. Right now in this country we're fully in the midst of this system. Nothing ever gets done. Not on the state level and not on the federal level.

A major tax cut is initiated, but it only benefits the wealthiest Americans. Yet it sounds good to the masses, regardless of their income level. And then the politicians can say that this was a campaign promise fulfilled. But this is really nothing more than a shiny object, and one that will last for only a few years. Then it disappears, and nothing was ever achieved long-term. Absolutely nothing. Taxes go back up, and society makes up the difference in the shortfall of money.

What ever happened to all of the talk about *not leaving massive amounts of debt for our children and grandchildren?* The Republicans were a deficit hawk party, and then they created more debt through tax cuts. Finding a sustainable solution to all of our country's debt would have made sense. But that's not what they did. Instead, the Trump-led Republicans followed their campaign promises of reducing taxes. And the people who actually saw their taxes reduced were not the true electorate, but those massive donors who helped put these candidates into office: the rich, the powerful, the well-heeled.

Regular people, Republicans and Democrats (and everyone else), won't ever see the true benefits of that tax cut.

There is clearly a massive and chronic problem in the United States with wage gap and wage stagnation. It's real, and I saw it every day with the people I served as mayor. I see it every day now as a private citizen. The people at the top of the food chain are continually fed more, and those at the bottom of the chain are at best fed the same, and more likely fed less. Until we find the way to break the culture of campaign promises and start addressing real issues, then we are going to continue to have big problems.

Local government cannot cure poverty. And it can't cure crime. Both issues are intrinsically linked, and mixed together with things like lack of education, unemployment, and racism. None of this is being addressed on the national level. There's a lot of lip service given, sure. But there are no viable programs out there. In order to have programs that are sustainable, the Democrats and Republicans have to work together. Right now they couldn't work together to choose the same restaurant for lunch. Not that they'd eat together if they could.

Because of this situation, this reality, I have major problems with both parties. Even though I served as mayor through a nonpartisan electoral system, I'm a Democrat. A lifelong Democrat. I believe in Democratic principles and philosophies. But the Democratic Party now sufferers from the same inertia as the Republican Party.

While the Republicans were attacking the ACA head-on, the Democrats chose to double down on letting the GOP do so as a political strategy. They didn't acknowledge that there were flaws in the ACA and then offer solutions to remedy those flaws. The Democrats had the opportunity to put forth a positive message and approach as to how the ACA could be fixed. This was a chance to juxtapose the Republican message of dumping the ACA entirely. Yet this huge opportunity–to work toward a positive solution–was missed by the Democrats. Rather than offer equitable solutions to the problems with the ACA, the Democrats waited for the entire situation to blow up in Trump's and the Republicans' respective faces. It was not a move to do something for the people who needed it the most. I have a real problem with this.

As a society we know what our problems are. Our leaders, however, are not finding solutions to these problems. They're not even *working* to find the solutions. What they are doing is working to be reelected. Whether Republican or Democrat, whether on the state or federal level, they all spout the same bullshit. They all follow their party's line. And these party lines are leading us off the cliff.

I'm asked constantly if I'm going to get back into electoral politics. My answer is an unequivocal NO. I ran for, was elected, and then reelected mayor of Kansas City as a nonpartisan. I wasn't beholden to any political party or special interest group. Instead, I had the freedom to act based on the facts and the data at hand. And with this, I was able to lead.

Chapter 11

Boot Camp

Marine boot camp was the most physically challenging experience of my life. They ran our asses to death. The drill instructors would come into our Quonset hut in the very early morning while we were still asleep, and announce that we had five minutes to "shit, shower, and shave." It didn't matter that I actually didn't have any need for a razor. First and foremost—there was no "I" in this equation.

Sir, the private doesn't shave, sir. Well, the private was going to shave, even if he had to take the blade out of the razor and scrape the shaving cream from his tender face. Then we'd go off, still half-asleep, on yet another punishing predawn run. After lunch it was the obstacle course, which still gives me nightmares. It was in a word, brutal. And then more running, always more running.

And if even just one of us screwed up, like the recruit who defied orders by smoking on our first day, it would be a five-mile run just before bedtime.

You lived by their code—the code of the United States Marine Corps.

Our drill instructors were straight from a Marine recruiting poster. Come to think of it, every drill instructor I saw looked this way. They all must have been cloned from some crazed gung-ho WWII prototype.

We had Sgt. Bland and Staff Sgt. Dennington, both of whom had already served two tours of duty in Vietnam. They were hard as nails. Sgt. Bland was a wiry black guy, 5-10, probably 180 pounds. Tough as hell. Staff Sgt. Dennington was a thicker built 6-1, with a square jaw, blue eyes, and blond hair. Absolutely no give in him whatsoever.

Every day was filled with our two drill instructors teaching us weapons, and drill, and the philosophy of "leave no man behind." There was constant physical training, and constant mental abuse.

Rare was the occasion when we were called by our actual names. Instead, we all had nicknames assigned to us by Sgt. Bland and Staff Sgt. Dennington. There was Private Bitch Lips, Private Bastard Eyes, and Private Ass Hole. Sometimes these nicknames were interchangeable. Never once did they call us Marines. This was crystal clear: we weren't Marines until we finished boot camp, *if* we finished boot camp. And this was to be understood at all times.

The insults and abuse were spouted just inches from our face, to of course increase the intimidation factor. And God forbid that we actually made eye contact during the shouting and berating. *Get your Goddamn eyeballs off of me! Are you looking at me?!*

Worse still was to use the word "you." The drill instructors would immediately convert this to "ewe," and ask us if we thought that they were sheep. And then they told us what we surely did with sheep, and what they would do to us if we were sheep. None of it was pleasant.

Very quickly, the separation among all of us opened widely into two distinct groups. I thankfully was in the group that was adapting and progressing. Not that I loved any of it mind you, but I could do all of it. And so I did. But there were other kids who were overweight, unathletic, mentally weak, or just simply not cut out for life in the Marine Corps. And these kids were failing miserably.

Our drill instructors were looking to see how we dealt with those kids who were dying on the vine. What were we going to do with them? How would they be treated by the rest of us? Would these weak links be helped or abandoned?

Very quickly we learned to support those who needed it the most. Because if just one person failed, then we were all punished. So, our good deeds were not out of kindness or altruism, but rather self-preservation.

If you finished the obstacle course and looked back to see someone lagging far behind, then you would go back and help them. Occasionally the drill instructors would change things up and order you to ignore them, and leave this person to their own devices. As much as we needed to help the weakest, slowest, and most incompetent of our group, they also had to develop a sense of self-reliance. It was an amazingly tricky dynamic and a delicate balance, all created with the intent to keep us from getting ourselves and each other killed when it counted for real.

Initially, we weren't allowed to blouse our boots. The Army tucks their pant legs into their boots, but the Marines use metal springs that clip around the boots so that the pant legs could then be pulled in underneath them. But seeing as weren't actually Marines, at least not yet, this was forbidden. And we were forbidden from starching our caps. To the drill instructors, we were all a bunch of idiots who didn't know jack shit. The truth is that they were right.

We were required to drill incessantly. It never stopped. The drill field must have been the size of five football fields. Absolutely massive. And it was constantly filled with companies and platoons doing nothing but drilling. There was a drill competition that we all had to pass at the end of boot camp, but that seemed like years away.

In this first phase of boot camp we were required to march arm in arm. We literally locked arms with those to our left and right, and marched as a group. There was no individuality at all. We'd catch a glimpse of the guys in second- and third-phase drilling, and wonder when we would ever be that sharp. Or God help us, if we would ever be that sharp at all. These were guys our age who had literally beaten us to boot camp by a matter of weeks. But they seemed like hardened veterans to our naive eyes.

In second phase the drill instructors started assigning us to leadership billets. They picked from our ranks the squad leaders and the platoon guidon. For some unknown reason, the platoon guidon was the most coveted position. Mystifying, as being the platoon guidon was a bitch. The job entailed being the lead man in formation, carrying the platoon banner. Go out for a five-mile run while carrying an eight-foot flagpole. Now whatever you do, don't let the flag dip. Hold the flag high and straight at all times. All the while setting the pace at the front. This was the gig.

Try running even one mile without swinging your arms, and you'll get a small glimpse as to what being a guidon is like. Not for the faint of heart.

But being the platoon guidon meant that at the end of boot camp you would be directly promoted to Private First Class, while everyone else was just a Private. And that first stripe meant a higher pay grade. It was also better than being a Private. Money and prestige are motivating factors for most. They certainly were for me, so I became the platoon guidon. Crazy now, I know. But it was fun…sometimes.

Perhaps worse than the physical training and drilling were the inspections. They were an absolute bitch. Your rack had to be made up so that the drill instructors could literally bounce a quarter off of it. And if they couldn't, there was no request to do it over. Instead they would rip all of the bedding off, and furiously throw it to the floor. There was a set, perfect way in which your lockers had to be organized. Dress uniforms must be immaculately starched, with shirt sleeves turned at a precise angle. There was a designated and consistent space that had to be maintained between the hangers. Shoes and boots were required to be shined so as to meet an almost impossible standard.

Every item in your locker had its predetermined and exact location: clothes, shoes, bedding, toiletries, personal effects–all of it. If even one thing was amiss, then the entire contents of your locker were tossed out in the most dramatic of fashion.

The same thing for your footlocker. Everything had to be perfectly rolled and folded. And yet nothing was ever quite right. I came to understand that there was no way to actually pass inspection. It was a rigged game. Instead of creating order, barracks inspections meant disorder, as everybody's stuff was strewn across the floor once the drill instructors had come through. And then you'd get ten minutes to put everything back together, and try again. So not only did you learn to do things as well as possible, you also learned to do them as fast as possible.

This need for speed extended to eating. When we'd go for chow in the morning the rule was that the drill instructors ate first, then everyone lined up behind them. Everyone, apart from the squad leaders and platoon guidon. They didn't get their food until everyone else had been served, with the guidon–me–always in last position.

Chow time officially started when the drill instructors began eating, so by the time I sat down at the table I only had the opportunity for a few bites of food. Once the drill instructors stood up and headed for the door, we all knew to stop eating and move outside for formation. This happened every single day. Those of us in leadership positions, and thus at the back of the line, learned very quickly to kick those in the ass who were not moving with expediency. Their lollygagging meant our empty stomachs.

The drill instructors weren't stupid. They knew that we had to eat. And it wasn't by accident that the squad leaders and platoon guidon were put at the end of the line. Sometimes they would read the room and linger a bit after their plates were empty. It was all just another covert exercise for us in problem solving. Literally everything that we did was, directly or indirectly, to prepare us for combat situations.

There was no such subtlety in our hand-to-hand combat training. This was always tough and often nasty. Now, pugil sticks look like fun. I can tell you from first-hand experience that they are not. In essence, a pugil stick is a giant Q-Tip made for beating your fellow man. For those of you old enough to have watched the TV show *American Gladiators* in the 1980s and '90s, you know what I'm talking about. Imagine a pole with large pads attached on both ends. This was our weapon, and our only protection was a football helmet and mouthpiece. No body padding, and certainly no athletic cup. Now take a group of frustrated and angry guys in their late teens and early twenties, give them a pugil stick, and the instructions, "Kill the enemy, and don't get killed!" Well, you can imagine what followed. We would wail on each other as though it was an actual fight to the death. Win, and stay in to face the next opponent. Lose, and you're out. The Marines wanted us to treat pugil sticks as a non-lethal version of a bayonet. Because in battle, you of course had a bayonet.

We also learned judo, with the requisite throws and chokes. The judo was incorporated into hand-to-hand fighting, and our arsenal of chokes were with bare hands, with a fixed object, or with a flexible object such as a piece of hose. Unlike being knocked out, getting choked out doesn't cause actual brain trauma (unless of course the choke is held for a prolonged period of time after the point of unconsciousness). But if you have never seen anyone choked out, nor been choked out to that point, it's definitely scary. We'd choke out our training partner, and then they would choke us out. Despite the supervision there would occasionally be someone who held their choke a bit too long, causing their now-unconscious partner to flop involuntarily on the ground while being revived. But this was all still better than inspection.

The entire experience of boot camp was brutal. Absolutely brutal. And first phase was the most brutal of all. This is not a memory from a period of my life that has grown fonder with time.

But I had completed one-third of boot camp, and while I wasn't thriving I was more than surviving. Being the platoon guidon had given me a sense of pride, as well as a sense of reassurance that I could make it in the United States Marine Corps. And if what the recruiter had told me was in fact true when I'd signed up for the four-year enlistment, once I left Southern California I'd be going someplace other than Vietnam.

Chapter 12

Data Instead of Polls

A **major driver** of partisan politics in the United States is polls. Elected officials at the state and federal levels feel that they best not act on an issue if polls say that the people won't like it. But polls are nothing more than a snapshot of an issue at a given point in time.

As mayors, we don't live by the polls. They were meaningless to me and to my staff. What we looked at were our Citizen Satisfaction Surveys. These were distributed and compiled every quarter, year after year. On a consistent basis we'd receive the data regarding what mattered to our citizenry the most. In these surveys people rank the issues that not only matter to them but also affect their daily lives. And the issues that are ranked the highest are the ones that we put forth the most time, money, and effort to address as local government.

Of course, as mayor I wanted to address every single issue that was reported. Even if something only matters to one person, it still matters. But Citizen Satisfaction Surveys allow administrations to prioritize, which is a reality of governing. When you continually see that people want the roads and bridges fixed, then it becomes imperative that the roads and bridges must be fixed. There's no ideology here, nor party politics. There's no polling or special interest groups to muddy the waters. Instead, this is direct feedback on which we took action, and on which all governments–local, state, and federal–can take action.

My staff and I heard directly from the people through our Citizen Satisfaction Surveys that the roads and bridges of Kansas City were a major problem. We used this information and other data to fashion a proposal for the purpose of raising more than $800 million over a 20-year span to address this need. While $800 million is certainly a lot of money, when looking at Kansas City, Missouri as a whole, the sum is actually a drop in the bucket. Our city spans 318 square miles, and has 6,300 lane miles of road. It also contains more than 3,000 miles of underground piping, hundreds of bridges, and $6 billion of deferred maintenance.

Under Missouri law, a vote is required to sell GO (General Obligation) Bonds. These bonds are paid for with property tax dollars, and by raising property taxes. But everything is made much more difficult and complicated because of the election schedule mandated by Missouri state law. The vote is held on the first Tuesday after the first Monday in the month, with the required approval percentage depending on the month and year in which the election is held.

The voting requirements are:

February election: 2/3rds majority in all years
April: 4/7ths majority in all years
June: 2/3rds majority in all years
August: 4/7ths majority in even-numbered years
  2/3rds majority in odd-numbered years
November: 4/7ths majority in even-numbered years
  2/3rds majority in odd-numbered years.

Frankly, I have no idea why there is such a confusing and convoluted schedule, but it is what it is. My Chief of Staff Joni Wickham and I worked for months with our City Manager Troy Schulte, and our Finance Director Randy Landes, to put the GO Bond package together. Troy worked with our Director of Public Works Sherri McIntyre and our City Attorney Bill Geary, in order to create a priority list of projects and fashion the legal ballot language. We then proposed a package of projects to the City Council, which consisted of a single vote to approve everything listed. This consisted of flood control, the construction of a new animal shelter, and repairs to roads, streets, bridges, and sidewalks, in addition to bringing all city property into compliance with the Americans with Disabilities Act (ADA).

While we vetted the proposal with the City Council, we submitted it to outside bond counsel for review. Much to our chagrin, bond counsel advised that we could not legally submit the entire list as one ballot issue, because of the differences in the types of projects we had proposed. The lawyers insisted that we had to submit three separate and independent ballots to the voters.

Question 1 consisted of $600 million for repairs to roads, streets, bridges, and sidewalks. We decided to divide that issue with $450 million allocated for repairs to roads, streets, and bridges, and $150 million for fixing the sidewalks. My Mayor Pro Tem Scott Wagner created a viable plan to address the thousands of miles of city and residential sidewalks on a priority basis.

Question 2 targeted flood control, and proposed spending $150 million in order to claim an additional $500 million in federal matching funds to address flooding issues in the Brookside residential, Westport commercial, and Dodson and Swope industrial areas.

Question 3 was for $50 million, $14 million of which would be the city's share of a public-private partnership (P3) used to build a new animal shelter. The balance would be set aside to address an unfunded federal mandate to bring our city property into ADA compliance.

An already complex campaign had become far more complicated than we could have imagined. On December 7, 2016, I took the matter directly to the voters through my blog. The campaign to pass these three ballot measures was brutal. From December 2016, until the day of the election on Tuesday, April 4, 2017, I campaigned almost nightly and virtually every weekend in an effort to get the GO Bond package passed.

Each of the three issues on the ballot needed 57 percent (4/7ths) of the vote to pass, which was a high bar indeed. We also had to push through the head winds of negative media, skeptical voters, and the ever-present CAVE people, whom I referenced earlier in this book.

In our campaign, we reminded voters that for a number of years their responses to the Citizen Satisfaction Survey had consistently listed the projects we were proposing as their highest priorities. Thankfully, our message reached the public, as Question 1 passed with 68 percent of the vote, Question 2 with 64 percent, and Question 3 with 68 percent.,

The passage of these three separate property tax increases illuminated some important differences between local government on the one hand, and state and federal governments on the other. These ballot issues were approved because we based our approach on facts, data, and direct information from the citizens. The people told us what was important to them, and we created a sustainable plan to address the longstanding and habitual chronic infrastructure problems they had identified. Both the state and federal legislatures continually talk about repairing infrastructure, but they fail to take any meaningful action. Instead they adopt a partisan position so as to avoid raising the taxes that would allow them to better address this very real problem.

As local government, we have to deliver the services our citizens demand. Mayors know that we can't wait for our state and federal governments to save us. Thus, we have to be innovative in order to get the job done. Cities like to use Citizen Satisfaction Surveys in order to find out what our constituents think and want. State and federal legislators, meanwhile, generally prefer to rely on polls as a method of deciding whether taking action, and if such action might hurt their popularity, and thus their chances for re-election.

I like local government for numerous reasons, but first and foremost because we do things, and we get things done. For me, because of this environment in which we are able to operate, serving as the mayor of a major city is the best job in politics.

Chapter 13

Becoming a United States Marine

There are two incidents that really stand out for me from the final two-thirds of my time at Marine Corps boot camp in San Diego: one funny, the other not so much.

The funny one—although it wasn't funny in the moment—occurred during an inspection for a high-ranking Marine general. It was hotter than hell, we were assembled near the airport, and it felt as though we were sucking in scorching jet exhaust every time we took a breath. We're in our dress uniforms, sweating profusely under the Southern California summer sun, as this inspection is taking forever.

Suddenly, without warning, my stomach felt queasy. At first, I thought it was the heat, but in short order I realized that this was something more. As I looked around, I saw that I was not the only one struggling with this ailment. It became immediately clear that we all had a case of the trots. And if you don't know what a case of the trots is—I'll be more graphic: flooding diarrhea. We later learned that the culprit was the metal trays on which our food was served. Apparently at breakfast that morning the trays had not been properly washed and rinsed before being made available to us, thus leaving them with a thick film of soap and God-knows what else to contaminate our food.

During the entire duration of boot camp, this was the only time that we were allowed to go hit the head without asking permission. Our drill instructors quickly surmised that it was either break protocol or see all of us shit our dress uniform pants in front of the General.

On top of all of this, we had the misfortune of standing in a location inhabited by a massive population of ants, who found their way up our sweaty pant legs throughout the entire inspection. It was truly a horrible day.

But we got through it, passed inspection, and in a weird way felt somewhat like men again, in that we were able to use the bathroom without having to ask first. Strange times indeed.

While our drill instructors laid off of us for a few days after as a reward, they went the complete opposite direction when we messed up. And this leads to the not-so-funny incident that had a profound impact on the remainder of my service in the United States Marine Corps.

Not long after our triumph in the face of diarrhea and ant bites, we had another a drill competition, and this went poorly. We messed it up badly. Myself most definitely included, we were all just off that day, and now it was time to pay the price. Our drill instructors proceeded to work us hard out on the road next to our Quonset hut. They were relentless in making us do squat thrusts, push-ups, sit-ups, and jumping jacks.

Of course somebody under his breath made a smart-ass comment, which one of the drill instructors heard, causing us even more hell. We were then ordered to stand in an empty dumpster—the entire platoon—as the drill instructors screamed at us, while taking aim at the dumpster with their batons.

Even this was extreme for the Marines during this less-gentle era, and a passing officer was horrified at what he saw. The officer ordered all of us out of the dumpster, and then forcefully chewed out our drill instructors.

This invariably pissed them off even more, so it was back to more brutal physical training as punishment, albeit now outside of the dumpster. I was one of seven black guys in our platoon, and it was clear that a few of the white guys were far from racially tolerant. A small group of them, in fact, were outright troublemakers, led by a little Southerner named Maycock. For no reason that I could tell, other than I was black, Maycock hated me. So I then of course hated him. But in the scramble out of the dumpster and back to the road, Maycock and I found ourselves side by side for the continuation of the rigorous physical training. At this point we were too exhausted to care.

Suddenly, three of the black guys in our platoon stood up in unison and refused to do any more of the exercises. The reason they gave was that our drill instructors were racists. Now keep in mind that one of our drill instructors, Sgt. Bland, was black. And keep in mind that every member of our platoon—white, black, and Hispanic—was being forced to do this relentless physical training as punishment for having screwed up our drill competition.

But in that moment, none of that mattered. The three protesters were now calling the other black members of our platoon to stand up and join them. "Get up Sly. Stand with us brother. Goddamn it Sly, stand up!" was all that I heard. Giving in to peer pressure, and now moving to join them, I suddenly felt the hands of Maycock on me and heard him say, "You'd better keep your black ass down here." And so I did.

The protesters were all sent to the brig as the result of their insubordination, and then made to start boot camp all over again. It wasn't as though they would do their time in the brig and then be sent home. I remember seeing them back in first phase, just as we were set to graduate, and thinking how close I had come to that being me.

And the reality is that this would have been me if not for the intervention of Maycock, who had been my sworn enemy. Whatever his prejudices, in that moment he protected me. And he saved my ass. Perhaps he had developed a respect for me because I had never backed down. Or perhaps it was him just taking care of a fellow

Marine. I never asked him why he did it, but I certainly thanked him. And from that point forward, Maycock and I were friends.

It turned out that this act of rebellion was a very big deal. That night our company commander met with our drill instructors, who then met with the remaining black members of our platoon individually. Sgt. Bland called me in to their quarters when it was my turn, and as I stood there braced and standing at attention, he immediately put me at ease.

I was told to sit down and speak freely. Sgt. Bland and Sgt. Dennington both asked me earnestly if I thought that they were prejudiced. "Sir, no sir," was my formal but still truthful response. They then asked me if I understood why they acted toward us as they did. On this question I wasn't as clear in my answer.

Sgt. Dennington said to me, "War is our business, and we're good at it." Sgt. Bland then added, "And it's our job to make you good at it."

They then proceeded to tell me stories of what they had experienced in Vietnam. They told me flat out what it was like to be in a war theater, to be under fire, to have your life truly on the line; and then they let me know that their experiences could soon be mine and everyone's from our platoon. And they told me that whatever I imagined, it was nothing like what it actually was in real life. Discipline is everything, and we have to learn these lessons here at boot camp; otherwise it will be too late on the battlefield.

These two hardened and battle-tested Marines wanted me to see their humanity and wanted me to fully understand why they did what they did. They weren't sadists, or bullies, or thugs. They were men whose job was to prepare us so that we didn't die, and that we didn't screw up so that our fellow Marines died. This wasn't a game or a big charade. It was truly life and death.

As I walked back alone to my Quonset hut, I thought, "Yeah, I get it now. I get it."

Despite my new-found perspective I still had my frustrations with our drill instructions. From the moment that we arrived at boot camp we had been forbidden to call home. Not to wives, girlfriends, kids, parents, grandparents, siblings, anyone. Only letters were permitted. And God help you if you received a letter with something extraneous such as "XOXO" or a hand-drawn heart next to your name on the envelope. That meant 25 push-ups for every offending character or symbol. Very quickly, loved ones back home were told to cut that shit out. Just name and address only!

And we learned to pity anyone who received a birthday cake that was not big enough to feed the entire platoon. The drill instructors would make the offending cake recipient eat their entire cake in one sitting, as well as its container. And on their birthday no less.

Perhaps worst of all were those who were sent Dear John letters from their wife or girlfriend. Word of this breakup would always get out quickly, probably because our drill instructors were reading every incoming and outgoing letter, and the tormenting would start.

During our runs, the drill instructors would gleefully lead us in chants such as, "Ain't no sense in going home, Jody's got your girl and gone."

And forget even thinking about a day off. There was no leave from the base of any kind. This was your home, 24 hours a day, seven days a week.

But the hope of a respite came when we had to train on the rifle range. Our drill instructors told us that if we all qualified, then we would be allowed our first phone call home. This was a true team-building exercise, as we were all motivated not just to do our best, but to help each other do their best.

I was really struggling while shooting from the prone position, until a member of my platoon taught me how to use a small dot of whiteout on my rifle sight to steady my shot. It worked, and I qualified on the rifle range, as we all did.

Our drill instructors then lined us up, and asked if we were ready to now call home. "Sir, yes sir," came our enthusiastic response in unison.

They then started to go up to us individually and ask, "Private Shit Head, where are you from?"

"Pittsburgh, Pennsylvania, sir!"

"Sir, the private is from Pittsburgh in this direction, stand over here."

"Private Scumbag, where are you from."

"Sir, the private is from Monroe, Louisiana!"

"That's in the South, so stand over here."

"Private Maggot, where are you from?"

"Sir, the private is from Kansas City, Missouri, sir."

"Face this direction, and stand here."

Once they had completed this with all of us, we were then told that we were facing home, and to call out to our mothers. We were literally ordered to yell, "Momma," over and over again. This was our call home.

At times like this, I tried very hard to remember my talk with Sgt. Bland and Sgt. Dennington, and how there was always a method to their madness.

As we progressed through our third and final phase of boot camp, we began to develop a real bounce in our step. I even became a bit salty, and found myself looking down at those hapless idiots in first and second phase. We were good, we were sharp, and we knew that the drill instructors were truly proud of us.

But it wasn't until the night before graduation that the drill instructors actually acted like we were real people. And it wasn't until immediately after our graduation ceremony that they actually called us Marines

We were given t-shirts emblazoned with the phrase, "USMC: War is Our Business, and We're Good at It." It was of course what my drill instructors had said to me previously, and I quietly smiled, now realizing that they hadn't made up this phrase.

Graduation itself was a very big deal. There were hundreds of us assembled for the ceremony on the drill field, with a crowd numbered in the thousands on hand, containing our families, friends, and loved ones, as well as numerous officers, politicians, and even minor celebrities.

After the ceremony we were all given our MOS–Military Occupational Specialty. What you didn't want to hear was anything beginning with an "O", as this meant infantry combat. I was informed that my MOS was 5811–Military Police.

As I breathed a massive sigh of relief, I was told not to get too comfortable. There were MPs in Vietnam, and I could most definitely be going there. But first I was heading to infantry training (ITR), then on to my specialty school. Only after I had successfully completed specialty school would I learn my permanent billet.

But this day was too special, too momentous, for me to now worry about something that was beyond my control. I knew that I could be heading to Vietnam, and heading to a war zone.

But I also knew that I was now a Marine, and I headed back home to Kansas City to be with my wife and son for 10 days of leave. Truly, I felt as though I could run through a brick wall.

Chapter 14

City Services

Every city government deals one way or another with the issue of trash. This is far from glamorous of course, but it is reality. Whether the sanitation service is through the local government or private enterprise, garbage ultimately falls back on the city. Litter, landfills, recycling, collection–whether residential or commercial–all of it is tied together, and it is always a big concern for the people. Our Citizen Satisfaction Surveys clearly showed us this was the case.

In Kansas City we use contractors for our waste disposal services. The problem arose from these contractors not finding enough drivers to operate all of their trucks. So of course the trash then started to pile up. There wasn't proper efficiency. And the citizens rightly complained. There were plenty of applicants for the driver jobs, but many of the prospective job candidates had been in prison. Thus they weren't being hired by our contractors, or even considered for employment. They couldn't even get a job interview.

Rather than look at the polls, check with the special interest groups, or consult with my political party as to their ideology on the issue, we found a practical solution. And that solution was to ban the question on the job application that asked if the prospective employee had ever been convicted of a felony. Make no mistake, this issue does come up under the system that is now in place, but it only comes up if the applicant has moved forward to their final job interview.

What we were seeing was the elimination of numerous good and qualified people at the initial job application stage because of this question. And the dilemma for the job applicants who had been convicted of a felony was whether to be honest, knowing that almost certainly that would be the end of the hiring process, or lie, and then hope like hell that nobody ever found out. This was a lose-lose situation.

These applicants generally had gone to prison for a drug conviction rather than for a violent crime, served their time, and then been released. Told to find a job, they began the search but were usually blocked immediately by this one question. This was certainly the case in the quest to hire the badly-needed trash truck drivers.

In some cases there were people who had no history of violence whatsoever, and had been out of prison for a decade or more. They had been leading trouble-free lives, and trying to do the right thing. Yet they could not get a job, often for the sole reason that they were an ex-con. The job process would end almost as soon as it started for them. There was never even a first job interview. So, by eliminating this question on the initial application, we solved the problem.

And this then solved the intertwined problem of our citizens complaining about trash piling up and not being collected in a timely fashion. Drivers were hired, and the trash trucks now ran at full capacity.

What we created was a new system where individuals were hired or disqualified from employment based on the individual circumstances of their case. It's now no longer a check-this-box, one-size-fits-all system. Common sense is what it is as well. Certainly this new hiring process takes more time. But it allowed us to create a system that is much more humane and much more practical for all parties involved.

We extended this program beyond the trash truck drivers to our city jobs as well. People who wanted a job with the city were being told "No" because of a conviction from years prior. This has now ended. When someone declares themselves as a convicted felon on an initial job application, it often becomes the only thing that the person doing the hiring sees. Eliminate this question, and this ex-con suddenly becomes just another job applicant. And if that person is a qualified candidate, able to move through the rounds of job interviews, then the position will be offered to them on those merits. It won't be taken from them because of an unrelated crime for which they have long since paid their debt to society.

If people are not given the opportunity for employment, then there's likely a predictable path that they will follow. If a person can't work, then what are they supposed to do for money? They want things, and if they don't have the money to buy them, well, then they might just come and take your things. All of this isn't being soft on crime. It's being practical. And truly, it all comes through nonpartisan politics.

The vast majority of city governments across the United States (Kansas City, Missouri of course included) are set up with a nonpartisan mayor. Now, I don't know the reason for this historically, but I do know from first-hand experience that it works.

As mayors, as local government, we simply have to perform. There is no luxury of engaging in long-winded debates on monetary policy or tariffs or anything else. Not that I would want that luxury anyway. It's clichéd, but in this case it's true: as the city, failure is not an option.

The trash has to get picked up every week, the snow needs to be cleaned from the streets, and the tree branches need to be cleared from the intersection. If these things don't happen, then the phone starts ringing at City Hall. We have to perform.

Problems often arise from limited budgets and very little assistance coming our way from the state and federal governments. Therefore, we have to be innovative in how we do things as a local government. We have to find ways to get more things done with less money. And this reality leads to real innovation.

Mayors are, through necessity, very good at creating public/private partnerships. We openly welcome the private sector to become involved. An example of this during my time as mayor was our Smart City initiative, where 54 continuous blocks were outfitted with free Wi-Fi.

Private parties came in with millions of dollars, looking for ways to develop and sell their products. And we afforded them this opportunity to use our initiatives for the purpose of product refinement and display. They were able to build their product base, and we were proudly able to become the technologically-smartest and best-connected city in the country.

We had to find a way to do things, but we simply didn't have the money to do them on our own. And we recognized that there was a need from companies such as Sprint, Verizon, and AT&T to experiment with new innovations in Wi-Fi.

Twenty-five interactive kiosks were placed throughout the city, completely free of charge. These kiosks allow users to do things such as access city services, view a calendar of events, and obtain local business information. The city didn't pay for the kiosks– private enterprise did. And 50 percent of the advertising revenue sold in conjunction with them is given back to local government.

Plus, a tremendous amount of data has been generated through the Smart City initiatives. There are of course privacy limitations and restrictions, but the majority of it is accessible to everyone on our city's open data port. So, if you own a bar downtown at 12th and Main and want to know the best time for Happy Hour, the data will tell you. There are sensors that determine how many people are standing at that location at any given time. It's practical data, non-invasive for the individual, and revenue-generating for the city and private businesses, big and small.

This entire environment allows city staff–the bureaucracy–to engage in innovative thinking. When I was mayor I encouraged my staff to think, and I never punished failure. You cannot have a scenario where a person advocates for a new idea, and if it doesn't work they are fired as a direct result. Then, of course, no one else will ever come forward with a new idea of their own. Instead, my attitude was that if something was tried and didn't work, well then let's attempt to fix it. Is there something else that we can do? Is there something that we missed?

And if an idea does work, then that person must be rewarded. This encourages them, it encourage others, and it encourages creative and innovative thought.

Keep in mind that unlike our counterparts who are elected to state and federal positions, we actually show up for work every day. The people know where to find us, and they know how to contact us.

What we do directly affects the people of our city, and what they do directly affects us as local government. Ask a person who their state senator or state representative is, and they likely will have no idea. But they all know who the mayor is, especially when something needs to be done.

We are correctly held accountable, because we are directly accountable to the people—and in a completely nonpartisan way. Local government is about getting the job done, and getting problems solved. The debates and rhetoric are left to those who work at the state capitols and in Washington, D.C.

Chapter 15

Life in the Military Police

After graduating from boot camp, I felt unbreakable. Nobody could mess with me. I wore my uniform everywhere during my 10-day leave back home in Kansas City. After all, I'd sweated my ass off to earn the right to call myself a United States Marine, and now I wanted everyone to know. This had absolutely nothing to do with the politics of the Vietnam War. This was all about pride in personal accomplishment.

Returning to Southern California for Infantry Training Regiment (ITR), this time at Camp Pendleton, I felt fully prepared. Long gone was the scared and disoriented kid who had made that same flight to San Diego for boot camp just months before. Unfortunately, just as before, I had no idea what I was about to experience.

A motto of the Marines is "Every Marine a Rifleman". At ITR, we trained as if we were a combat-ready infantry platoon. I laughed to myself thinking that boot camp had been physically demanding. A three-mile run now would have been a delight. That would have been a warm-up exercise for what we were doing daily at ITR.

It didn't matter to the Marines what your MOS was. Nobody cared that I was going to be an MP. Everyone went through infantry training. And no matter where you were eventually headed, everyone was being trained for combat.

The absolute worst things about ITR were the mountains we had to climb. The most daunting and brutal ones were Mount Smokey and Mount Motherfucker. If they had different and official names I never learned them. The first time we saw them we all had the same reaction—*You want me to climb that?!*

Now keep in mind that this wasn't true mountain climbing, in that we were not scaling the face vertically. Rather these were long, arduous hikes up dirt trails. We climbed in company strength, hundreds of us at the same time wearing boots and helmets and with our full packs, weapons, and rations. Very quickly I figured out not to be in the back, because that meant constantly eating dirt.

These were Marines who had all graduated from boot camp and were presumably in the best shape of their lives. Yet guys would collapse and break down in tears. Their bodies, and sometimes their minds, would just break.

Everyone was ordered to walk over these fallen Marines. Make that walk on, as they passed by on the dirt trail. Everyone, that is, except for the squad leaders, which is what I was. We were responsible for everyone to make it up the mountain. So I was constantly helping one or more of my fellow Marines up Mount Smokey and Mount Motherfucker, as I struggled to keep from collapsing myself.

The one thing that terrified me during ITR was Drownproofing. I wasn't a strong swimmer, so this was the worst thing in the world to me. The only time during ITR that I flat out refused to do something was when it came to Drownproofing. *Kick me out*, because there was no way in hell that I was going to do this. Everyone was amazed that I was able to talk myself out of this, but I somehow did. They assigned me extra weapons training as an alternative, which I happily accepted.

There were elements of ITR that I did enjoy. One of these was the War Games that we did over three nights. The culmination, after reaching our end point on the side of a hill, was shooting up old discarded tanks, vehicles, and weapons. They let us shoot light anti-tank weapons, .30 caliber and .50 caliber machine guns partially loaded with tracers, and shoulder-mounted weapons. In the darkness of night it looked as though we were producing a ribbon of white hot lead. I felt more than ever that I was actually a Marine. It was an extremely cool and satisfying experience.

We also had intensive weapons training, which included .45 calibers, M4s, and M16s (which are real AR-15 rifles), and hand grenades. Once during hand grenade training, the guy standing next to me pulled the pin in his grenade and then accidentally dropped it behind him. As he froze, our drill instructor removed it in a heartbeat, in an almost unconscious action. I never again saw the guy who dropped that grenade. What they did to him, I could only speculate. But it made me that much more careful.

There was also ship boarding, which sounds really easy until you actually go through it. Using rope ladders, we had to climb down from a large fake ship into actual boarding vessels. The key, I found, is to never look down. Not all of my fellow Marines learned this lesson.

But just below our mountain climbs on the sheer misery index was the gas chamber. We'd enter with our gas masks on, only to find our drill instructors standing inside without a gas mask. They would then announce that they would tell us when to take our gas masks off, and sing the Marine Corps hymn. Under no circumstances could we leave the gas chamber until we had sung the Marine Corps hymn in its entirety. The first time in the gas chamber, I thought, *How hard can this be? The drill instructors don't even have a gas mask.*

Moments later I was desperately gasping for air and singing the hymn as fast as humanly possible. But by the third time through the gas chamber, you learned how to control your breathing a bit and get through it. Make no mistake, the gas chamber was still horrible, just not as horrible as before.

There were two things that were great about ITR. One was liberty, something that we never received during the entirety of boot camp. I was now able to go off base with my fellow Marines and experience the nightlife of nearby Oceanside and San Diego.

The other was that I graduated with another stripe. I was now a lance corporal and headed to Ft. Gordon, located just outside of Augusta, Georgia, for Military Police training with the Army.

The Marines farm out a lot of training to the Army and Navy, which is why I was sent to an Army base to become an MP. I was one of 10 Marines in the company, and all of us were immediately given leadership billets. At first I thought it was odd that we're coming to an Army base as Marines and now leading the Army guys in our company. Very quickly I found out why: their basic training was nothing in comparison to our boot camp and ITR. The Army guys had almost no weapons training, other than having fired a hand gun and rifle. They hadn't had much hand-to-hand combat training. And most amazing of all, they'd actually received liberty during basic training. Remember, we didn't even get a phone call home, and were punished for overly affectionate letters from our sweethearts.

Very quickly, though, we became a very tight unit. It didn't matter if you were in the Army or in the Marines. We were all in this together.

One night a group of us were at a pizza place in Augusta, and a few local bigots took exception to the presence of me and a black Army soldier. The scene turned into something out of a bad movie, as it was military vs townies. And it wasn't a fair fight. We were a racially harmonious wrecking machine unloading on a bunch of small-minded white racists. Then we quickly departed, and I haven't been back to Augusta, Georgia, since.

Compared to boot camp and ITR, MP training was a breeze. My only real stress was that upon graduation I would be receiving my orders, and Vietnam remained a real possibility. Remember, I had enlisted in the Marines in the first place because the recruiter had told me that enlisting rather than being drafted greatly increased the likelihood that I would be stationed outside of the war zone. But the possibility of assignment to Vietnam still remained.

I was then hugely relieved to learn that my orders were to report back to Camp Pendleton in California, where I would be stationed with the First Marine Division Military Police.

While this seemed like a blessing, the reality of the situation was that it was boring as hell. I was basically a glorified security guard. I definitely appreciated that I wasn't in Vietnam, but I also felt that I could, and should, be doing so much more with all of my training.

Our jurisdiction was limited to the Division area. Nothing ever happened, and if it had, then we would have had to call the Base MPs. Thankfully, I soon after received orders to join the Base MPs, which I absolutely loved.

My jurisdiction was now the entire base at Camp Pendleton, and I was quickly promoted to corporal. It was a lot like being a small-town police officer in a town of 20,000 people. And like a small-town police officer, a big part of the job was traffic control. I often would park on the side of Rattlesnake Canyon Road, near the MP station, and run radar in search of speeders.

There were definitely out-of-the-ordinary occurrences to break up the daily routine. One speeder, who was especially belligerent, quickly calmed down when I pointed out that he was wearing nail polish while in uniform, and that I might have to testify to this infraction.

While answering a domestic violence call, my young partner had a gun pointed at his head by the wife of a drunk Marine. I told her and her Marine husband very calmly, "I'm not dying tonight. But if that gun isn't put down, then you are."

The worst incident while I was a Base MP at Camp Pendleton involved an accident call. A Marine had lost control of his motorcycle on the highway, gone off the road, and then been decapitated by a steel cable which held a street light in place. I, along with a number of my fellow MPs, had to search the brush for his disembodied head. In a moment of true dark comedy, the youngest MP among us ran gleefully from the darkness to the road, yelling, "I've got it! I've got it!", as he held the head by its hair.

The overall stability of my life as a Base MP allowed me to move my wife Karen and young son Eric from Kansas City to Southern California. We rented a small duplex apartment off base in Oceanside. It was a pit, but it was literally all that we could afford on my meager corporal's salary. Karen was now pregnant with our second child, Malik, and the prospect of me actually going to Vietnam was now extremely remote.

The comfort and security of my day-to day-life as a Base MP at Camp Pendleton did lead me to make a few less-than-stellar decisions. During the 1972 Presidential Election, I campaigned door-to-door in the area for George McGovern in his bid to unseat President Richard Nixon. This, I promptly discovered, is against the rules, and I was threatened with court-martial. I apologized profusely and told them I didn't know that this wasn't allowed; that was true, but still not a great excuse. They accepted it though, and told me that if I did it again there would be serious consequences.

Strangely, not long after my support of McGovern was revealed, I was asked if I wanted to go on presidential security for Richard Nixon. I asked what this entailed, and was told that I'd be part of the team guarding his private residence in San Clemente, California. Acting as a complete smart ass, I responded, "So you're going to give me a gun, and then ask me to guard Nixon?"

No one saw the humor.

I was promptly called in by my commanding officer, who let me know that he was supposed to court-martial me, and asked me why he shouldn't. My only defense was that I was joking. He told me that it wasn't funny, and that nobody was laughing at my veiled threat to assassinate the President of the United States.

It was determined that I would not be court-martialed, and I would of course not be placed on presidential security. I would however be placed on beach patrol, which entailed spending every Friday, Saturday, and Sunday night on the beach trying to catch illegal immigrants who were attempting to sneak across the U.S.-Mexico border. It was not a pleasant assignment at all, but obviously a much better option than being court-martialed.

Upheaval again entered my life, and this time in a major way, when completely unexpectedly I received orders to ship out to the Marine Corps Air Station at Iwakuni, Japan for a 14-month deployment.

There were already severe strains in my marriage with Karen, and now I had to tell her that I was moving to Japan, and that she and the kids couldn't come with me. Had it been a two-year deployment I would have been allowed to bring them. But the rules were that it would be me, and me alone, relocating to Iwakuni.

Keeping her and our boys in Oceanside wasn't really an option. She'd never fully settled in Southern California, and I knew that she was homesick and really missed her parents. The only answer was to move her back to Kansas City, to which she readily agreed. We hurriedly packed up our tiny duplex apartment and made the drive back home.

During this leave I contacted my father and made arrangements to visit him and my mother. I hadn't seen either of them since that fateful day of my choosing the band over the Chiefs game when I was 16 years old. But I now felt that they should know their grandsons, and that my sons should know them.

Nothing was ever said about me leaving home and the aftermath that followed.

Five years had passed since I had last been in their home—my home. But it seemed as though I had lived there in another life. Since leaving, I had graduated from high school, gotten married, joined the Marines, and become the father of two boys. And now, alone again, I was heading to Japan during the height of the Vietnam War.

Chapter 16

A Streetcar Named Success

During the first year of my first term as mayor, I was approached by City Councilman Russ Johnson about his passion project–a modern streetcar for Kansas City. I liked Russ, knew that he was very smart, and understood him to be a transportation geek, in the nicest sense of the term. Russ told me all about his big picture plans for this streetcar, but conceded that it wasn't getting done. He then told me that to be brought to fruition, he needed somebody to lead the effort, and that somebody was me. In essence–*Tag, you're it.*

I was happy to take this on, as I truly felt that a streetcar would be a great thing for our city. As mayor I was able to use the power of my office to inform and persuade people on this issue. Thankfully, a number of people, Russ very much included, had laid the groundwork for me well before my election. There were dozens upon dozens of meetings that I attended, many of which grew contentious. But I believed in the benefits that a streetcar would bring, so I took on the project, fully aware that there would be a great deal of pushback.

For the streetcar to be built, a Transportation Development District (TDD) would have to be approved by vote. This would allow for the TDD to then levy a 25-year, one-cent tax on all retail sales made in the district, as well as a series of property reassessments. The areas of the city that would fall into the TDD, because they would be housing the streetcar lines, were Downtown, the Crossroads Arts District, and the River Market.

Under Missouri law, a city can establish a TDD within a discreet area, with discreet boundaries. But for a project to be approved, only the people who actually live within the TDD are eligible to vote. And rather than going to your local polling location, those residing in the TDD have to request a ballot, fill it out, and then have it notarized.

The pro-streetcar groups took full advantage of this system, as they organized community events, meetings, and parties to inform and lobby residents about the benefits of this modern public transportation system.

Resistance, and even hostility toward the streetcar, came largely from the business owners within the TDD. Most of them lived elsewhere in the city or, as was often the case, in the wealthy metro area suburbs located on the Kansas side of the state line. They were furious that they faced higher sales taxes and property assessments without the ability to vote.

Beyond this there were the CAVE people—the usual stream of contrarians you get anytime something new is proposed—be it a streetcar, or a stadium, or a neighborhood revitalization, or a new airport terminal.

We heard arguments that the streetcar was outdated technology, and that our focus should be on driverless cars. First off, this wasn't a 1930s- style streetcar, but one that used state-of-the-art technology. Secondly, I've seen a lot of modern streetcar systems across the country, but I'm still searching for the first driverless car on a street in Kansas City.

We also had the naysayers who claimed that only drunks, drug addicts, and homeless people would ride the streetcar. *And why would we spend taxpayer money on them?*

The hits just kept on coming. *It will be a white elephant. It will be used by tourists only. It will be a burden for our city.*

It became commonplace to be harangued at City Council meetings by business owners from the TDD, as well as by random people who just didn't like the idea of a streetcar. But there was also a great deal of support.

This was my first real battle in office, and I was happy to wage it. Seeing this as only about a streetcar was both naive and simplistic. This was about economic development and redevelopment, as with the streetcar came riders. And those riders would spend money within the TDD.

In December 2012, the streetcar measure passed comfortably. Because of the system mandated by Missouri law, there was only a pool of 550 voters, and they were overwhelmingly in support.

I can now state confidently, and quite proudly, that our city's streetcar is the most successful of its kind in the United States. Of course I'm going to say this, but the numbers back up my claim.

There is now 58 percent more in sales tax collection in the TDD since 2014, and there is now more than $2 billion in development within the TDD boundaries. Plus there have been over 6 million passenger trips on the streetcar through May, 2019. And oh, our city's streetcar is completely free to ride, and it came in $250,000 under budget.

Because there is no charge for ridership you can get on and off as much as you'd like without hassle or issue. Board at Union Station, and then step off at the next stop along Main Street. And when you exit you're going to spend your money right there. Then get right back on board for the quick return trip.

You can ride the streetcar all day long. The data has proven that riders, no matter where they're from, will get off at a streetcar stop and often buy something.

If you were to see photos of the streetcar route today compared with five years prior to its construction, it looks like a different city. The construction of office buildings, shops, restaurants, bars, condos, and apartments is truly remarkable. Those of you reading this who are Kansas Citians know exactly what I'm talking about.

Construction happens along rails. It's just that simple. All of those new housing units didn't just pop up in the TDD because it seemed like a fun place to build. They were constructed because of the new life breathed into the area by our city's streetcar. We actually had a team of real estate developers come from Colorado and walk the streetcar route. They wound up building two high-end apartment structures, both of which contain street-level restaurants and retail stores. The land they purchased had been supporting surface parking lots, which were generating little money for the tax base.

Even those Kansas City residents who have never ridden the streetcar, and never will, are beneficiaries of its success.

The first place that I saw a modern city streetcar system was in Charlotte, North Carolina, when my friend Anthony Foxx was mayor. He was its champion, and it wound up providing a massive positive economic impact. I duly took note.

Foxx went on to be appointed Secretary of Transportation during President Obama's second term. He was instrumental in the awarding of a $20 million Tiger Grant for our streetcar in 2013. This was the biggest Tiger Grant awarded during the entire year, and the only one awarded for a streetcar. To make things even better, Foxx personally delivered the grant to Kansas City.

Now I'm not the type of person who likes to say, *I told you so.* But it's a very good feeling when former opponents come over to your side of the issue. Not because of ideology, but because of reality and practicality.

One of the earliest and most vocal opponents of the streetcar was Keith Novorr, the owner of the venerable Kansas City institution, Michael's Fine Clothes for Men. This business-wear and formal-wear retail establishment opened in 1905, and has been in the same location ever since—just south of downtown at 19th and Main. But as the area started to fade, Michael's began to lose its hipness. Its customer base was pretty much reduced to older men who had been going there since they were kids.

Now Michael's is hip again, because it is located directly on the streetcar route. The sales numbers have increased dramatically, and there is a brand new and vastly younger clientele. Novorr is so pro-streetcar that he has actually done commercials touting its merits.

There's now an initiative to extend the streetcar south, all the way to the University of Missouri-Kansas City (UMKC), which is located just off the Plaza (one of our city's premiere shopping and restaurant/bar districts). If successful, this expansion will link the streetcar with its current southernmost stop, located at Union Station. The proposed expansion would span more than 50 city blocks.

And yet for all of the undeniable success of the streetcar, there are still opponents. I had one person tell me they were against the streetcar expansion because it would bring into their community riders who would rob the houses. This person lived in Brookside, a higher-income and highly-desirable neighborhood located near UMKC.

First, Brookside is already well-served by public transportation, as there are a number of bus stops in the vicinity. I doubt that the criminal element would restrict themselves to streetcars.

Secondly, is anyone really going to ride the streetcar (or bus for that matter) into an expensive neighborhood, break into a home, steal a bunch of things, and then jump back on the streetcar (or bus) with their bounty for the return trip? This is of course laughable. This concern is nothing more than a dog whistle for race. They don't want certain types of people in their neighborhood. I get it, but it's bullshit.

The larger issue is that if people don't like something, they'll come up with a thousand reasons why. None of the reasons have to make sense. And our phenomenally successful streetcar is not exempt from this line of thinking.

The outliers, though, are fewer and fewer as the streetcar continues to create revenue, development, and jobs. It's tough to argue with positive economic impact, and most now don't. What I find amusing is how many of the original streetcar opponents, many of whom were extremely public in their dissent, now want to take credit for this overwhelming success. According to them, it was entirely their idea in the first place.

Because I don't care about getting credit—I care about getting results—this doesn't bother me at all. But while I got behind the streetcar with everything I had early in my first term, it is important to me that people understand it wasn't my idea. The initial streetcar plan was in motion well before I even announced my candidacy. The real credit goes to people like Russ Johnson, David Johnson (a streetcar and transportation activist and advocate), and other innovative and big-picture thinkers, from both the public and private sectors.

In addition to all of the economic growth directly brought about by the streetcar, there is something much more human to consider. Public transportation is one of the pillars of equity in a society. When there is adequate public transit, then people of lesser means don't have to spend nearly as much of their meager income as they would otherwise. In Kansas City, and most major cities nationwide, people spend about one-third of their total income on transportation. Then factor in gas, insurance, maintenance, parking, and tolls—not to mention the cost of purchasing a car itself. It can be devastating to someone living at or below the poverty line.

But with good public transportation, such as a modern, safe, and clean streetcar system, a larger portion of a person's budget can be spent elsewhere, on things like food, housing, health care, and education.

Another benefit has been the increased density in the TDD, which includes our downtown. People in close proximity is a good thing, because it's easier to deliver services more efficiently than when they're scattered across the 318 square miles of our city.

I'm often asked how much longer the streetcar will be free to ride. People seem mystified that there is not a charge now, and even more so that there won't be a charge at least in the foreseeable future. But when you look at the numbers, there's no mystery about it. Our city's streetcar is fully funded by a one-cent retail sales tax and property reassessments within the TDD.

Because of the tremendous growth in tax collections and the increase in property values, the funding is solid. So the maintenance and contingency fees are funded, and two more cars have been purchased.

Since the official launch of our streetcar in May 2016, we've had mayors and their representatives, from Tennessee, Ohio, Louisiana, Arkansas, and elsewhere, come to Kansas City to study our streetcar system. They want to know exactly how we did this, and how they can replicate our success.

One of the most satisfying things for me in regard to Kansas City's streetcar program occurred during one of our U.S. Conference of Mayors meetings in Washington D.C. I was speaking with David Holt, the mayor of Oklahoma City, about his plan to institute a charge to ride his city's streetcar. Immediately I told him to be careful that his ridership didn't drop, and reminded him of our policy to never charge.

"Yeah," he responded, "people keep telling me that we need to keep it free, just like Kansas City. Every time that I mention our streetcar, I keep hearing that we need to do things 'just like Kansas City.'"

I had always viewed issues in regard to how we compared to other cities across the country. Now I was being told that Kansas City was the benchmark for how others compared to us.

Chapter 17

Iwakuni and Subic Bay

Here's one word to describe the time of my life in Japan at Marine Corps Air Station Iwakuni: *boring*. My already shaky marriage was now completely falling apart, with Karen and the boys now back in Kansas City, and me literally half a world away. The job of an MP in Iwakuni was painfully boring. There was literally nothing for me to do. All my fellow MPs and I did day after day was drive around the seawall in old trucks.

I was now a sergeant, but that bump in pay didn't matter in my daily life, as I always sent the bulk of my money to Karen. This left me in a constant state of being broke. So I basically just stayed in the barracks during my free time, and I ate virtually all of my meals in the chow hall.

Other than playing the occasional game of softball, I either just worked or sat around and did nothing. The guys I worked with as an MP were cool, but I never really made any deep friendships. I just wasn't in the mood.

One night, at a particularly low moment, I decided to go by myself to the NCO club. I thought, *Screw it, I deserve some fun.*

I've never been a big drinker, but that night I really indulged. And I let loose on the slot machines as well. The result of the evening was that I lost my entire two-week paycheck playing slots.

It was all gone, and I had absolutely no idea what to do about it. Incidentally, this proved to be the last time that I ever gambled.

Not long afterward, when I called home one night a guy answered. I hung up, and then said out loud to myself, "Well, that's the end of that shit." The good news was that at least I wasn't around to deal with all of the conflict that goes with the end of a marriage. I certainly wasn't blindsided by the end of my relationship with Karen. And while I did experience breakup depression, I vowed to myself that I would move on quickly with my life. There really wasn't an alternative.

Fortunately, my daily life as an MP started to become a bit more interesting. Not exciting certainly, but at least there were now things to do other than just drive around that damn seawall.

We started going on prisoner runs, picking up Marines who had been arrested elsewhere in Japan and transporting them back to base. Not only did we get to see far beyond Iwakuni, we got to do so driving brand new Dodge D100 pickup trucks. They were vastly superior to the old beater trucks that we had been driving on base, and they were a hell of a lot bigger. On one run a fellow MP tried to squeeze through a narrow alley and the truck got stuck. It was completely wedged between the buildings on either side, and had to be dragged out by a tow truck.

The closest call with the massive Dodge D100 came on a narrow mountain pass. I was driving down and realized that my truck took up four-fifths of the road. Slowing down, I then looked out the driver side window and noticed that it was a straight vertical drop down the side of the mountain. There were no safety barriers or hard shoulders. Just the edge of a cliff! It was far scarier than any of the Marine prisoners whom we transported.

I attempted to learn some Japanese, and even began to venture out of my barracks into the nearby villages and cities. On one occasion three of my fellow Marines and I took the train to Tokyo, my first-ever visit there. After one meal and some souvenir shopping, we were all out of money. We then hastily and dispiritedly departed Tokyo without even a glimpse of its renowned night life.

A much better outing was to the Iwakuni Cherry Blossom Festival. Our job as MPs was to essentially make sure that the hundreds of Marines in attendance didn't get so drunk that they then embarrassed themselves, the Marine Corps, the United States, and Japan. No pressure. But we were treated wonderfully by locals, who really made us feel welcome and appreciated. A number of the women brought us lunch, which was packaged in beautifully wrapped ornate boxes. They were incredibly proud, and I could tell how much they wanted us to enjoy our meal. Inside the delicate packaging was a bed of rice, topped by a lone fish eyeball. I smiled at them, and thought, *I'm not eating this. Where's McDonald's?*

I do have two very fond but starkly different memories of my time in Japan. One is from the day I arrived, flying over Japan while still seated on the military cargo plane. Looking out the window, I spotted the biggest and most spectacular mountain that I had ever seen in my life. It was Mount Fuji, and I quickly realized that I was only seeing the top of the mountain, which was visible above the clouds. The plane then further descended, and we could now fully experience Mount Fuji in its entirety. It was truly magnificent.

My other truly fond memory from Japan is of something that was also amazing, and far more unexpected. There was a small family-owned restaurant located just off the base. I'm telling you that this little place in Iwakuni, Japan served the best BLT sandwiches I've ever had. Before or since. Homemade bread, fresh bacon, thick tomatoes. To my palate, which had now been subjected to years of military food, this was the best meal in the world.

I really felt like God was smiling on me when I received orders, completely to my surprise, that I was going on Temporary Assigned Duty (TDY) to Subic Bay in the Philippines. I could hardly contain my delight. Like all Marines, I had long heard the stories of Subic Bay, which was the military equivalent of Sodom and Gomorrah. As a newly single man, I felt like I had just won the lottery.

I was assigned to shore patrol at Subic Bay in a mixed unit of Navy and Marines. My commander was a Naval officer, and my executive officer was a Marine Corps captain. This turned out to be just what I needed at this time in my life, and it was the most fun that I'd ever had in the Corps.

The Filipino women absolutely loved American men, even more so if they were Marines. If there was ever a cloudy or rainy day while I was in the Philippines, I don't remember it. I do remember that this felt like something akin to a beach vacation, where it was always warm and sunny.

There were four of us who worked together in a unit, and with that we were also roommates. Gonzalez, Gulley, Gage, and me. We absolutely loved each other, so much so that we actually had t-shirts made that read "The Four of Us."

We went absolutely everywhere together, for work and for play: two Marines and two sailors turned loose in Subic Bay.

But as much as I loved my new life, I was fully aware of my often dire surroundings. As an MP on shore patrol, we had two nights on duty followed by two nights off. Our only weapon was a night stick–well that and the Filipino police.

People in this country who talk about police brutality were clearly never in the Philippines during the regime of President Ferdinand Marcos. These police officers had all types of weapons and weren't shy about using them. Most brutal of all were Marcos' private police, called the Philippine Constabulary. These guys didn't wear uniforms, and were flat out mean. Even the regular police were afraid of them. This was the time of martial law, and very questionable civil rights.

As part of our orientation for beach patrol, the local police took us on a ride along and then gave us a tour of their jail. They'd bring in a prostitute, and then toss her in the drunk tank. A pickpocket would have all of his fingers broken. Inmates were beaten and humiliated. Really horrific stuff.

On numerous occasions we encountered bar fights that seemed straight out of a John Wayne movie, with tables and chairs flying everywhere. Once we witnessed a heated argument between a Filipino civilian and a member of Marcos' Philippine Constabulary that appeared to be about a woman. Without warning, the Philippine Constable pulled out his gun, shot the other man in the chest, and then walked away. There was absolutely nothing that we could do.

From our base into the city, we crossed a bridge above what was known as "Shit River." I don't know the river's official name, but I definitely know why it received this nickname—because it was literally a river filled with human shit. Girls outfitted in long white dresses would ride in boats and shout to the U.S. Sailors and Marines who were passing on the bridge above. They wanted us to throw them money, and when we did the young boys of the village would jump out of the boat and into Shit River to retrieve the coins. It was truly the saddest thing that I have ever seen in my life. And this was every single day.

There was definitely brutal poverty in the Philippines, but there we also encountered people enjoying a middle-class existence. In particular was a wonderful family who ran our favorite restaurant, which was located just off base. We went there so often that a genuine friendship was formed.

The husband and wife had two beautiful daughters who were around our age. They were absolutely stunning, but we knew better than to pursue anything romantically with them—and so we didn't. We really liked and respected the entire family, and they began to take us around Luzon, the Philippine island on which Subic Bay is located. We'd go on picnics, fishing excursions, and sightseeing trips with them. It was always a great time and a welcomed respite from military life.

When our executive officer was looking for a place to host his birthday celebration, their restaurant was of course our only choice. He was a good guy, but a squared-away Marine who had dressed for this occasion in his full uniform.

Because we were so comfortable at our now-close friends' restaurant–which was our regular hang out–we absolutely let loose that night. Beer turned into hard liquor, which turned into shots of tequila, which turned into us all becoming completely shit-faced. The entire shore patrol was in attendance in full-on party mode.

We were all so drunk that we decided to hold down our executive officer on the floor and dump pitchers of beer on him. Then we bundled him into one of our vehicles and drove him back to base, where we deposited him at his residence–the Bachelor Officers Quarters (BOQ). We then drove back off base, tracked down a local prostitute whom we all knew, and told her to get in. Back on base to the BOQ, we opened his door and shoved her inside. We then left, laughing hysterically.

The next day, our executive officer called us in, and he wasn't laughing. He told us, "You had your fun last night. Well I guarantee you that you're not going to have any fun today."

He then proceeded to run all of us for hours. The entire shore patrol. I never once puked from physical activity during boot camp or ITR, but I puked on this occasion. Actually, I puked multiple times. No doubt the massive quantities of alcohol that I had consumed the night before didn't help matters.

When our punishment was over our executive officer laughed, and everything was good again. Nothing more was said, and there were no further repercussions. But on that day, vengeance was a bitch.

By far the most interesting experience that I had while at Subic Bay occurred on New Year's Eve 1974. The entire Seventh Fleet was in from the U.S. Navy, and well as ships from the navies of Great Britain, Australia, Germany, and Russia, just to name a few. It was wall-to-wall sailors and marines from a vast array of international militaries. And they were all drunk.

My grandson, Race, stands outside the house I shared with my father, mother, and brothers, LaFrance and LaVance. The house is located at 44th Street and Montgall Avenue in Kansas City, Missouri.

A day in the backyard with my brothers LaFrance and LaVance circa 1963.

I was feeling it on this night in 1968, as lead singer of the Amelia Earhart Memorial Flying Band.

Here I am serving as a shore patrol officer in the Philippines in 1974.

A house party gig for the Amelia Earhart Memorial Flying Band near Loose Park, circa 1968. We were well dressed indeed.

An artist's sketch depicts me cross-examining a witness during the nine-week, Sam Dowdy federal trial in 1990. Sam Dowdy was the only one of 12 defendants acquitted of criminal charges.

I was really excited to be at the Negro Leagues Baseball Museum, to unveil the plans for the MLB/Kansas City Royals Urban Youth Academy.

Licia and I met while attending Rockhurst College, and have been married since 1981.

My wife Licia—make that Dr. Licia—on the day that she earned her PhD. She's joined by our kids Aja and Kyle.

Go Chiefs! At home with the family on an NFL Sunday in 2018.

My son Malik was with me for a birthday party at Chicken & Pickle. He plays Pickleball. I don't!

Three James men: Kyle, Eric, and me; while Malik was serving in Iraq.

I love reading to kids, and so I often bring along a book to share during my visits. During my two terms as mayor, I visited 140 schools in the Kansas City area.

A great day with my daughter Aja, grandson Race, and the other kids at Notre Dame de Sion school. Check out all of those bowties!

Army veteran Charles Brown has been my barber for the past thirty years. A trip to see him at 7 Oaks, on Kansas City's East Side, is always a pleasure.

The full-size "Mayor Sly" puppet presented to me at the annual West Bottoms Association meeting in April, 2019.

Key members of the Cub Scouts stopped by City Hall to give me advice on economic development and the budget.

My Chief of Staff and business partner Joni Wickham. I've seen this look many times. It means that she thinks that I've lost my mind!

Missouri Governor Mike Parson and I like to show off our Kansas City socks.

My friend and Kansas City rap icon Tech N9ne, as he enjoys his own Tech N9ne Bou Lou beer at Boulevard Brewing Company.

Even I look good holding the Kansas City Royals 2015 World Series trophy! This was an outstanding night at the Kauffman Center for the Performing Arts.

Partying with "Queer Eye!" Reality TV stars Bobby Berk, Tan France, and Karamo Brown are frosty dudes. Kansas City was the backdrop for the Fab Five's third season.

I formed an instant friendship with master cellist Yo-Yo Ma when we first met in 2017.

I loved stopping at Casey's General Store on I-70 to talk to this coffee group, every time that I travelled to mid-Missouri.

On March 25, 2019, I got to take the first whack at the old KCI Terminal A, to make room for the new single terminal.

On the Spring Training field in Arizona with Kansas City Royals multiple time All-Star and Gold Glove winner Alex Gordon.

Kansas City resident Derron Black disrupts my second State of the City Address at the GEM Theater in the historic 18th & Vine District in March 2013. Moments later, he was tackled by my security team and arrested.

I was there with Tom Gerend, KC Streetcar Executive Director, and Donna Mandelbaum, KC Streetcar Communications Director, when the first streetcar was delivered on November, 2, 2015.

My first trip to the White House in June 2011 was with a contingent of mayors from the U.S. Conference of Mayors to meet with President Obama, Vice President Joe Biden, Senior Advisor Valerie Jarrett and Chief of Staff Bill Daley.

I've got to admit, it was pretty frosty being in the White House Press Room at the podium, answering questions from the White House Press Corps with Mayor Marty Walsh of Boston and former Fresno Mayor Ashley Swearengin.

I had the pleasure of greeting U.S. presidential candidate Hillary Clinton upon her landing in Kansas City for a campaign stop in September, 2016.

Former Kansas City, Missouri, Mayor Kay Barnes and I really enjoyed our evening, as we dedicated and renamed the Convention Center Grand Ballroom in her honor.

These two frosty brothers always had my back: Mayor of Columbia, South Carolina, and 2018 President of United States Conference of Mayors, Steve Benjamin (left); and U.S. Secretary of Transportation and former Mayor of Charlotte North Carolina, Anthony Foxx (center).

My daughter Aja was with me to see the Grammy Award winning Boyz II Men when they played Kansas City's Kauffman Center for the Performing Arts.

Photo by David Hathcox © 2019

Ok, I admit that I was star struck! It was great to meet Lady Gaga.

I had the honor of throwing the "first pass" to former Chiefs wide receiver and return specialist Dante Hall, prior to Kansas City's NFL playoff game against the Indianapolis Colts at Arrowhead Stadium on January 5, 2019.

It was an honor working with Dayton Moore (seated to my immediate left) and so many others on the MLB / Kansas City Royals Urban Youth Academy project.

A moment of fun with the citizens who attended one of our city budget meetings.

It felt like I had come full circle as I delivered my final State of the City address at my alma mater, Rockhurst University, in Kansas City on March 26, 2019.

As MPs our jurisdiction was the base as well as Magsaysay Drive, the long main street of near-by Olongapo City, which terminated in a T-junction. On this street were countless bars, restaurants, and shops, as well as scores of street vendors serving monkey meat and all sorts of other crazy local food.

Normally this street was packed. On this particular December 31st, it was so crowded that no one could move. And in this situation we were tasked with keeping order!

Out of the thousands of drunken belligerents we encountered, the most memorable was an Australian sailor who was walking around with his pants and underwear around his ankles, fully exposed, and calling out for women to join him.

We told him that he had to pull his pants up or else we'd arrest him, and off to the brig he'd go. "No worries, mate," was his barely intelligible reply. Ten minutes later, there he was again, pants and underwear again bunched at his feet.

Of all the different nationalities represented with these sailors and Marines, the biggest conflicts were not between the Russians and the Americans, but rather the Brits and the Aussies. They were continually taunting and fighting each other.

Our New Year's Eve, both day and night, largely consisted of running from bar to bar and restaurant to restaurant, breaking up brawls and dragging the completely hammered participants to the brig.

When we were finally off-duty after midnight, all of us headed to the NCO club on base. The renowned American R&B and funk band Tower of Power was playing, and it was truly the place to be. Beers only cost 25 cents and there were women absolutely everywhere. The place was absolutely packed, and unlike the bars that night in Olongapo City, everyone was there simply to have a great time. Soon we moved from drinking beers to Brass Monkeys. It was some type of yellow fruity drink with rum that made inhibitions disappear that much quicker. The highlight was when Gage–all 6-5 of him–got up on the dance floor by himself and got after it. Everyone at the NCO club watched in awe as this big man put on a show. I'm telling you, Wilbur Gage could really dance. Gage and his favorite band, Tower of Power, all hailed from Oakland, California. It was an extremely happy coincidence that they were reunited at Subic Bay.

I loved the Philippines so much that I offered to re-enlist for four years if the Marines would guarantee that I would be at Subic Bay for two years. I was told no deal. Everyone apparently loved the Philippines and wanted to be there as well. Then I countered with a six-year re-enlistment for the guarantee of two years at Subic Bay. But the Marines weren't willing to make that deal happen either.

So when my TDY to Subic Bay was up, rather than returning to Iwakuni, Japan, I was sent back to Camp Pendleton in Southern California for the final month of my original four-year enlistment.

My gamble had worked, and I would never see Vietnam. I would never see a battlefield or war zone. Upon being honorably discharged I headed promptly to Kansas City.

I was 24 years old, a divorced father of two young boys, and a Marine Corps veteran who had spent the past 13 months living in Asia. And like countless young men and women before and since, I had absolutely no idea what I was going to do next.

Chapter 18

Innovative Leadership and Partnerships

I learned early on in my tenure as Mayor that if we wanted to push our city forward, we could wait for glacial change and help to come from the state or federal government, or we could find a way to get what we needed through innovative approaches and partnerships. That concept was not unique to Kansas City, in that most mayors feel the same way. Unhampered by partisan politics, and driven by the daily demands of our citizens to provide additional services (more efficiently and faster), mayors are adept at sharing ideas and solutions.

Perhaps no single mayor was more sharing than New York City's Michael Bloomberg. As he was completing his third and final term in office, Bloomberg let it be known that he would make members of his staff available to selected cities, so as to provide expertise in a wide range of subjects. He also offered up personnel from his organization, Bloomberg Associates.

Even more impressive, Mayor Bloomberg did this at no charge. I jumped at this opportunity and wrote to him immediately. Our formal engagement with Bloomberg Associates (BA) commenced in August 2014, and ran through December 2016. Both Jim Giles, my legislative director and liaison with BA, and I remain in contact with members of the Bloomberg team.

BA brought a fresh set of eyes to Kansas City, to examine our processes and assets. Kate Levin worked with Visit KC to integrate arts and culture informational opportunities, in an effort to further promote our city. She helped create the strategy and mission for the newly-created Office of Culture and Creative Services. Adam Freed worked on sustainability with our city staff in order to develop an infrastructure plan for a 70,000-acre development area, Twin Creeks, located in the northern part of city. In addition to working on public infrastructure issues in the area, the team helped stage an international design competition for a linear park in the development tract.

Katherine Oliver worked with media and technology, and was key in helping to develop our first Digital Roadmap. She partnered with both my communications director and the city manager to host KC Digital Lab for all city departments and communications staff. This in turn led to the formation of SMART (Social Media Advisory and Research Team). Rose Gill Haven worked with us in municipal integrity, and helped to develop a cross-sector approach to problem-solving. She also advised on KCStat.

George Fertitta gave excellent advice on how to increase the tourism sector of our economy by identifying and applying industry-best practices. And Linda Gibbs provided broad scope consulting to us on a number of topics.

The Bloomberg Associates personnel from New York loved Kansas City, and we loved them. They were collaborative without condescension. And they were genuinely interested in helping us improve our systems and processes, while simultaneously recognizing the areas in which we were advanced. They opened some new doors for us, and as a result our city was invited to be one of the inaugural participants in "What Works Cities," an initiative to help cities improve the lives of citizens through data-driven policies.

Since 2017, only thirteen cities have been certified by "What Works Cities." In 2019 Kansas City was one of seven cities to be certified, and during that year we moved from Silver certification to Gold.

In addition to the very productive partnership with Bloomberg Associates, we had what I consider to be an almost perfect P3 (public-private partnership) in the historic 18th & Vine District. It was ideal, in that it combined several areas in which we concentrated a lot of time, effort, and resources in our administration of youth engagement, education, mentorship, out-of-school activities, and economic development. On September 25, 2015, Kansas City Royals General Manager Dayton Moore, representatives of Major League Baseball (MLB), the Players Association (MLBPA), and I met at the Negro Leagues Baseball Museum. We came together to announce our joint effort to build and finance the Urban Youth Baseball Academy (UYA) at Parade Park in the 18th & Vine District.

Months before that public unveiling, Dayton had approached me with his concept. He was passionate about building the UYA in order to serve the kids of the urban core. In partnership with Boys and Girls Clubs and Reviving Baseball in the Inner City (RBI), the vision of the UYA was to use baseball as a vehicle to reach kids by providing high quality coaching, mentorship and programming. All of this was in an effort to teach character, teamwork, and citizenship—as well as baseball.

If some kids with talent managed to get into a college program or even professional baseball, that would be fabulous. But the primary goal was to reach the kids—both boys and girls. I was already aware of Dayton's deep commitment to helping those in need through his foundation, "C" You in the Major Leagues. He had raised funds, including through his annual celebrity softball game, and educated followers and benefactors through a speakers program. Dayton had also run a mentorship program. He's a man who believes deeply in being a positive force, and he puts his beliefs into action. So when Dayton pitched me on the idea, I knew that he was both serious and totally committed. Without hesitation, I agreed to work with him.

Our immediate goal was to build a facility and infrastructure, so that we could support, mentor, coach, and teach 800-1000 kids each year, ages six through 18. Royals owner David Glass announced his support of the operation of the facility by pledging up to $500,000 per year for 20 years. I committed to helping Dayton with community outreach, and also by raising the $14 million of funding needed above the Glass commitment.

Carolyn Watley, President of CBIZ, was my choice to head our fundraising efforts. She and I then enlisted Kansas City Royals legend and Baseball Hall of Fame member George Brett; five-time Major League Baseball All-Star Joe Carter; Matt Roney of Kit Bond Strategies; Michael Carter, owner of Carter Broadcast Systems; and Terry Bassham, CEO and President of Kansas City Power & Light (KCPL), to round out the committee.

Royals Director of Baseball Operations Kyle Vena acted as Dayton's representative, liaison, and point person. Attorney David Frantze was the liason for David Glass, and also provided legal and financial advice. My friend Dave Bower, the mayor of Raytown, Missouri and an architect with Populous (a firm famous internationally for building sports venues around the world) was enlisted to design and build the Academy. City Manager Troy Schulte and Kansas City Parks Director Mark McHenry facilitated the city's role in the construction and infrastructure work in the park.

As design work began and the desired features of the UYA came into clearer focus, the price tag increased from $14 million to $21 million. We knew that work was cut out for us on this very worthy project.

In response to the additional money needed, we devised a multipronged approach to fundraising. The state of Missouri contributed $2 million, thanks to help from our city lobbyists Bill Gamble and Sam Panettiere, as well as State Senators Kiki Curtis and Jason Holsman. In October 2015 we travelled to St. Louis and made a presentation to the Missouri Development Fund Board (MDFB), in which we requested $3 million in tax credits. Our request was granted, and then we sold the credits to private persons and companies in order to secure their investments in the UYA. During the 2015 World Series, played between the Royals and the Mets, Dayton flew back from New York in time to attend a "friend raiser" held at JJ's, one of my favorite restaurants, owned by David Frantze's brother Jimmy.

For the 2016 Royals season opener, the marketing geniuses at VML came up with a truly brilliant fundraiser for the UYA. People paid $30 each to be part of a "baseball relay team," which travelled the nearly 9.5 miles from Union Station, located just south of downtown Kansas City, to Kauffman Stadium. Union Station was significant, as the previous November an estimated 800,000 people attended the World Series championship celebration for the Royals. For this event, in conjunction with the 2016 season opener, more than 2,500 people registered to be part of this unique "relay team," which tossed a baseball a few feet to the next person until it had reached the Royals home. Some people made a picnic of the event, and others came to entertain those who waited for the ball to reach them. And many more came just to be there. "Relay The Way" was widely covered by the national media, and was such a success that VML won a Clio Award, given for innovation and creative excellence in advertising.

The UYA was ultimately built in Parade Park, located directly behind the Negro Leagues Baseball Museum. Bob Kendrick, the museum's director and an incredibly sharp dresser, was an immediate and enthusiastic supporter. As we moved forward he also served as a source of historical information to us and the donors.

Bob recognized, as did I, that it was great to have black, white, and latino boys and girls playing baseball and softball 100 yards from the museum's doors. Proving once again that Kansas City is one of the most philanthropic cities in the county, millions of dollars in private funds were raised in order to build this outstanding facility. In addition to support from the Kauffman Foundation and numerous business leaders, several Royals players made sizeable contributions as well. Those contributing at the highest monetary level were allowed to designate honorees for the three baseball fields and one softball field at the UYA. Chosen were iconic Kansas City sportswriter Joe McGuff, legendary Negro Leagues umpire Bob Motley, 2015 World Series MVP and Royals great Salvador Perez, and the Women of the Negro Leagues.

The UYA also contains a 38,000-square foot indoor facility and an educational press box, which was quietly financed by country music superstar Garth Brooks. Groundbreaking occurred on April 21, 2016, and the UYA officially opened on March 29, 2018. Since then it has hosted hundreds of games and teams, in addition to community events and functions.

It's the home of the UMKC NCAA Division 1 softball team, and a location for mentoring and tutoring sessions, along with baseball and softball instruction led by former professional player and current UYA Executive Director Darwin Pennye. And it's also the site of the Queen of Diamonds fundraising game that brings attention to girls softball.

Dayton Moore's commitment to the ideals of the UYA has only increased since our first conversation. I'm honored to serve on the Board of Directors with Dayton, as well as Kyle Vena, Carolyn Watley, former UMKC Chancellor Leo Morton, and Carlos Casas, Google's head of business activities in Kansas City. Dayton always talks in terms of the UYA's primary goal of building leaders. This isn't surprising when you understand that quality leaders like Dayton truly understand and appreciate the need to build leadership and character in all children.

Chapter 19

Lost then Found

In **April** 1975 I returned home to Kansas City from the Marines. After so much responsibility and so much structure in the military, I reveled in being able to do nothing more than bum around for a few months. This stretched through the entire summer, but come the fall I knew that to follow through with my goal to attend law school I had to make a move. I enrolled at Penn Valley Community College, located in midtown Kansas City, where I spent two semesters. The following fall I transferred to Rockhurst College, a private Jesuit school located not too far from where I had lived growing up.

I figured the only way to get the true college experience that I sought was to live the dorm life. Attending college in the city in which I grew up, it would have been far too easy to live off campus and then utilize Rockhurst only for the academics. But I wanted to truly live the life of a college student, even though I was seven years older than the average freshman, with far more life experience.

My roommate was Pat Condon, a red-headed Catholic from Chicago, and we had a blast together. Both Pat and I pledged the Tau Kappa Epsilon (TKE) fraternity, as Greek life was the primary on-campus social outlet. Pat was a huge Notre Dame fan, which made me think back to my very brief academic recruitment by the school when I was at Bishop Hogan, and he was one of the most imaginative people I'd ever met. For our Halloween party at the TKE house Pat dressed up as a "blind date." His costume consisted of a suit of brown trash bags stuffed with newspaper to add considerable size to his frame, plus a hat, dark glasses, and a white cane. I realize now it was far from politically correct, but at the time we laughed our asses off.

Our main fraternity rival was Sigma Alpha Epsilon (SAE), which we all called "sleep and eat." For reasons never clear to me Pat dubbed them "sick elves," which then became "booting dwarfs," and the name stuck. It was clear that this really bothered the SAE guys. So seizing on the momentum, Pat made t-shirts for all of us in TKE that featured multiple cartoon dwarfs throwing up.

Because neither Pat nor I had enough money for a state-of-the-art stereo system, we came up with the idea of placing our own small radios on opposite ends of the dorm room. We'd then tune them to the same FM station and create an improvised high-fidelity sound. This was always a hit at our parties, of which there were many.

After life in the Marines, and living in Asia, I found the college experience to be exactly what I needed. I fully embraced being a student at Rockhurst. As an English major I was excelling academically. I had my roommate Pat and our TKE brothers for everything that I could want socially. I even started playing intramural football and was a member of the Student Senate.

It was at Rockhurst College where I met Licia, whom I married in 1981. I saw her one day in the cafeteria, and I immediately noticed she had extremely long hair. Rather than making my move directly, I ordered one of our TKE pledges to go ask if he could measure her hair. Rather than bristle, she accepted this unusual request in her good-natured way, which allowed me to then come over and introduce myself. We've been together ever since.

Since I was the oldest guy in my fraternity (and seemingly the oldest person on campus), added responsibilities seemed to naturally fall to me. And of course it wasn't just because of my age, but what I had done in my life before enrolling at Rockhurst. When the cops would come to tell us to turn down the music or break up a fight or deal with a drunk fraternity brother or friend, I always, and I mean always, would be the one to intervene. I'd be the negotiator, the voice of reason, and the seemingly responsible party. And after all, having been a Marine MP, I knew these situations all too well, albeit from the other side. *Yes sir officer, you won't have any more problems with us tonight. Absolutely officer, the music will be turned way down. Sir, we're all about to head home and go back to our studies.*

These incidents ultimately became my first mediations.

Our main athletic rival while I was at Rockhurst was Benedictine College. For one particularly crucial basketball game between our two schools, my fraternity chartered a bus to make the trip to their campus, located in Atchison, Kansas. Of course this was a party bus, complete with multiple kegs of beer. We were all toasted before the game even started. Afterward, as we made our way out of their gym and back to our bus, my close friend (then and now) Johnny McMaster started taunting a group of the Benedictine football players who had been in attendance. Fully living up to his nickname of *Johnny Disaster*, he was about to incite a full-on brawl. After telling him multiple times to "Shut the hell up!" to no avail, I finally picked up Johnny and carried him to the bus. No way was I going to let the drunken bravado of a bunch of brawny teenagers lead to me getting my ass kicked.

At another basketball game against Benedictine, this time on our campus, someone decided to bring a whole burnt chicken to taunt our rival, the Ravens. This was our prop for the continual chant of "What do we eat? Raven meat!" that we repeated continuously. Of course we were well warmed-up after our pre-game party, as was always the case. It was almost inevitable that the burnt chicken would be thrown on the court. The administration was so furious that we were actually suspended from attending future Rockhurst athletic events. Finally our suspension was lifted, but under the condition that we did not act out in any way. In response we created the *silent cheer*, where we'd flail our arms, pump our fists, move our lips, and generally pantomime hysteria and euphoria at key moments, all while never actually making a sound. I'd like to tell you that the silent cheer was my idea. Unfortunately I'm not that imaginative, but I did give it my full endorsement and participation.

I really loved my time at Rockhurst College. It was an extremely "frosty" and much-needed experience—perfect for me, in fact, at that time in my life. I studied everything from Beowulf (in the original Olde English—with a little help from *CliffsNotes*) taught by Frank Sheeran, to religious doctrine with Father "Buddha" Nash. We called him "Buddha" because anytime someone disagreed with him on an issue of religion, he'd have them write a paper on Buddha. My favorite class was Shakespeare with Father Oldani, an upper level course with only 12 total students. It was intense and detailed, and we all knew that if you weren't fully prepared you were better off staying home. My first date with Licia was at a performance of *Hamlet,* which I was required to attend for this class.

During my entire stint as a full-time student at Rockhurst, I also held a full-time job. First, I worked at Rainbow Mental Health Center in Kansas City, Kansas, as an aid in charge of the adolescent cottage—five days a week from 11 p.m. to 7 a.m. I'd get off work, go to campus for my classes, sleep in the afternoon, party in the evening, then go in for my shift. Somehow, I was never exhausted.

Eventually I left Rainbow Mental Health Center and worked for a really nice older lady named Virginia Hart, who owned a very high-end antique store. She lived in Mission Hills, Kansas, (for those of you not familiar with the area, this is one of the wealthiest and most exclusive suburbs in the Kansas City metro), and her customers were the elite of the city. Imagine paying $10,000 for a chair–and doing so in 1977! My job was to personally deliver the antiques to the customers' homes– venturing into neighborhoods that seemed like a dream. Mrs. Hart genuinely was one of the kindest and warmest people I've ever met in my life. I really cared for her, and she cared for me.

Between these two jobs I worked for a couple of seasons as a beer vendor at Royals (now Kauffman) Stadium, and it didn't end well. In fact, I was fired. Working at a gig where you get to be at the stadium every day and watch baseball might seem like fun, but being a beer vendor was truly brutal. It's always hot, the beer container is heavy, people are always yelling, your feet hurt, you never stop moving, and you absolutely never get to see actual baseball being played. Toward the end of the second game of a doubleheader with the New York Yankees, I'd had it, and along with two of my coworkers I moved to the far reaches of the upper deck down the left field line. We filed into the empty seats, and helped ourselves to the remaining unsold beers while we counted the money. Our supervisor spotted us, ran up immediately, and was absolutely livid. The other two beer vendors apologized and then exited quietly. Meanwhile, I sat there drinking my beer and listening to his venom. Remember how I told you earlier in this book that I've always had a smart-ass streak? Well, my supervisor launched into a diatribe about my high degree of unprofessionalism and my utter lack of work ethic. He then asked me in a flat-out yell, "Name me one goddamn example of where you can drink on the job?!" Without missing a beat, I replied, "Bartender." Needless to say, that was the end of my employment at Royals Stadium.

I graduated from Rockhurst College in four years, cum laude with a B.A. in English. From there it was on to the Syracuse University College of Law, where I had received a fellowship. My fellowship had been arranged by Robert Jackson, one of the deans of students at Rockhurst. He was also one of the top black lawyers in Kansas City, and had worked extensively in prison law. This fellowship paid for my tuition and books, plus it gave me a living stipend. On top of this I had the G.I. Bill, which was paying me another $500 per month. This allowed me to have a better financial situation than when I was working full-time as an undergrad. So Licia and I, along with our Irish wolfhound puppy Arklow, loaded up a moving truck and headed east from Kansas City.

In Syracuse I rented a tiny studio apartment that didn't even have its own bathroom. The toilet, tub, and shower were located in a separate room down the hall, for use by all of the building's residents. We had just enough room for our bed, a refrigerator, and a stove. And really nothing else. Arklow slept with me, as she really didn't have any other options because she was so big.

I enjoyed Syracuse, but it never seemed a perfect fit. Annoyingly, I was required to take classes separate from the College of Law, which made no sense to me. I was there to become a lawyer, and that involved studying the law full-time. Anything else academically seemed like a waste of my time, so I rarely attended these outside mandated courses. Toward the end of the school year law firms from around the country came to interview us for summer clerkships. The only Kansas City firm that signed up, Blackwell Sanders, wound up not coming. These clerkships were key, as they often led to a job offer if things progressed well. The only firms that interviewed us were from the East Coast, and I had no intention of settling in that part of the country. My mind had long been made up that I wanted to return to Kansas City after law school, so I figured that I needed to find a school closer to home.

I transferred to the University of Minnesota, which worked in my favor geographically, and whose law school ranked higher than Syracuse's. Mistakenly, I thought that its location in Minneapolis would not be as cold and snowy as Syracuse, which was of course not the case. Happily, I had my credits transfer, and I received the same fellowship that I had at Syracuse. Financially and academically, I was covered.

During my first year at Minnesota I was able to get a job in the law school's Legal Aid clinic, which I loved. It was real work, complete with my own caseload. Even though we were students, Legal Aid actually let us represent clients in court, albeit under the close supervision of attorneys. The vast majority of my Legal Aid cases were of the domestic variety, and even though I was thriving, I quickly realized that I didn't want to practice family law upon graduation. It was too painful and there was too much emotion. People were just too emotional in these situations. I had a client in a seemingly life-or-death argument over who would receive the sheets and pillow cases. There was a constant stream of vindictive nonsense involved in these cases. It was great at the time for me as a law student, but not a direction in which I wanted to steer my professional life.

While at Minnesota I joined the Third World Caucus, which initially seemed to me like a quality and worthwhile organization. But before my second meeting I met two white students, who entered the room with me. Prior to the meeting they told me they were fully aware they didn't fit the organization's profile, but they believed in the values and principles of the Third World Caucus and felt that they could contribute as members. But when they entered the room everything stopped cold, and they were told to leave. White people weren't welcome. I spoke up immediately and said that if they weren't allowed to join, then I wanted nothing to do with this organization. To me this was just another form of discrimination. The Third World Caucus was explicitly for blacks, Hispanics, and Native Americans only, and that was that. My stance didn't make me very popular with the minority faction of the student body, but I didn't care. I saw bullshit, and I called them on it. After all, how were we to learn from and about each other if we excluded segments of our community from engaging with us?

Toward the end of my first year at Minnesota, I'd decided to attend Georgetown University to pursue an LLM in criminal law, which is a Master of Laws post-law school graduate degree.

But my old friend Robert Jackson from Rockhurst, the man who had originally gotten me my fellowship at Syracuse, told me that he had signed me up to interview with a number of prestigious law firms. His reasoning was that it was now in vogue for major firms to claim that they were actively trying to hire "qualified" minority applicants, and I had the highest grade point average of all minority students at the University of Minnesota Law School. So, he explained, if they were being truthful and really committed to integrating their firms, then I was exactly the person whom they would hire. I agreed, but only as a social experiment. I was still committed to going to Georgetown to continue my education.

First up was a boutique firm in Minneapolis that was not a good fit for me at all. They were Order of the Coif, Law Review, gentile smart-guy types. Not at all whom I saw myself spending time with in my career.

A firm in Chicago that specialized in entertainment law and counted the band Aerosmith among its superstar clients really intrigued me. I interviewed with the senior partner, whose office was so big that it contained two separate seating areas with multiple couches. But an offer never materialized.

Bryan Cave, the largest law firm in Missouri and located in St. Louis, wanted to hire me, but on the condition that I rotate through numerous departments at six-month intervals. The money was big, but I had no desire to spend time in areas such as banking law, construction law, and trusts and estates. Beyond that, it seemed too impersonal. Walking through the offices, I met two young associates and struck up a conversation. After a few minutes of pleasant conversation, I asked them how to get back to the office of the senior partner who had been conducting my interview. "Who's that?" they both asked.

Apart from private firms, I interviewed with the Minnesota Attorney General's office, which made me an offer. But I passed, as it just didn't seem like a career move that I wanted to make. Not to mention that I had decided I couldn't live in a place where you had to plug your car into a block heater on extremely cold winter nights. No doubt this was a prestigious job and the money was decent, but I just didn't feel that I would be happy doing this type of work. Numerous people told me that I was "crazy" for turning it down. Instead, I thought of myself as selective, and felt that I had earned the right to be this way.

Finally, I flew home to Kansas City and interviewed with Blackwell Sanders, one of the city's best firms. Blackwell Sanders had no rotation requirement and a great reputation as a trial law firm, and trial law was exactly what I wanted to do. The day I returned to Minneapolis I received a call from Tom Wagstaff, a partner in the firm. He made me an offer, and without hesitation I accepted. Wagstaff seemed astounded, and told me that that this was the first time anyone had ever accepted an offer over the phone. He wanted to make sure that I didn't need time to think things over.

I told him that there was nothing to think about. I'd always planned on returning home to Kansas City, and I felt that working at Blackwell Sanders would allow me to thrive as a lawyer. No longer did I have a desire to go to Georgetown and continue my education; I was ready to become a lawyer. And that was that. All that was left for me to do was successfully complete my second year at Minnesota, my third and final year of law school in total. Oh, and a meeting with the head of the firm, Bill Sanders.

It wasn't until a trip home for Thanksgiving that I had the opportunity to meet Bill Sanders. I felt that this was just a formality, but nonetheless it was still incredibly important for me to make a great impression. Sitting in his office, I noticed that unlike every other office at every other firm I had entered, no diplomas hung on the wall. I soon learned that this was because Bill Sanders had never actually graduated from law school. He attended the University of Chicago Law School, but then left to serve in the Korean War. But he was so brilliant and so driven that he was able to still pass the bar, and become a massively successful attorney.

Bill and I talked for more than an hour. He was genuinely curious about my time in the Marines, and told me about his military service. We discussed my future at his firm, my career goals, my life in general. And when we were finished, Bill took me around to every office at Blackwell Sanders and introduced me to every employee, from the secretaries to the paralegals to the attorneys. It was astounding, and it was outstanding.

Once I had graduated from the University of Minnesota Law School, I began my full-time employment at Blackwell Sanders. And just like every other lawyer there, I didn't hang my diploma on the wall. Bill wanted his clients to know that he only hired great lawyers. He didn't want them to see Harvard in one office and the University of Kansas in another, and draw conclusions based on those pieces of paper.

I took my place at this prestigious and progressive law firm as their first-ever black lawyer. Their first-ever black employee, in fact. "If anyone here ever gives you any trouble about being black, let me know, and I'll fire them on the spot," Bill had told me.

"Boss, I've been black a long time," I assured him with a laugh, "and I can handle that in my own way."

Chapter 20

The Buck O'Neil Bridge

I've already talked a lot in this book about the need for mayors, and for local government as a whole, to innovate. And why at the city level we *have* to innovate. Well, here's an example for you of this innovation, and the subsequent efficiency in action.

The Buck O'Neil Bridge in Kansas City was a bad bridge. This was unfortunate for numerous reasons, including the fact that it was named for such a great man. Originally known as the Broadway Bridge, it was re-named in honor of Buck O'Neil in 2016. For those of you who don't know, O'Neil was a legendary player and manager for the Kansas City Monarchs of Negro League Baseball. He also became the first black coach in Major League Baseball when he was hired by the Chicago Cubs in 1962, and beginning in 1988 he served as a scout for the Kansas City Royals. Additionally, O'Neil was one of the founders of the Negro Leagues Baseball Museum, located in Kansas City's historic 18th and Vine District.

Unfortunately there are no such accolades for the bridge that now bares O'Neil's name. Opened in 1956, this key bridge to our city had long been a crumbling mess when I was first elected mayor. It was in horrible condition and in need of serious repair. Beyond this, it contained far too many twists and turns, was virtually unwalkable (at least safely), and as it emptied into Downtown Kansas City it didn't meet the intersections properly. The Missouri Department of Transportation (MODOT) told my office that they only had $50 million dollars available and were on a "maintenance-only program." I found this curious, as well as interesting. Was this why the Missouri state government had enacted corporate tax cuts: so that they would have less or no money for bridges and infrastructure in need of major maintenance and repair?

This $50 million of state money was not going to adequately address the severe issues of this failing bridge. Keep in mind that 44,000 cars per day cross this bridge. To repair it as best we could with the $50 million would mean complete closure for two years. This is where political ideology has absolutely no place in local government. And why it can't have a place. The Buck O'Neil Bridge leads right into the heart of Downtown Kansas City. Closure meant rerouting an average of almost 310,000 cars per week, and partially cutting off the north part of the city from the south.

Many of the people impacted would be work commuters. This isn't just inconvenience, as lives would have to be rearranged. People would have to leave earlier for work, which meant that the issues of childcare would certainly come into play for many of them. Who would watch the kids for the extra time vacated by the parents for their new commute? They would have to leave home earlier than before, and would arrive home later in the evening.

Suddenly an issue about a bridge becomes an issue about childcare. The big picture problems always lead to the everyday life problems that directly affect the citizens. And then there are all the considerations of commerce, tourism, and special events that would be disrupted.

If the inconvenience to commuters wasn't bad enough, the southbound entrance to the Wheeler Downtown Airport was at the foot of the bridge. That posed a number of problems. First, if the bridge had to be closed for two years, we would have to build and man a fire station at the airport, because fire trucks and ambulances would not be able to quickly respond in cases of an emergency. Additionally, Children's Mercy Hospital used the downtown airport, and their services would be impacted. And we doubted that the companies with corporate planes, whose business sustained the airport, would put up with the inconvenience for such an extended period of time. There was realistic and genuine concern that they might move en masse to other airports in the area, and possibly never return.

So this idea of closing the bridge for two years was completely unacceptable. In response, City Manager Troy Schulte, his staff, and I started looking for options as well.

We knew that fixes and repairs were short-term solutions. But we also knew that the cost of a new bridge would exceed $200 million, and this is before factoring in the potential tariffs on steel. Clearly a new Buck O'Neil Bridge was what we all desired. But the city didn't have $200 million, and if MODOT did they weren't going to send it our way.

The state of Missouri finally came back to us and said that if they really stretched their budget and moved things around, well then they might just be able to provide $100 million. Great, but where was the other $100 million plus going to come from for the new bridge? And keep in mind, the Buck O'Neil Bridge is, and always was, a state-owned bridge. It just happens to be located in our city.

Predictably, the issue of the Buck O'Neil Bridge fell directly to us as local government. The state of Missouri was not going to offer solutions, and certainly the federal government wasn't either. MODOT wasn't the culprit here. They are a state agency, and have to work with the budget that the legislature provides. The City Council opposed use of any of the bond money from the GO (General Obligation) Bond initiative that had recently passed.

Working with this perceived $100 million-plus shortfall, we were able to allocate $60 million from our Public Improvements

Advisory Committee (PIAC) program. This money could have, and really should have, been used for local issues–not a state-owned bridge. But there was no other realistic choice.

Then we were able to work with surrounding municipalities and get a number of them to agree to channel some of their Federal Surface Transportation Program (STP) funds toward the bridge project. This meant another $40 million.

So there was now $100 million secured through our area local governments. This meant under the best-case scenario we had exactly half of the money needed for the new Buck O'Neil Bridge. All the while, we kept thinking that the state of Missouri was going to find a way to get out of paying their promised $100 million.

Thus, with all parties staying true to their word and costs not getting out of control, *we* found a way to pay the $200 million price tag to build our new bridge, which is really not even ours! But this bridge was incredibly important to us, so we found a way to solve the problem. Now we just have to get it built.

As local government we knew that the state and federal governments were not going to help us find the answer. This was up to us and us alone. Working to raise the $200 million for the construction of the new Buck O'Neil Bridge stands as one of the proudest achievements of my time as mayor. And it stands as a clear example of the great government collaboration for the mutual good. Two municipalities who agreed to contribute were partners indeed. We had the need at the city level to undertake a massive and sorely-needed project, yet without the required funds. But we found a way, just the same.

This doesn't happen enough on either the state or federal level. As the local government of Kansas City, we were not unique in this problem solving. Mayors and local governments do this every day across the country.

How many times have you heard talk of federal infrastructure projects? Yet where are they? Where is all of this money that is supposed to be available from the state capitals and from Washington, D.C. ?

The federal government has talked about allocating 20 percent of the needed funds for infrastructure issues, with the other 80 percent coming from the private sector. This is absurd, as there is no private profit motive to fix a stretch of interstate or build a bridge. And of course if the private sector can't make any money, then they aren't going to come up with any money to get involved. Thus these proposed public-private partnerships don't make much sense, unless you can charge a toll on a road or bridge–which you can't legally do in Missouri. They fail before they even start.

We all hear the campaign promises about roads and bridges, but after the election these promises are forgotten. They are campaign promises and nothing more. There is no plan and there is certainly no action.

Local government works because we are focused on finding pragmatic sustainable solutions to problems. State and federal governments don't work, because they are guided by ideology rather than pragmatism. The party that is in power lets it be known that things will be done their way. And of course, the minority party vehemently objects. Nobody ever works together. Nobody ever comes together to address issues and solve problems.

To draw an analogy, this situation is like the dad coming home from work every day and telling the kids *it doesn't matter what your mom says, this is what's going to happen–period!*

When this occurs, it means that mom and dad aren't getting along very well, and they won't get along moving forward. And the kids are left bouncing around from idea to idea, uncertain whom to follow and what to believe. This situation creates insecure kids and a high level of dysfunction.

And this is where we are now as a country: full of insecurity and mired in dysfunction.

Chapter 21

Blackwell Sanders & Michael Keith Samuels

Licia and I moved back to Kansas City after I graduated from the University of Minnesota Law School in May 1983.

Even though I was happy to be back home, I really had enjoyed my time in Minneapolis. The law school was tough and highly-rated, and the people and the city were progressive. Throughout law school, I'd played intramural baseball in the graduate school league. My final game took place the day after graduation. Even in May, it was so cold that I wore long underwear under my uniform, earmuffs with my cap, and a winter glove in my mitt as I played right field.

During the game I doubled to right center, and moved up to third base on a long sacrifice fly to right. While on third, I took an aggressive lead that gained the attention of the very good catcher on the medical school team. He threw a low bullet to the bag, which forced me to dive back head first—which turned out to be a big mistake. The infield dirt was like sharp, nubby concrete. I left some skin on the frozen ground, and I was once again reminded of one reason I was glad to be leaving the Twin Cities and heading back to the relatively warm climate of my hometown.

Upon our return to Kansas City, I began studying for the bar exam and started work at Blackwell Sanders. I talked the firm into prorating my salary over that summer, so that I could take time off from work to prepare for the bar in July. The bar exam is a nerve-racking two-day torture, as failure would not only be embarrassing, but also potentially job-threatening. No rational person ever wants to take the bar more than once.

Once I'd decided as an undergrad at Rockhurst that I wanted to go to law school, I quickly settled in on the idea of becoming a trial attorney. For me, this was the practice of law. I now had a job at Blackwell Sanders, which was known as a trial firm. Not all law firms have this designation. Some firms are more accomplished in tax or corporate practice.

Blackwell Sanders was split down the middle between trial attorneys and corporate attorneys. In our first meeting Bill Sanders said that he saw me as a trial attorney, which was exactly what I wanted to hear. Early on he placed me in attorney Jim Horn's trial team. Horn was a senior partner who ran insurance defense for the firm, and who went to trial constantly.

Jim and his team, which included Bill Sanders Jr., handled car wrecks, slip and falls, accidents—that type of thing. And they were really good at trying cases. It was an honor to be placed with Jim and to immediately begin doing exactly what I wanted to do in my law career. As an associate, I was trying cases before most partners in other firms ever had the opportunity.

I'd be given a $10,000 automobile case, while a partner at another firm would have a $10 million commercial or business litigation case. In all likelihood, the one going to trial was mine. Theirs would reach settlement, and usually only saw the inside of a courtroom on motion practice. While they weren't generally big or high-dollar, I was trying numerous cases per year.

I worked on the trial team during my entire time at Blackwell Sanders, and both my cases and caseload grew progressively bigger. This was ideal, but still exhausting. As an associate at a large law firm, any large law firm, it's all about billable hours. They are everything, and you work your ass off. And of course, your billable hours are tracked in meticulous fashion. In the early 1980s this was done on a prehistoric word processor. I always pitied the poor word processors who had to do this thankless and mind-numbing work.

We'd be able to check our billable hours to see how we were doing and if we were hitting our targets. I quickly realized that for me to hit my billable hours I'd have to work long hours, go home, and then start all over again. Whereas corporate lawyers were often able to bill in hour-long increments, working for insurance company clients required me to bill in tenths of an hour. This was not what I had in mind when I first entered law school. So I decided to do something different. I'd go home in the evening, have dinner, and spend time with Licia and the kids. Once everyone had gone to bed, I'd go back to the office and resume my work.

Without fail, Bill Sanders was always there late at night. Often it would be just the two of us in the offices of the firm well past midnight. This shared time allowed us to grow close, as we'd eat together, share a cup of coffee, sometimes just talk. On one occasion, Bill asked me if blacks and Mexicans get along. "Why don't you go ask them?" I responded in my typical smart-ass fashion. The reason for his query was that Bill had a case where one of the litigants on the other side was Hispanic. And what it came down to was that Bill wanted some color at his table in the courtroom.

I told him that I wouldn't be window dressing; that I wouldn't just sit there silently and be black. For me to join him on this trial, he was going to have to give me something to do. Bill agreed, and he let me do a few small things. The next time I got to do even more. And this pattern progressed.

On one case, Bill turned to me and said that it was time for me to do voir dire–jury selection. Stunned, I told him that I didn't know how to do voir dire. And he told me that I'd better learn quickly. I proceeded to do a really poor job, because I had absolutely no idea of what I was doing. Then, as I was continuing to flounder, Bill said, "Okay, now watch how I do it," as he smoothly took over.

Later, on a particularly big trial, Bill assigned me as second chair. This was a really complicated case, and it was truly exciting to be included. But then on Monday morning Bill turned up at the firm hobbled, as one of his horses had stepped on his heel over the weekend. He informed me that my second chair duties would now include pushing him around in his wheelchair. This is going to look great, I thought, *The lone black lawyer pushing his white boss around the courtroom!*

But I really liked and cared for Bill, so I went with it. So much so, in fact, that I was able to get my hands on one of the white jackets that the bus boys wore at Annie's Santa Fe, one of our regular lunch stops located on the Plaza. We won't get into how I got the jacket, but let's just say that I borrowed it forever.

The next day when I came to the firm, I was wearing this stark white jacket, and I called out to Bill, "Come on Mister Sanders. I'm gonna put you in yo' chair, and take you down to trial."

Yes, it was racial, but it was funny. And we all had a laugh.

Bill was a genuinely kind man, and he was a brilliant man. He had the ability to take the most complex case and break it down to its core elements, so that it was easily understood.

I did, however, have my frustrations while working at Blackwell Sanders. Our firm was retained by a woman named Sue Miller, who was the plaintiff in a wrongful death case. This was extremely unusual for our firm, as we almost exclusively did defense work. But Blackwell Sanders took this case, and it was assigned to me. Sue's husband had suffered a heart attack, and the medical alert system installed in their home failed to work. Because no one ever responded, Mr. Miller died of the heart attack. Sue felt that had the medical alert system worked, her husband's life would have been saved. Thus, the lawsuit.

I worked my ass off, including taking a great deposition from the medical alert system people. And I'd developed a rapport and a high level of trust with Mrs. Miller. But when it came time to go to trial, I was told that I would be second chair. And then, when the trial started, I quickly discovered that I had been relegated to third chair. My case, on which I had devoted my time, energy, and emotions, had been taken from me, and without proper explanation.

To make matters worse, Sue Miller and her family kept asking why I wasn't leading this case. They made it clear that they wanted me. I followed the company line, and assured them that more experienced trial attorneys had been assigned and that they were in great hands. "But we want you," Sue Miller and her family kept telling me.

My role during trial was extremely limited, but acting as the good employee I kept my mouth shut and did what I was told to do.

The case, which I felt that I absolutely could have won, was lost in the end. Mrs. Miller received nothing, as the defense prevailed. That night back at the law firm, Bill Sanders stormed into my office and threw the time sheets for the case down on my desk. "Look at all of this goddamn time that you wasted on this case," he yelled at me. "And now we're never going to get paid for any of it."

The case had been taken on contingency, and since the ruling went against us there was no money to claim for the firm.

I told Bill in no uncertain terms that I did what I was supposed to do: I put together a great case. And then, just before trial, my case was taken from me by your lawyers, who lost it. Right there in my office, we had it out. I was on the verge of getting fired. And I thought that this would be my final night at Blackwell Sanders.

Instead Bill exiled me to the firm's Kansas office, located in the Kansas City suburb of Olathe. We didn't speak for weeks afterward, as we remained furious at each other.

Having been relocated, I suddenly had no idea what my job entailed at Blackwell Sanders. In fact, none of us did at that satellite office. Supposedly we were to work on a case involving a pet food plant that had a multi-million dollar lawsuit, for some reason which I honestly didn't understand then and still don't. Nothing was properly explained to us. So we all just sat there, spinning our wheels, waiting for guidance and direction that never came.

Finally I'd had enough, and called Bill. The other lawyers in the Kansas office seemed terrified, and pleaded with me not to bother him. This was the first time that Bill and I had talked since our blow up in my office. I asked him directly, "Exactly what the hell are we supposed to be doing out here with this case?"

Bill actually provided instruction, but it was all scut work–low level stuff. We could have done it in half the time allotted, with half of the people assigned. But they were sparing no expense on this case. A scale model of the pet food plant had been created, and it was elaborate, intricate, detailed, and utterly amazing. It must have cost at least $100,000, and it was massive.

After much time, effort, and money spent, the case went to trial, and Bill lost. Immediately afterward, I went down to his office at the Kansas City headquarters and threw a stack of time sheets on his desk. "Look at all of the goddamn time that you wasted on this case," I told him. "We're never ever getting this money back." Bill looked at me directly in the eyes without saying anything.

"Now how does that feel?" I asked him earnestly.

"Not very good," he replied. "And I know that you've been waiting to say this. Now let's go get a whiskey."

And with that, we went to his home, drank late into the night, and rekindled our friendship.

Now back in Bill's good graces, he assigned me to work a huge agricultural case with him as third chair. Penny Johnson was second chair, and the opposing counsel was a lawyer who was a known asshole.

There was a huge argument over documents, and finally the opposing lawyer said that he'd produce what we had requested. The caveat was that they'd have to be reviewed at his house. Bill

Sanders called me into his office and asked me to accompany Penny Johnson on this field trip. When I asked why, Bill told me that he didn't trust the lawyer alone with Penny.

When Penny and I arrived at the house the lawyer brought out his antique menstrual cup collection, in some horribly misguided attempt to impress Penny. We're trying to review the documents, and he kept redirecting our attention–Penny's attention really–back to these menstrual cups. It was totally inappropriate. Finally, I told the lawyer that we'd like for the documents to all be shipped back to our firm, and that we were leaving.

At trial, the lawyer was cross-examining one of our witnesses. Suddenly, he turns to me and says brusquely that he needs a certain defense exhibit. As third chair I was in charge of documents for our team, so the request was appropriate. His demeaning and rude tone, however, was not. As I maneuvered through the massive sea of boxes and paperwork, the lawyer said to me, even louder and more aggressively, that he needs this defense exhibit.

"I'm looking for it," I responded.

"Well then hurry up!" was his shouted reply.

With that, right there in federal court, I told him to "hold your damn horses."

All hell then broke loose. The lawyer was practically foaming at the mouth, as he ranted to the judge about how I needed to be sanctioned right there for saying such a thing to him in front of the jury. The judge, fully aware of his character and reputation, told him to calm down. I wouldn't be sanctioned; he was to get over it and resume his cross-examination at once.

At the end of the day, as we're walking out of court, this lawyer ran up to me. Jabbing a finger in my face, he screamed, "You don't ever talk to me like that again. Ever! Do you understand?"

Steeling my gaze, I responded, "Your name isn't on my damn paycheck, so you need to get the fuck away from me. I don't care who you are. I'll kick your ass."

He stepped back, stammered, and then walked away. Bill

Sanders then said to me, "I don't think that you should have said that. He's mean and vindictive."

"Sorry boss," I told him, "but you know that I don't take shit. And anyway, I'm not afraid of him."

I was then confronted by the lawyer's two associates, who had been assisting him at the trial, and I thought, *Here we go again*.

But to my pleasant surprise they said, "I know that he's our boss, but the guy is the biggest prick in the world."

"Yeah, and nobody has ever talked to him like that. We're so glad that you did."

We went on to win this case, which of course made the lawyer even angrier with me. Oh well.

Immediately following our successful verdict, the judge, Joe Stevens, asked me to report to his chambers. I had noticed throughout trial that he had been staring at me, but I figured that it was all related to the issue with the documents.

So I was ready to discuss this further when I met him face-to-face. Instead, Judge Stevens said that he wanted to appoint me to defend a guy on a federal criminal case. "But I'm not a criminal defense attorney," I protested. He retorted that it was a straightforward case, I would have support, and that he knew that I could handle it.

"But why me?" I queried. "There are a lot of great criminal defense lawyers in the city, and there are also public defenders here who can do this."

"Mr. James, the defendant keeps firing his lawyers. And as a black man, he's now insisting on having a black lawyer. And, well, you're the only black lawyer I know."

The case was The United States of America vs Michael Keith Samuels. My client was a severely mentally-ill young man who had been diagnosed as a paranoid schizophrenic, and had recently gone off of his medications.

Samuels became convinced that Soviet Union government officials were speaking to him through his television, in an attempt to control his mind. These imagined conversations led Samuels to write a letter to then President Ronald Reagan, addressed to the White House, and signed by Samuels himself.

It read in full:

To Ronald Reagan and all the other Presidents of the Honkeys who stole the land from the Indians. Stop fucking with me or I will kill you with no clothes on.

Michael Keith Samuels

The letter was of course turned over to the Secret Service, Samuels was arrested and charged in Federal Court, and he had been in jail ever since.

When I first met with Samuels he was not stabilized on his meds, and was completely psychotic. All that I could do is listen to him, nod my head, and tell him that I understood.

Then Samuels told me that he wanted to sue the United States government. I responded that this isn't possible, but he insisted that he'd sue them anyway. I again told him that I understood.

He then handed me a bunched up ball of handwritten papers which read:

I Michael Keith Samuels sue the United States Government for $1,000,000,000,000,000...

A full 20 pages containing nothing but zeroes and commas then followed.

After meeting with Samuels, I filed a motion with the court claiming that he was incompetent to stand trial. He was clearly unable to assist in his defense, he was psychotic, and he needed professional treatment. What Samuels did not need was a federal criminal trial and prison.

Medical professionals who had treated Samuels previously gave statements that he was of no danger to anyone. The medical consensus was that Samuels could be stabilized once back on his medication, and his psychotic and paranoid behavior would cease.

Judge Stevens, however, ruled that Samuels was competent

to stand trial while he was taking his meds. Samuels was then moved to the Medical Facility for Federal Prisoners in Springfield, Missouri, and the case was transferred to that city for the trial.

My immediate thoughts were: *Oh great, I'm a black lawyer in my first criminal case, defending a psychotic black man who threatened the life of President Reagan, and I get to do so in Springfield, Missouri. What could go wrong?*

I continued to try to have Samuels declared incompetent, but Judge Stevens would never budge. The pressure on me was tremendous, as I really felt that I had my client's life in my hands.

On the first day of trial, Samuels sat down next to me at the defense table, and I could see that he was overly medicated. He was drooling, continually nodding off, and unable to speak coherently beyond an occasional "How we doing, Mr. James?"

The key moment in the trial came when I cross-examined a psychologist who was a witness for the prosecution. I'd literally stayed up all night preparing for him. Once he was on the stand, I felt as though I was tearing him apart. But I realized later that I wasn't being wise about it. I became so angry at this quack that I was fully on the attack. Meanwhile, he answered my questions calmly and matter-of-factly. Juries most definitely notice these things.

I asked him, "Doctor, don't you admit that a man who is psychotic would be unable to form the requisite intent to actually do what he says that he is going to do?"

The psychologist's response was, "Well, Lawyer James, I'm just an old country boy. But I can tell you that a dog can have both fleas and ticks."

"What the hell does that mean?" I snapped back.

"Just because he's psychotic don't mean that he ain't dangerous."

When the judge sent the case to the jury, the foreman stood up and asked if they actually had to deliberate, since they had already made up their minds.

I knew exactly what this meant.

Fifteen minutes later, after being ordered by the judge to deliberate in the jury room, a verdict of guilty was returned.

Ultimately, I filed an appeal with the Eighth Circuit Court of Appeals, which ruled that Samuels never should have stood trial. He was released from federal prison and sent to a halfway house. For many years after, I'd hear from Michael Keith Samuels. He'd ask me for $10 so that he could buy cigarettes or a bus pass. I'd mail him a check for $25.

Eventually his calls came with less frequency, until they finally stopped altogether.

Chapter
22

Leadership Not Legacy

Politicians are continually asked about their legacy, but legacy has never mattered to me. As I wrote earlier in this book, I've always been about "we" and "us," rather than "I" and "me." And legacy seems to be about "I" and "me."

I believe the most important thing that we did long-term during my eight years as mayor of Kansas City was to focus on education and kids. Nationwide, our population is aging to the point where pretty soon we're going to have more old people who aren't working than young people who are. My generation, the baby boomers, are terming out, and the population has not kept pace with it.

If we're going to be prepared for this new reality of smaller numbers of young people supporting larger numbers of old people, then the young people must have skills. The time to start developing these skills starts before birth, as this is when prospective and soon-to-be parents should be educated about brain development in newborns through five year olds. The biggest cerebral explosion takes place during that time when the brain is 85 percent to 90 percent formed.

For many lower-income kids, there is already a 30-million word gap with higher-income kids, by the age of three. This has to

197

be cured. Pre-K education needs to begin at age four. And the five year olds must be kindergarten-ready.

All of this flows directly into third grade reading proficiency. As I've already detailed in this book, this is a critical crossroads for kids. If they are behind with their reading at third grade, the chances for success in later life are significantly diminished. This fact simply cannot be overstated.

My administration made it our priority to look at this timeframe and try to really make a difference in kids' lives. This isn't simply an altruistic platitude. The benefits to society are massive. There is a return of seven dollars on every one dollar invested in quality pre-K. Crime rates go down, and employment rates will go up.

Kids who have quality pre-K educations are 80 percent more likely to go to college than their non-pre-K counterparts. And without pre-K, the likelihood of third grade reading proficiency drops dramatically. Then these kids who are behind in their reading in the third grade are 31 percent less likely to graduate from high school. You can see where it often goes from there.

When you have all of this data, when you now know all of these things, it's impossible to sit back and do nothing. At least it was impossible for me. Even though none of this is in the City Charter, as mayor I wasn't going to act as though this was none of my business. It's vital to our city, and to every city for that matter, to build the workforce of the future and the citizens of the future.

Sadly, the schools can't be relied upon to remedy this situation on their own. Hell, most schools don't even teach civics anymore. And they barely teach government. Other programs had to be created outside of the traditional school structure, so we created them.

Of all the things accomplished during my eight years in office, the focus on our kids is by far the most important, and the one most likely to pay long-term dividends.

I'm often asked if I'd like the new airport in Kansas City named after me. My answer is always the same: *I don't care what they name it, as long as we get it.* I feel the same way about our pre-K and third grade reading proficiency initiatives. And I absolutely don't care who gets or takes credit. Instead, I'm looking for the programs to be put in place and then thrive. This has never been about me as mayor. It's always been about making sure that every child, regardless of zip code, race, or socioeconomics, has an equitable chance at success. This is truly about us as a city.

Taking credit is at the heart of the difference between politics and leadership. Finding others of like minds to get things accomplished is what it should always be about. This for me is leadership.

When I was at Marine boot camp, I never once heard our drill instructors focus on themselves. They were teaching us how to focus on each other. Their goal was to make us responsible for and to our fellow Marines. It was instilled in us that we had to help the weakest in our group succeed. Clearly, it would have been much easier to shit-can them or ostracize them or forget about them completely. But what we came to understand is that the weakest person just might be who you need to save your ass in combat. So we treated the struggling among our group like we needed them, and we built them up. Everyone was given multiple chances for success, because ultimately it was in their and our best interest.

I believe in leadership. I'm not a fan of partisan politics and partisan politicians. And at the state and federal levels, I see a lot of politicians, and not nearly enough leaders. I am a big fan of GovLeaders.org, which is a group of representatives from the NSA, EPA, FERC, VA, NASA, FDA, HHS, FDA, Reserve Officers Association and the Graduate School, and USDA. They began to meet together monthly in July 2001 with the mission to "re-energize the practice of leadership for the public good."

I was fascinated when I read their paper, "The Leadership Dilemma in a Democratic Society." In it, these leaders asked a number of pertinent questions, including: "Is there a natural conflict between our elected constitutional process and structures which directly affect the practice of leadership for the public good?"

This leads to other important questions, such as: "Can we describe these structures in ways that would help us learn together and begin the journey of creating more ideal public sector workplaces?"; "How can we overcome the barriers inherent in our system of governance, which no longer serve us well?"; and "Who cares about the practice of public sector leadership?"

Through a series of diagrams and discussions, this group made a powerful point that accurately describes our current political atmosphere, which should give us pause. The Constitution, they reminded, requires elections. And in those elections, candidates try to differentiate themselves from one another, including the incumbents. We know that in almost all campaigns, candidates are prone to make campaign promises. And, of course, they often criticize the campaign promises, programs, and performance of their opponents, even if some of those promises, programs, and their performance have merit. Think "Obamacare."

Once elected, they further observed, the elected then acts through their appointees and the bureaucracy to fulfill those campaign promises as quickly as possible. They strive for the "short-term fix," often ignoring or abandoning in the process potential long-term solutions to problems. In this way, they can say when they run again, "I promised you I would say, 'build the wall' and I did, so re-elect me!"

GovLeader.org further points out how this process of running against incumbents creates distrust of career civil servants, as they are perceived as keepers of the status quo, and thus suspected of resisting new initiatives. This distrust leads to suspicion regarding attempts to educate the appointed officials, and reduces the speed of the learning curve in both groups.

This immediate focus on fulfillment of short-term campaign promises then simply becomes an added duty for the career civil servant, and the highest priority for the elected's appointees. The pre-existing long-term work is then left to lower-level civil servants, who are deprived of resources that are diverted to the campaign promise goals. And the civil servants are further deprived of upper-level leadership.

All of this contributes to poor morale and lowered productivity within the organization. As more and more elections take place and different elected officials come and go, the civil servant is left to lurch from one campaign promise goal to another. And our country is denied viable, sustainable solutions to long-term problems. Look no further than the issue of health care.

The brilliant analysis put forth by GovLeaders.org accurately defines the problem with partisan politics and elections. It also clearly and boldly illustrates why the chronic problems of this country and the 50 states never seem to be adequately addressed. And it shows why local, nonpartisan government works better than its federal and state partisan counterparts.

I truly believe that being mayor of a major city is the best job in politics. Mayors are forced to get things done, think long-term, and solve everyday problems every single day. It's leadership at its most basic and effective, plain and simple.

If there were more real leaders, then the games that are being played on the citizens wouldn't exist. These politicians are locked into an ideological war with no end in sight. Party has, in many instances, been elevated over country. Sadly, winning has become everything.

As elected officials, we are in the service business. We are public servants. Period. And if the politicians can't accept this fact, then they need to find a new line of work. The public is not our servant, which seems to be continually twisted.

It's been a huge benefit to be a nonpartisan mayor, because I've never been beholden to a political party or political ideology. As mayor, I was only beholden to the people. Had the mayor's office been tied to partisan politics, then I would have been the wrong man for the job. You know by now that not only am I a smart-ass, I'm also an independent thinker. In my role as mayor, and in my life, I've always tried to do what I thought was the right thing.

I'm open minded, I analyze data, and I try to listen to others. But in the end, I try to always act according to what I truly believe is right and just.

My hope for Kansas City is that we've learned the lesson that as long as we work together, then we can build things, and do things, and get things done. This shouldn't be forgotten. It would be a terrible thing to see us turn politically and ideologically tribal. We've had that previously in the city, and it was not a great time.

I genuinely hope that the people who follow me in leadership positions actually act as leaders. We need elected officials who work toward building up our entire city and our entire region, as opposed to being ultra-competitive with their peers and rivals.

We have to continue to make strategic investments and build foundations. And foundations by and large rest with the people. Competing interests lead to inefficiency, and often serve as a barrier to success. Life is too damn complicated to be separate. Things work a lot better when there is unity and focus on a common goal.

Kansas Citians are pretty cool people. We're friendly, philanthropic, welcoming, and we step up time and time again. I was really moved while attending our city's Ethnic Enrichment Festival, my final one as mayor. There is a parade of flags, and people from those nations (either directly or by heritage) all walk together, dressed in their traditional clothing. Albanians, Indonesians, Chinese, Serbians, Argentines, Haitians, and so on. I thought, *If we can all get together here with different people from across the globe; eating food, listening to music, and getting along— well then why can't we do that every day?*

We shouldn't have to wait for the Ethic Enrichment Festival one day a year to appreciate other people's cultures, and interact with those who don't look or sound like you. We can do this every day.

I think about this a lot, for not just society, but for politics as well. Being divisive is easy. Getting to really know and understand someone who differs from you in appearance, or thought, or beliefs takes a lot more. And one thing that it absolutely takes is leadership.

Chapter 23

The United States
v Samuel Dowdy Part 1

Following my representation of Michael Keith Samuels, Judge Joe Stevens appointed me to another case. And this one proved to be the most complex, most high profile, and most important of my entire legal career.

I immediately thought, *What the hell have I gotten myself into now?* I also thought that Judge Stevens must have been genuinely impressed with my work on the Samuels case, or else he still didn't know any other black lawyers.

On February 20, 1990, Kansas City Fire Department Captain Gilbert Dowdy and 10 others were indicted on 27 counts, including conspiracy to distribute drugs.

This case was immediately front-page news.

Judge Stevens appointed me to represent Gilbert's brother Sam, one of the other 10 defendants in this federal case.

It was even more daunting when Judge Stevens gave me the additional responsibility of liaison counsel for the defense. I found this to be a very heavy responsibility, considering my relative lack of criminal practice experience, plus the fact that I had no idea of what being "liaison counsel" meant. Most of all, I was acutely aware of the fact that, just as with Samuels, I was again responsible for what would happen to my client's life.

As the case moved toward an inevitable trial, seven of the defendants pled guilty. I quickly realized that I had no real idea of how to approach this type of trial. So I made two critical and crucial decisions.

First, I convinced the firm to allow me to enlist an associate, Mike Furlong, to assist me. This was no small task considering that we were only going to be paid for court-appointed attorneys at the federal rate, which was considerably less than our normal hourly rate in private practice.

Secondly, I decided to approach this criminal case just as I would a major civil case, in that we would read every document and track down and interview as many witnesses as possible to prepare our defense.

Ultimately, this second decision led me to all but abandoning my case docket, in order to work on this case virtually full-time for over a year.

The first thing Mike and I did was to extensively interview our client Sam Dowdy. He vehemently and repeatedly denied any involvement in the alleged drug conspiracy. Sam was a struggling small businessman whose primary source of income was doing home repairs in Kansas City's black community. He was convinced that he'd only been indicted for the purpose of testifying against his brother Gilbert–something that he adamantly refused to do.

It didn't take too long to learn what it meant to be liaison counsel. We were charged with coordinating and filing all of the motions for the defense. We also took on the task of reviewing documents, then summarizing and reporting the significant ones to the entire defense team. By law, we were entitled to review all of the evidence the government had against our clients. Furlong and I met with Linda Parker, the Assistant U.S. Attorney (AUSA) who would try this case, so that we could request access to all of the discovery. She showed us into a large room which was filled with a dozens of boxes stacked on tall shelves, and told us, "Good luck."

Mike and I looked at each other and swallowed hard. We knew that it would literally take months of full days for the two of us to go through all of these documents, in order to determine the relevancy and significance of each one. And once this was accomplished, we'd then have to report our findings to the defense team and start the process of tracking down the witnesses discussed in these thousands upon thousands of pages.

After only a few weeks of reviewing these documents Mike and I thought that our eyes might actually start to bleed. Most of what we found was fairly routine and mundane–things like phone bills of the eleven defendants dating back several years, bank statements, car titles, plane ticket stubs, and receipts for purchases of expensive clothes, watches, and jewelry. But buried in all of this were two items that concerned us.

The first was a stack of Sam's bank records that showed multiple cash deposits going back a number of years. We knew that drug transactions are almost always conducted in cash. Clearly only an idiot would leave a paper trail of bank records implicating themselves in cash drug deals, and Sam was no idiot. It struck Mike and me as odd that most of the deposits were in relatively small, irregular amounts, such as $3,489.29 or $2,918.52. There were no records of $5,000, $10,000, or $20,000 amounts, which you would expect to see in the type of long-standing, large-scale, drug-selling enterprise that the government was alleging. This was really odd.

But we knew the other detail Mike and I uncovered could be extremely damaging to our defense of Sam. There was a single sheet of paper, handwritten by Gilbert's girlfriend Vicki, which clearly documented a drug transaction in specific amounts of money and kilos of cocaine. The scariest part for us was that at the bottom of the page, Vicki had written, "Gave Sam $10,000.00." Mike and I looked at each other in a mutual *Oh shit!* moment.

After we recovered, we went to meet with Linda Parker to see if she would tell us anything about what the government had on Sam. Linda explained that the bank records evidenced drug activity because of the numerous cash deposits, and Vicki's handwritten note proved it. When I asked her what else she had on Sam, Linda flatly stated, "That's all I need."

Mike and I now knew that our entire defense clearly depended on explaining the documents that we'd found. If we had a chance to save our client Sam, it would have to come in the form of explanations for the bank records and what we came to refer to as "the Vicki Note."

When we asked Sam about the bank deposits, he explained to us that the majority of his work consisted of remodels and renovations on homes located in the predominately black neighborhoods on the east side of Kansas City. And, Sam continued, most of his clients distrusted banks and preferred to pay in cash. This rang true from my own childhood experiences. Sam was adamant that all of the bank deposits were from these legal transactions, and had nothing to do with dealing drugs.

"That's great Sam," I told him. "Now you need to give us as many names of past clients as possible."

True to his word, Sam produced a long list of names, and Mike and I began the arduous task of tracking these people down. It was critical to know the type of work that he'd done for them, the dates on which it had occurred, and how much they had paid him. We then met with everyone we could find, and collected from them all of the information that they'd provide. From there, we began the painstaking task of matching this information to Sam's numerous bank deposits in preparation for trial.

The Vicki Note, however, proved to be much more problematic. Sam could not explain why his name was on a piece of paper documenting what clearly appeared to describe an illegal drug transaction. But he did tell us that he sometimes borrowed money from his brother Gilbert when he needed it for his business. Beyond this Sam just kept repeating, "I have no idea. You'll have to ask Vicki". The problem was that Vicki's lawyer would not let us talk to her, no matter how often we asked and how much we argued with him.

We were not completely satisfied. Where would a fire captain get this type of money? Sam explained that Gilbert owned a popular nightclub called The El Capitan, and they did a booming business—a lot of it in cash.

As the trial approached, Linda Parker notified us of a key witness named Carolyn, who was now in the witness protection program. She had allegedly been part of the entire drug conspiracy, and would say in court that our client had indeed been involved. Although our request to take her deposition before trial was denied, Linda did allow us to interview Carolyn on the Saturday before the trial, which was set to begin on Monday.

So less than 48 hours before we were set to be in the federal courthouse, Mike and I met with this striking, tall, confident black woman. She walked calmly into the interview room, sat down, and arranged herself comfortably into a chair. Carolyn was well-dressed and on her left hand flashed an extremely large diamond engagement ring.

Very quickly we went to the heart of when, what, who, why, and how. Carolyn stated that she had been a "drug mule" for the group, and once Sam was present when she was delivering her load of illegal narcotics to Gilbert. Furthermore, Carolyn said that on this occasion she saw Sam put a kilo of cocaine into one of his tennis shoes and leave with it. This was of course damning information.

As the interview was winding down, I found out that Carolyn was engaged to a prominent lawyer who had given her that impressive ring. She was very proud of this expensive piece of jewelry, and eager to talk about it. I just listened intently.

As we grew closer to the start of trial, our firm became more and more concerned about the amount of time and energy that Mike and I were spending on this low-paying federal criminal defense case. I was Sam's court-appointed lawyer, and in this role I enlisted Mike to help me. Sam never could have afforded us at our regular rate. Not even close. Thus, just before the trial was to begin the firm pulled Mike and did not give me a replacement. It was now on me, and me alone, to defend and prove that Sam Dowdy was not guilty.

When I reported to the courtroom on Monday, I saw that Sam and I had been assigned seats at the counsel's table with my friend Carol Coe and her client, Sam's brother Gilbert. But I was immediately concerned with this location, as Carol and Judge Stevens had already engaged in a number of loud and contentious arguments throughout pre-trial proceedings. It got so bad, in fact, that Carol had already been cited twice for contempt of court–and ultimately there would be seven contempt citations against her. I demanded a different and separate seating arrangement for Sam and me. I was genuinely worried that sitting so close to Carol, with the anticipation of more fireworks to come between her and Judge Stevens, would prejudice Sam in the jury's eyes. Happily we were given our own table, placed as far away from Carol and Gilbert as we could get in the crowded courtroom. It was a small but important victory. And on day one of this trial I'd take any victory I could get.

Generally at trial, attorneys will stipulate to the authenticity of routine documents. In this case, however, Carol flatly refused to stipulate to any documents. This then required the prosecution to bring in various custodians of records to testify that the documents had been kept in the regular course of business, and that they were true and accurate copies of the originals. Judge Stevens was absolutely livid. Carol's refusal to stipulate would require that an additional group of witnesses would have to be called to testify about the documents, thereby extending the trial. Judge Stevens and Carol argued vehemently, but Carol refused to budge. She refused to change her mind on this issue, no matter how much Judge Stevens cajoled, yelled, begged, and threatened her.

But Carol's stubborn decision turned out to be a blessing for the defense and all of the lawyers on this side, myself most definitely included. We were silently grateful. This new course of action with the custodians of records allowed us to ultimately poke small holes in the prosecution's case and slow down their presentation. For example, all of the phone providers were now forced to send records custodians as witnesses. On cross-examination, we were able to get them to explain under oath that some of the phone calls the prosecution claimed were conversations in furtherance of the drug-dealing conspiracy could actually be, and probably were, unanswered calls. Even though they showed up on the records as lasting for one minute, it was impossible to tell if these calls were ever completed because of 60-second billing cycles.

Records custodian after records custodian traipsed into the courtroom to testify. It was clear that many were annoyed they had to be there at all. Others were visibly nervous. One was a tall blonde woman from California, wearing a white blouse, beige riding pants, and shiny riding boots. She testified that the titles to all of the expensive and exotic cars that Gilbert had allegedly purchased with drug money were authentic. After her brief direct examination, I rose to cross-examine her.

"I only have a couple of questions," was my opening remark to her.

Then I asked, "Do you know Sam Dowdy?"

"No, I don't think so," she replied.

"Well, would you recognize him if you saw him?"

"No."

"So you never sold Sam Dowdy any cars according to your records, did you?"

After looking through the stack of pages piled up in front of her, this witness flipped her long blonde hair out of her eyes and again answered, "No."

I then turned to the jury and smiled, trying hard to subconsciously persuade them that here, at least, Sam was not involved. My hope, of course, was that the jurors would become increasingly convinced of this, as I asked the proceeding records custodians a similar set of questions, designed to separate Sam from the herd of his co-defendants.

"You don't have any records showing that Sam bought (fill in the blank), do you?" I repeated this for jewelry, property, electronics, clothes, and other expensive items. Although I felt that we had gained some momentum, Carolyn's statements and the Vicki Note were looming, and crying out for plausible explanations.

On the big day of her testimony, Carolyn, wearing fashionably expensive clothes and sporting her big diamond ring, strode into the courtroom. Linda Parker walked her through a long, thorough, and damaging direct examination designed to bury the defendants. She again told her the cocaine in the tennis shoe story, in an attempt to implicate Sam. When my turn came to cross-examine Carolyn, I knew I had to destroy her credibility as a key witness for the government.

"Good morning Ma'am," I said.

"Good morning Mr. James," she responded, with a confident smile that let me know she believed that the upper hand was hers.

"I can't help noticing that beautiful ring on your hand. Where did you get it? It looks like it's about a carat."

She beamed back at me and proudly said, "It's actually two carats." Carolyn then turned to see if the jury was impressed. And some were.

After establishing that she was engaged to a wealthy lawyer, I started my attack.

"Now, it's my understanding that you claim you were a 'mule' and carried cocaine for this alleged conspiracy, is that right?"

"Yes,"

"During this time, were you using cocaine yourself?"

"Yes," was her reply, this time with feigned embarrassment.

"I also understand that at some point you decided to cooperate with the government and testify against all of these defendants. Is that also correct?"

"Yes."

"In exchange for your cooperation and testimony, you were offered immunity and placed in witness protection. Is that correct too?"

I asked this while looking straight at the jury.

"Yes."

"Are you still in witness protection as you sit here?"

"Yes."

"Do you still use cocaine?"

When I asked this question, Linda Parker jumped out of her chair and shouted, "Objection, Your Honor!"

"May we approach the bench?" I asked calmly.

"Yes you may. Come up," responded Judge Stevens.

At the bench Linda argued that my cocaine-use question was irrelevant and prejudicial. I argued that it was absolutely relevant to the credibility of this witness. Judge Stevens overruled Linda's objection, and ordered Carolyn to answer my question. Now, looking directly at her, I could see that she was both fuming and confused.

After a long pause, Carolyn finally answered with a weak "Yes."

The jury was now on full alert and leaning in.

"Tell me, please!" I then resumed. "How is it that you are able to get cocaine, an illegal drug, while you are in the witness protection program?"

With this question, I'd broken one of the cardinal rules of cross-examination, because I didn't know the answer myself. But I figured that now it didn't really matter how she responded. Any answer Carolyn gave would be damaging. However, I wasn't prepared, and neither was anyone else in the courtroom, when she responded that the U.S. Marshalls got it for her.

There was an audible gasp from the jury, as well as the crowd of people who packed the courtroom. I could also hear snickering from the other defense attorneys. Glancing away from Carolyn and toward Linda, I saw that the Assistant United States Attorney was keeping her head down in a failed attempt to look like the answer didn't hurt. But I knew, as did my fellow defense attorneys, that Carolyn was now dying inside.

Seizing the moment, I bore in further.

"You mean the United States Marshall Service supplied you with cocaine?" I asked incredulously, while drawing out the phrase *United States Marshall Service.*

Again she answered, "Yes!"

After absolutely and emphatically beating this point into the ground, I decided to move on.

"Now the only thing you have testified to about my client, Sam Dowdy, was that you actually saw him put a kilo of cocaine in his tennis shoe, is that correct?"

"Yes."

Unbeknownst to Carolyn, I'd instructed Sam to wear tennis shoes to trial that day, because I didn't believe that what she had claimed was physically possible. I now walked toward the plastic-wrapped bricks of cocaine, which were staged on the evidence table. After retrieving one of the one-kilo bricks, I handed it to Carolyn and asked her if this was the same size and shape as the brick of cocaine that she said Sam had placed in his tennis shoe.

She testified that it was.

I then asked Sam to take off one of the tennis shoes he was wearing and give it to me. He did, and I then presented it to Carolyn in the witness box.

"OK, here is a kilo of cocaine and here is one of Sam's tennis shoes," I said to her. "Now show the jury and me how he put the kilo in his shoe."

I literally held my breath while I watched her struggle to shove the hard, tightly-wrapped brick kilo into the shoe. When it became clear that she couldn't do it, I looked at the jury and said, "Doesn't fit, does it?"

Carolyn stared at me directly, and answered, "No."

Somewhat theatrically, but not over the top, I then looked at the jury again, and shook my head.

I hid from the jurors a smile that I showed to Sam as I sat back down beside him.

We hadn't won anything yet, of course. I now felt we were most definitely winning, but this trial–the biggest of my life and one that could ruin Sam's life–still had a very long way to go.

Chapter 24

Education

I based my tenure as mayor of Kansas City on the 4-E Agenda: Education, Employment, Efficiency, and Enforcement. I arrived at these objectives after talking with numerous citizens and learning what seemed to matter most to them. In essence they are the four objectives that people want to see addressed head-on.

In this book, I'm going to spend ample time on each of the 4-Es. And I want to start with education, because for me it is the absolute priority.

Under our charter, the City actually has no official role in education. None. The word education is in fact not even mentioned in the city charter. This is in part because Kansas City contains 15 separate school districts, plus numerous private and charter schools. And all of them are their own little kingdoms. As the city, we can't favor one school or school district over the other–ironically not even the Kansas City Missouri School District (Kansas City Public Schools or KCPS).

So what we decided to do was go directly to the kids of our city, rather than deal with the myriad of schools and school districts. One of our major initiatives has been pre-kindergarten (pre-K) education.

This has unfortunately been a major fight. The school district superintendents want to control the money, and they don't want to see it spread outside of public schools and public charter schools. And yet only 35 percent of our city's kids are in a pre-K education program. So this leaves more than 4,800 kids every year who aren't in quality pre-K education.

And of that 35 percent, only one in four are actually involved in a public school or public charter school pre-K education program. The rest are getting their pre-K education at everything from private schools to mom-and-pop operations.

But these superintendents want to control all of the money made available for the city's pre-K programs. This doesn't solve the problem for more than half the children who need it.

Of the 43 States that allocate money for pre-K programs, Missouri ranks 42nd and contributes $17 million in actual disbursements. While I was mayor I was told by the Missouri Governor's office that there was a chance that the state legislature would allocate up to $16 million more for pre-K. But a total of $33 million for all of Missouri is a drop in the bucket. It's nowhere close to what is needed. It wouldn't even fully cover the needs of Kansas City.

In the numerous conversations that we had with the school superintendents, I seldom heard them talk about the kids. They said a great deal about budgets, legislature, and experts. And they talked constantly about how much money would be available and who would control it. But not much about kids other than their students.

I'll never buy into the mindset of "if it's not my idea, then it's not worth doing." And yet this was what I continually encountered. The reality is that the ideas out there–their ideas–are not working. We're not getting smarter as a country. Our kids are not catching up with their counterparts in the rest of the world. At best we're treading water, and at worst we're drowning. And it's largely due to this incredibly frustrating level of close-minded bureaucracy.

There is no political will in this country to do the right thing when it comes to education. And there's largely no political help to do the right thing.

During my time as mayor I learned that pre-K education is not just important, for poor kids especially, it's a virtual prerequisite for academic achievement. Pre-K education leads directly to third grade reading proficiency. And third grade reading proficiency is truly the critical benchmark for childhood development and success in later life.

In 2010 the Annie E. Casey Foundation published a report entitled *Early Warning: Why Reading by the End of Third Grade Matters.* Three years later, an updated report was published under the name *Early Warning Confirmed: A Research Update on Third Grade Reading.* The results of these two reports are staggering, and formed the foundation of my views on this subject. According to these reports, students who do not read proficiently by the third grade are four times more likely to leave high school without a diploma. Furthermore, 82 percent of those students who fail to reach third grade reading proficiency come from low-income households.

I know that it's easy to look at third grade reading proficiency as an arbitrary statistic. Why does it matter more at third grade than say fifth grade, or ninth grade? But educators will tell you that children learn to read up to the third grade, then read to learn thereafter. This may sound trite or cliché, but it's true, undisputedly spelled out by volumes and volumes of research.

If kids lack proficient reading skills in the third grade, the harsh reality is 75 percent are likely never going to catch up. Consider that 49 percent of prisoners nationwide failed to graduate from high school. Consider also that kids who do not graduate from high school are six times more likely to live in poverty.

Pre-K education flows into third grade reading proficiency. A report published by the Abecedarian Project, which was conducted to study the benefits of early childhood education, found that those who had received pre-K education were four times more likely to graduate college. A separate study by the Child-Parent Center Program found a long-term return to our society of $8.24

for every dollar invested during the first four-to-six years of school, including pre-K.

When I took office as mayor of Kansas City in 2011, I discovered that only 33 percent of our city's third graders were proficient in reading for that grade level. I was absolutely outraged. What outraged me even more was that nobody seemed bothered about this staggering fact.

If your car only started one out of every three times, you would damn well do something about it–and do it immediately. Yet the reality that two out of three third graders in our city were not reading at their appropriate level was met with apathy. It was just accepted, with little more said or done.

As a response, in my first year as mayor, I created Turn the Page KC. Our mission was to mobilize the community to achieve reading proficiency at grade level or above for all third graders in Kansas City, Missouri. Six years later, our third grade reading proficiency was up to 55 percent. But I don't want any congratulations. The average for all third graders in the state of Missouri is 62 percent. Just better than half means that while we have definitely made sizeable improvements, we still have a very long way to go.

Earlier in this book I described the sacrifices that my father and mother made so that my brothers and I could receive a high-quality education. And I described how education was always the utmost priority in our household. This core philosophy extended to my two terms as mayor.

Later in this book, I'll delve deep into my initiative to create $30 million in annual funding for all four and five year olds to have access to a pre-K education, funded through a 3/8 cent city consumer sales tax.

You'll no doubt expect that I had opposition proposing a tax increase. What very well might surprise you is that the fiercest opposition came from the school district superintendents.

Under our plan the $30 million annually would have been used to help all families afford high-quality pre-K instruction, as well as provide investment in pre-K programs to ensure that as many as possible are high-quality.

Kansas City, Missouri families with a four- and five-year-old would have been eligible for a discount on pre-K tuition the year before the child begins kindergarten, with the amount of the discount depending on their income and the quality of the pre-K program.

I feel that there is no better place in which to invest our city's tax dollars than our children and the high-quality pre-K programs. These can prepare them to be kindergarten-ready, and in the future they result in proficient third grade readers who are better educated and sufficiently prepared for a rapidly-changing workforce. Both the short- and long-term benefits of this investment are well-researched and proven.

I'll never back down from this belief. Ever.

Chapter 25

The United States
v Samuel Dowdy Part 2

My "Trial of the Century," in which I was defending Sam
Dowdy in U.S. criminal court, dragged on for weeks.
Even after my *Perry Mason moment* with the government's star
witness Carolyn, I could not relent or relax. Sam was still on
trial.

The evidence against Sam's brother Gilbert mounted, and
some of the defendants started to plead out. My client now almost
appeared to be an afterthought, which confirmed his earlier belief
that he had been charged for the sole purpose of pressuring Gilbert.
The prosecution, however, still had the bank deposits, which I felt
could be explained. And of course they still had the Vicki Note,
which I knew was going to be problematic.

The government played the bank deposits card first. Assistant
United States Attorney Linda Parker called FBI agents to the
stand, and had them walk through impressive charts that showed
all of the cash deposits that Sam had made, going back numerous
years. There was line upon line of deposits, almost none of which
were in nice even sums.

The FBI agents testified that these deposits were clearly drug-
related, because there was simply no other viable explanation for
this many cash transactions.

I of course knew that there was another logical source for those deposits—Sam's customers from his home renovation and repair work. But apparently the FBI was blissfully unaware of this.

I was ready to pounce on these agents during my cross-examinations, but I remembered what my mentor Bill Sanders had beaten in to me over the years. His philosophy was that you should only destroy a witness when the jury wants them dead. If you attack a witness whom the jury doesn't want to see go down, then you do so at your own peril. These were respected federal law enforcement officials—not the cocaine-using Carolyn. Thus I had to proceed with caution and care.

I calmed myself as much as I could, and with one major goal in mind I rose for my first cross-examination of an FBI agent. It was imperative that I respectfully set up the government for the knockout punch, which would ultimately be delivered when I called Sam's repair and renovation customers to the stand. I knew that they would blow the government's theory completely out of the water.

As I did with Carolyn, I again broke a cardinal rule of cross-examination. This time I had the FBI agent repeat his theory about why the deposits could only be a part of a drug conspiracy. He then recited almost word for word what he had said when questioned by Linda during his original testimony.

It's dangerous to have damaging testimony repeated, but I wanted the government's theory nailed down so tightly that they couldn't move away from it when I finally sprang my trap.

The prosecution had added up all of Sam's small cash deposits from over the years, so that they could present one large total to the jury. This was designed to show that my client was a big-time, dangerous drug dealer. My goal was to cast doubt on each and every deposit, so that I could ultimately obliterate the large total.

During my cross-examination I was able to get this FBI agent to overconfidently state that, based on their thorough investigations, he was sure that the deposits were all from the sale of illegal drugs.

"And you're sure of that, are you, sir?" I asked forcefully but with respect.

"Yes. There is no other source for these deposits," the FBI agent replied.

"Each and every one, right?"

"Yes," he replied.

"So if there are some legitimate sources of those funds, your theory would be wrong, wouldn't it?"

"The FBI isn't wrong, sir."

I decided to let that proverbial bird sit out on its limb for a bit, and reserved the right to recall him as a witness when we started our defense.

As the trial continued the prosecution continued to pile evidence on top of Gilbert. They were determined to bury him. Things really went south when Vicki changed her plea and agreed to testify.

I was now really worried because her written note, which read, "Gave Sam $ 10,000.00," was the most damning evidence against my client.

I still had no explanation for it, and neither did Sam.

It came to the point where I was now begging Vicki's attorney to let me talk to her. Finally, I broke him down, and the night before she was set to testify he called to say that I could speak with her for 30 minutes.

Vicki was a beautiful young woman who was in serious hot water. I genuinely felt sorry for her, and hoped that the court would be lenient in light of her willingness to now testify for the prosecution and against her boyfriend Gilbert. She was in a tight jam, and Vicki, her defense attorney, and I all knew that the best way for her to get a good deal was to be as helpful to the prosecution as possible. And this of course meant being as damaging as possible to the remaining defendants–Sam and Gilbert most definitely included.

When I finally interviewed Vicki, it became evident to me that she knew absolutely everything. Once she testified, it was pretty much "game over." It was clear why the prosecution had saved her to the very end. Her testimony was their big finale. But the fact that she was such an insider and would produce such damning testimony was actually great for Sam. Because as she buried her boyfriend Gilbert, she would simultaneously be exonerating his brother Sam.

Vicki told me that Sam was not a member of this criminal conspiracy, and that to her knowledge he didn't use drugs. She told me that she had never seen him put a kilo of cocaine in a tennis shoe, or anywhere else for that matter.

"What about this note though, Vicki?" I asked her.

Her answer provided the simplest and most helpful explanation that I could have asked for.

"Sam needed to borrow some money from Gilbert," she stated earnestly. "Gilbert said OK. When Sam came to get the money, I wrote that I gave him $10,000 on a piece of paper so that Gilbert would know what I'd done."

I wanted to hug her! In one fell swoop, Vicki put another nail in Gilbert's coffin while simultaneously lifting the lid on Sam's. I had to make sure she had absolutely nothing else incriminating that she could say about my client. Once I felt confident that she didn't, I rushed home, where I went to work writing and rewriting every single question that I would ask Vicki on cross-examination in court. I stayed up all night, but my exhilaration carried me through.

Twice in this trial I had broken cardinal rules when questioning witnesses. I now promised myself that I would strictly adhere to the script, and thereby leave no avenue for a last-minute surprise.

As I arrived for trial the next morning, I was so jazzed that it hadn't even occurred to me that I had not slept the night before.

Thankfully this didn't matter, as I stayed completely on course during my cross-examination of Vicki. Ending with a flourish, I had Vicki explain the infamous note, and repeat several times that Sam Dowdy was absolutely not involved in any way. Truly his only guilt was by association. It was Sam's brother Gilbert, and not Sam at all. There was silence in the court room, except for perhaps a little hissing sound that came from the air escaping the prosecution's balloon of a case against my client.

Now that we had shown that a kilo of cocaine wouldn't fit in a tennis shoe and that Vicki's note did not implicate Sam, all that remained was to blow away the prosecution's sole remaining theory. I had to give a credible explanation for those numerous cash deposits, and for this I was of course ready

Using Sam's list I'd been able to track down about 20 of his customers, and match up their dates and amounts of payments with the FBI's comprehensive charts. My plan was to bring a few of these people in to testify each day, so as to drag out the fact that the FBI's investigation was not as thorough as they'd tried to portray.

As I put each witness on the stand I had them testify about the jobs Sam had done for them, what they'd paid him, and when and why they'd paid in cash. Some said that they transacted all of their business in cash, while others stated that they'd cashed a check or money order first in order to pay Sam. And a few simply said that they didn't like or trust banks, which made me smile. As we matched their payments against the FBI charts, I'd draw a line through the entry–clear enough for the jury to see.

At the end of this progression of witnesses I recalled to the stand the FBI agent who'd originally testified, and then reminded him of what he'd previously said.

I then asked him, "Did you ever talk to my witnesses during your investigation?"

"No," he answered flatly.

"Any way you have to refute his (or her) testimony?"

"No, but these are isolated incidents that don't really disprove our point," was the FBI agent's counter.

"Ok, but regardless, if those bank deposits that I crossed off weren't from drug activity like you said, then they really shouldn't be on a chart that says they were, correct?"

"Yes."

The next day at trial, the prosecution brought in a corrected chart with a new and reduced total for Sam's total cash deposits, in an attempt to mitigate the damage caused to their case by the witnesses' testimonies. I then proceeded to go through the process all over again with more witnesses who had been Sam's customers. More testimony, more cross-offs, more explanations by the FBI agent. Then came another new chart and another reduced total. Rinse and repeat.

Eventually I was out of witnesses, but I'd clearly made my point. In order to finish this potentially damaging prosecution theory, I decided to recall the FBI agent one more time. Once again I established that when he first testified about this prosecution theory, he was certain that Sam's deposits were drug-related. This was a conclusion drawn from his agency's investigation, and one that he fully endorsed.

I reminded him about the original charts which detailed Sam's cash deposits, and the subsequent updated charts with the reduced totals.

Surely, he had to concede, it was now clear that these deposits were the result of a completely legal and plausible alternative scenario. And that scenario, of course, was that Sam Dowdy was involved in the legitimate business of home renovation and repair, for which a great deal of his customers paid cash.

The FBI agent admitted he had not interviewed any of the witnesses I produced, and he had absolutely no facts with which to refute their testimony.

I then asked him, "So sir, at the end of the day, you can't prove beyond a reasonable doubt that any of the remaining deposits on those charts are related to drugs, any more than the ones we crossed off, can you?"

"No, but I believe they are," he responded.

"Well, you believed the ones we crossed off were drug-related. And you were wrong on those, weren't you?"

Reluctantly and grudgingly, he admitted that was true. With that I sat down at our defense table and prayed that I'd done enough to keep my client, who I truly believed was innocent, out of prison.

After six weeks of an absolutely grueling trial, we were ready for closing arguments. Afterward the jury would deliberate, and ultimately decide whether our client would be going home or be going to prison. It was that cut and dried. By rule and custom the prosecution goes first in closing arguments. This is because the government, in this case the United States federal government, has the burden of proving guilt beyond a reasonable doubt. The defense follows the prosecution with their closing arguments, and the prosecution then has the opportunity for rebuttal.

The courtroom was absolutely packed, as this case had been a major news story for months. The media, just like all of us involved, knew that it was now coming to a highly dramatic close. This case wasn't just about Sam. It was about his brother Gilbert, and the remaining defendants who had resisted taking a plea deal. Nothing was guaranteed for anyone. It was now up to the jury, and the jury alone.

As I had long since learned in my career as a civil litigator, trial work is brutal. This is a universal truth. And this was certainly the situation in my criminal defense of Sam. In my year-plus commitment to this case, my days were routinely 12 to 15 hours long and constantly filled with tension. Surprises invariably cropped up and threw me off stride. I routinely applied what I learned in the Marine Corps: "Improvise, adapt, and overcome." And yet through all of the stress and frustrations, I loved it. I absolutely loved it.

What really struck me, in first defending Michael Keith Samuels and then Sam Dowdy, was that a civil trial is really about money or contractual obligations, while a criminal trial is about freedom and life. Even though neither of these men faced the death penalty, they did face a long-term loss of freedom, which of course would greatly alter and reduce their quality of life. I took my responsibility so seriously that I often had trouble sleeping. My fear was constant that I might not be good enough, and as a result my client would spend years of his life locked in a prison cage. It was a terrifying prospect.

By the time we reached closing arguments in Sam's trial the ranks of his fellow defendants had been severely depleted. This was largely due to Vicki's testimony, which led to a run on plea deals.

Linda Parker was an experienced and highly professional prosecutor. She summarized her evidence succinctly and explained why the jury should return guilty verdicts against all of the remaining defendants, including Sam, and especially his brother Gilbert. Linda wasn't flashy, but she was very effective.

When my turn came to close, I reminded the jury that everything the prosecution and its witnesses had said about Sam Dowdy was either proven to be false or an exaggeration.

"You remember Carolyn?" I asked rhetorically. "You know the woman with the big diamond ring and the cocaine supplied to her by U.S. Marshalls while she was in witness protection? You saw for yourself that the only evidence she offered about my client was a lie. She tried hard, but she could never get that kilo of cocaine to fit in my client's tennis shoe."

I laid out my case for why Sam had to be acquitted in as much detail and with as much passion as I could muster. Finally, I ended by challenging the prosecutor to respond. There was no doubt in my mind that this was a dangerous gambit. But it felt like one which had a better than average chance of success.

"You all have been sitting here for weeks as you watched us refute every theory the prosecution has raised against Sam Dowdy," I said while looking directly at the jury. "We have established more than just reasonable doubt. We have shown you that the government really has no proof at all that Sam Dowdy was involved in any alleged drug conspiracy. The prosecution's star witness flashed a big diamond ring given to her by a wealthy lawyer, when she came in here to testify. I don't have a ring like that, but I do have this ring my wife gave me when we were married in my second year of law school in 1981. This ring has never been off my hand."

I then took off the ring, a gold ring with three inlaid rows of onyx worn on my right hand, and displayed it to every member of the jury.

"We showed you that all the money the FBI said was drug-related, actually wasn't drug-related at all," I stated.

With that I pulled a $20 bill from my wallet. I then folded it and placed it on the rail of the jury box. Slowly I rested my ring on the $20 bill.

"Here is the ring my wife gave me and $20 of my own money," I announced. "If Ms. Parker can show you that anything I've said to you during this entire trial is false, then she can have this $20 and the ring that I've worn since the day I was married. Thank you."

Assistant United States Attorney Linda Parker was now in a bind. I knew that she could not refute what I'd said, but I didn't know how she would respond. Linda chose to ignore it entirely, which was a mistake. I watched the jury as they glanced back and forth between the $20 bill and my ring, still resting on that rail in front of them. As she delivered her rebuttal Linda barely mentioned Sam Dowdy. And she never touched or even mentioned my ring, sitting on the rail as a personal challenge.

I could tell the jury was waiting to see how Linda would answer my challenge, and they seemed disappointed when she failed to do so. Linda simply finished her rebuttal, thanked the jury for their attention, and sat down. Waiting for the precise moment, I slowly walked back to the jury rail, made a show of slipping my ring back onto my finger, then unfolded the $20 bill and put it back in my wallet.

Once finished I just glanced up at the jury, smiled, turned, and walked back to my seat. I had gotten the last word without actually saying a word. The trial was now over and the jury was sent off to deliberate.

Truly, and without ever really understanding it before, I now knew that I had become a lawyer precisely for Sam Dowdy.

While we waited for the jury to return, Carol Coe and I would often sit in the hall talking. Mostly she talked about her new daughter Ailey, a young woman I still see from time to time, as she works as a political aide for Missouri Senator Roy Blunt.

After five days of deliberation the jury finally returned a verdict of guilty for Gilbert Dowdy and every one of the remaining defendants. Every one, that is, except for Sam.

Chapter 26

Employment

Employment was the second "E" of my 4-E Agenda as mayor of Kansas City. Simply put, employment is economic development in all phases and forms. And through this we attempted to create a situation where talent, in the form of great workers and entrepreneurs, came to the city. In this era economic development is more about attracting talent than it is about moving businesses.

As mayor I discovered that the growth in jobs is with smaller companies. It's the high number of people employed by small businesses, as opposed to the small number of employees hired by big businesses.

We sought out people who were entrepreneurs, people who would come into our city and create a company. And that of course led directly and immediately to the creation of jobs. This proved to be extremely successful.

Through this line of thinking we created the Innovation Partnership Program (IPP), in which we entered into contracts with entrepreneurs who needed access to the various resources that we could provide. For example, businesses wanted to display or test their products, systems, and services with our residents. We provided the resources they needed free of charge, in exchange for their pledge to stay in our city and hire from our citizenry once they became successful. And we as the city were in return able to use their products, systems, and services.

This is how we came to partner with the data analytics people. They became IPP partners when they asked us if they could do a specific data analysis on potholes that would occur on our city streets. And now, through their work, we can predict within two days when a pothole is going to occur. And this has expanded to successful predictive analysis of when water mains are going to blow.

As you know by now, I'm a huge advocate of data. With our Smart City initiative, we have sensors in the roads and sidewalks, and on street lights and traffic lights along the streetcar route. These sensors collect data on cars and pedestrians that is accessible to local business owners.

And what we found was that businesses were able to design their marketing around this data, through data analytics, and make more money. This is not anecdotal. Rather, we knew that they were monetizing the data through the sales tax that we collected as the city.

I'm extremely proud of the fact that Kansas City, Missouri can now lay claim to being the "Smartest City in America". And by smart, I mean technologically smart. We have the largest contiguous free Wi-Fi area in the country, which we didn't pay for. Instead it was paid through our private sector partners such as Sprint and Cisco. They created and now maintain the free Wi-Fi networks, because of course they are seeking new customers for their related products and services. A classic win-win all the way around. And the group that wins the most is our citizens.

Especially in our poorer areas and neighborhoods, we found that a large number of kids had laptops and tablets they couldn't use outside of school because of a lack of internet in their homes. As the free Wi-Fi area continues to expand this problem gets rectified.

In everything we did with economic development our goal was to address equity rather than equality. They are of course different concepts. This was most readily visible with the airport project.

As I wrote earlier in the book, Kansas City International Airport opened in 1972 and remains a relic of that bygone travel era. The airport is simply ill-equipped to keep up with and meet modern travel and travel security needs. When voters approved in 2017 the construction of a new $1 billion single terminal that would completely replace the existing terminals, this was a much-needed and long-awaited move into the 21st century for our city's international airport.

The developer of the new airport, Edgemoor Infrastructure and Real Estate, set Minority-Owned Business Enterprise (MBE) and Women-Owned Business Enterprise (WBE) hiring goals that we felt were too high. They wanted 35 percent, which is a pretty sizeable number.

First of all, as Kansas City we don't have a huge excess capacity in terms of workforce. We're not New York or Los Angeles.

Secondly, it's not as though nothing else is going on construction-wise in the city. There are a number of other things being built, and workers are being siphoned off for those projects. So it wasn't as though the full contingent of MBEs and WBEs was just sitting idly on the sidelines, waiting to be hired. Many of them were already engaged.

But Edgemoor felt that they could meet their 35 percent target. Proactively, they created training programs and classes for potential MBEs and WBEs, covering things like: how to build your business, how to get a contract, what to do once you get a contract, how to get bonding, and the like.

Working with us, Edgemoor set up a bonding program where prospective MBEs and WBEs could use Edgemoor's own bonding credit with the city, which then allowed these emerging businesses to be bonded for the first time.

In the process, these MBEs and WBEs started doing other projects in the meantime, which of course meant hiring workers from our city's population. It all flowed directly into our Employment Agenda.

In our ongoing search to attract talent we created a program for entrepreneurs to compete for $50,000 and a free office space in Kansas City for one year. From the mass of submissions, received not only from across the U.S. but globally, 10 applicants were ultimately picked. The selection of the 10 was rigorous and thorough so that we were left with the best of the best.

After their year was up, we helped them relocate with like-minded companies if they weren't yet able to venture out on their own. We repeat the process each year. This has been a massively successful program that has led to the creation of numerous jobs.

EyeVerify, Inc., a biometric security technology company took a different path to success. EyeVerify competed in an international competition hosted in the U.S. by the Kauffman Foundation. It actually didn't make the cut to the finals, but was selected to replace one of the selected companies that decided to drop out.

EyeVerify surprisingly won the U.S. competition and then went on to win the international competition as well. They then opened shop in the area with 50 full-time salaried employees. In 2016 the company was acquired for a reported $100 million, but it remains based in Kansas City, where it opened its headquarters downtown.

This is a prime example of talent now being the currency of economic development, rather than business itself. As a city you are far better off trying to incubate and grow your small local businesses organically, rather than trying to attract established businesses from elsewhere. Every city has entrepreneurs. It's just what you do with these entrepreneurs that really counts.

When you attract, or some would say steal, an established company from another city, it can be a short-term proposition. As soon as the incentives that were given to them expire, then they start looking for a better deal. And if you can't or won't provide that better deal, then they are on the road again.

We experienced this with the restaurant chain Applebee's. When the company was purchased by two Kansas City businessmen in 1988, they relocated their corporate headquarters from Georgia to our city. In 1993 they jumped across the state line to Overland Park, Kansas, a Kansas City suburb but very much its own city. This was because of a very attractive incentives package. Three years later Applebee's moved to another Kansas City suburb, Lenexa, Kansas, because of a better deal still. In 2011, almost $13 million in incentives brought them back to Kansas City, Missouri. Now they are based in Southern California.

Applebee's had no loyalty. It was simply about what was best for them. Fair enough. But their history stands as a case study of how these massive businesses sometimes operate. And it underscores why investing in talent, rather than corporations, is the way to proceed. It's much better to build your next H&R Block or Hallmark (two homegrown Kansas City-based businesses) than trying to import your next Applebee's.

As mayor I was determined to bring to the table new people, and specifically young people, complete with their fresh ideas. And I made sure that they had their voices heard as loudly and clearly as the voices of the older established business people and bankers.

Generally the old guard has their way of doing things, which might not be the best way forward. Innovation is the key to opportunity. And opportunity creates employment.

Chapter
27

Kenner & James and
Almost the End

I **had met** Nancy Lucido at a Blackwell Sanders picnic shortly
after I started at the firm, and we became fast friends. Nancy
was a graduate of the University of Missouri Law School, and we
were in the same associate class. She had served her first year as a
law clerk for Federal Judge Howard Sachs, through whom she met
her future husband David Kenner.

Although Nancy and I were in the same class, we worked
in different areas of the firm's practice. Nancy handled a lot of
medical negligence cases with partners Tom Wagstaff and Larry
McMullen, while I was assigned to Jim Horn's trial team.

In 1990, Blackwell Sanders made Nancy one of their early
female partners, and made me their first-ever African-American
partner.

A few years prior, accounting firms and law firms had started
to merge into megafirms. Blackwell Sanders decided to jump on
this merger train and started vetting potential partners, primarily
targeting firms strong in corporate and business law. This was
intended to match up with our strength in litigation and trial
work. As the courting process played out, it became clear that the
firm I was a part of was morphing into something less comfortable
and recognizable than the one I had originally joined.

At a mixer for our firm and the Smith Gill firm, I asked John Phillips, one of the more senior partners, why we were going through all of this.

"Because bigger is better," John replied.

I retorted, "Just because they both begin with 'b' and have six letters, does not mean they are synonymous."

The merger with Smith Gill never happened, but shortly thereafter the firm brought in a big corporate rainmaker from another firm through a lateral move. This was when the Blackwell Sanders culture started to change. Contrary to popular belief, making partner in a law firm doesn't mean that you are set for life. There are always more senior partners who decide how much you are worth to the firm based on client attraction, and how many associates you can keep busy. Business generation was always more difficult for me as a non-golfing African-American. This was true as well for Nancy, largely the basis of her being a woman.

When the compensation committee decided to encourage partners to argue for their salary, and make a case as to why they should be paid more than another partner, Nancy and I decided to bet on ourselves. We both decided that we didn't want others to decide our value year after year. So together we left Blackwell Sanders in January 1993, and formed Kenner & James.

Nancy and I set up a loan with the SBA (Small Business Administration) to pay ourselves while we generated cases and waited for them to mature. Marilyn and Pete Lucido (Nancy's mom and dad), worked as our unpaid staff. Luckily, we were able to get some great referrals from friends at Blackwell Sanders, which helped us pay back the SBA loan within a year.

When Nancy and I left Blackwell Sanders, we switched from 100 percent defense work to 100 percent plaintiffs work. Instead of defending doctors, hospitals, drivers, and insurance companies, we were now suing them. And we became members of the Missouri Association of Trial Attorneys (MATA), so that we could hang out with all the other plaintiffs lawyers.

In June 1993 I was loading beer in my car before picking up Nancy for the drive to our first MATA Summer Convention, which was to take place in the Ozarks. As I walked back to the house to kiss Licia goodbye, I suddenly couldn't breathe, and hit the ground facedown. The next thing that I remember is being at St. Luke's Hospital, disoriented and with doctors staring down at me from all angles. I heard the doctors say "pulmonary embolism," "anemic," and "lucky to be alive."

Over the next few weeks, while in the hospital, my right leg started to swell so much that my skin started to split in places. The doctors couldn't diagnose the problem, even after exploratory surgeries.

I was groggy and disoriented from the constant intake of morphine and steroids. Licia was at the hospital with me around the clock. My father came to see me, and I heard him say through tears that "children aren't supposed to die before their parents."

But I was so drugged up that I don't remember everything that happened, or in what order it happened. I do remember, however, that my kids weren't around much. Diana and Bill Lund took care of Kyle and Aja while Licia practically lived at the hospital. It is funny how memory works. I do recall one day when the kids were at my bedside, I noticed that Kyle was missing his two front teeth. And Aja, who was on Licia's hip, smacked him hard on the top of his head with a plastic novelty McDonald's microphone. He cried, and I laughed.

After some painful tests, doctors getting confused as to whether I should be on 10 mg or 100 mg of prednisone, medical students standing around clucking at my enormous right leg, and a specialist talking about amputation, one of the doctors finally landed on a provisional diagnosis of retroperitoneal fibrosis. I was then life-flighted to the Mayo clinic in Rochester, Minnesota, where I met Dr. Luthra. He was the Mayo Clinic's expert on retroperitoneal fibrosis and told me exactly what was wrong. This came as a relief, as the days of the unknown were far worse for my family and me.

The Mayo Clinic is the most efficient medical operation I've ever seen. Two doctors and two nurses met Licia and me as I was being off-loaded from the plane. They introduced themselves, explained their roles, let us know who would be my primary contact, and then outlined their immediate course of treatment. For the next seven days I underwent numerous tests, including a painful nuclear uptake test where dye was shot between the toes of my right foot. But nothing was more painful than dealing with the effects of three weeks of morphine, and what that does to bowel movements.

It turned out that I had what they called a "lottery disease," meaning that I had about as much chance of getting retroperitoneal fibrosis as I did of winning the lottery. Basically, blood in my right leg began and then continued to clot until it collapsed the vena cava. This caused a pulmonary embolism, swelling in my leg, and excruciating pain whenever my leg was lower than my heart.

The steroids that I was given had made me want to eat everything that wasn't moving, while the steady doses of morphine made everything taste like I was licking a crowbar—except for popsicles. After eight days of a continued popsicle diet (red ones, blue ones, banana ones, every ones), more tests, and weaning off morphine, I was back on a plane bound for Kansas City. Before I was discharged, the doctors advised me that because of the steroids, I should avoid stressful situations and making important decisions. Apparently they had no idea what I did for a living, and they had no clue as to my basic personality.

Nancy had been holding our new firm together for weeks while I was hospitalized. Even after returning to Kansas City, I was far from ready to return to the office. Instead, I was at home with my right leg elevated and my eyes bugging out due to the steroids. And I was also going nuts with boredom, and feeling guilty that I wasn't carrying my weight in the firm. So, earlier than perhaps I should have, I convinced Licia and Nancy that I was fine to go back to work.

Soon after getting back to my office, I was on the phone trying to negotiate with an assistant Missouri Attorney General.

The conversation wasn't going well, and then really got out of control when the lawyer said something to the effect of "you'd better get your client under control." I reacted immediately, going off like a rocket.

"You'd better? You don't get to tell me what I'd better do while you're sitting down there in Jefferson City sucking off the teat of the state," I yelled.

Nancy walked in as I was about to let go with another barrage. She took the phone out of my hand and calmly told the lawyer, "He'll call you back."

She then hung up, and laughed at me for what seemed like a full minute. Nancy then suggested that perhaps I ought to go home. Without argument, I agreed.

Despite my early health issues, and thanks in large part to Nancy's hard work, our firm grew prosperous rapidly. We filed and settled a legal malpractice case on behalf of a doctor imprisoned because of poor representation. And we filed a medical malpractice case representing a mother whose newborn infant with a cardiac condition received improper treatment leading to a brain injury. These were exactly the types of cases that we wanted to take on in our new firm.

But an unexpected call that I received in 1996 had an impact on our firm, and on me, like no other before.

Chapter 28

Efficiency

The third of my 4-E Agenda as mayor of Kansas City was Efficiency. To me, efficiency starts with building trust in government. As the City, we had to be efficient with tax dollars and how we governed. The people demanded this, and it was our job to produce.

We also had to be efficient with our numerous departments and services. People don't want to encounter bureaucracy and be told *No*. Instead, they want to be heard, and to have their issues and problems—big, small, and in-between—resolved in a timely manner.

Governmental departments generally only focus on themselves, ignoring the departments literally next door. Public works only wants to do public works. General services only wants to do general services. And this follows down the line. Real efficiency is created when, as a city, you integrate all of the services into a team.

After looking closely at our various and numerous departments, we decided to shift the emphasis of how they function individually to council committees, which I formed and appointed to look at the big picture issues.

As an example, take neighborhoods and public safety. This isn't just the police. It's also fire, ambulance, sanitation, public works, and housing. And taking them together, we're then able to look at the problems and issues from a holistic standpoint. All of the departments that are involved with neighborhoods and public safety are brought together. Then once together, they can trade ideas. They can discuss what's working and what isn't. And they can work more efficiently.

When the various departments actually communicate, redundancy is eliminated. They find that if one department is doing something, then they are freed up to do something else. The first thing that we noticed was that Codes Enforcement would say that a fence was too high. Then Housing would go out and say that the same fence was badly damaged. And both departments would fill out forms, and then go to work on removing the fence.

I asked why two different agencies were taking separate routes to accomplish the same goal: tearing down a fence. It was obvious that whoever was there first should go to work on having the fence removed. Bringing in a second department with the same objective was redundant. And it was wasteful.

But by allowing the two departments to actually communicate and share information, then the goal would be accomplished in an efficient manner. And if Housing took care of removing the fence, then Codes would be available to go on to other issues and problems. There was a double touch that served as a prime example of government waste.

As mayor, I always sought government efficiency.

As part of this quest for efficiency we fully utilized the system of 311 calls. These are non-emergency calls for citizens to report issues such as damaged sidewalks, excessive litter, and abandoned cars. Many 311 calls are quality-of-life issues that absolutely should be addressed and resolved.

When numerous 311 calls come in from the same sector reporting potholes, for example, we know there is a systemic problem. The inefficient way of doing things, which had been in place previously, was to get a call on Monday, respond to the area on Tuesday, then get another call on Wednesday, and respond on Thursday three blocks away.

By charting our 311 calls we can then channel our resources and comprehensively attack the problem in the area, rather than case by case, and day by day. This saves money, it saves time, and it keeps everyone busy.

This targeting of efficiency led us to create KCStat. This is a data-driven, public-facing initiative focused on improving the efficiency and effectiveness of city services. We started KCStat in 2011, my first year in office, with the main focus on the areas of our residents' greatest concern, based on the complaints that they reported on 311 calls. These were street maintenance, water line maintenance, water billing and customer service, code enforcement, and animal control.

Two years later we began using KCStat to monitor the progress on the City Council's Strategic Priorities. The following year the Strategic Priorities were incorporated into the Five-Year Citywide Business Plan, and since 2014 KCStat has tracked the progress on the goals and objectives in that plan.

Monthly KCStat meetings were held to monitor the city's progress on a number of goals: housing; neighborhoods and healthy communities; infrastructure and transportation; planning, zoning, and economic development; public safety; customer service and communication; and finance and governance.

KCStat then put the measured indicators for outcomes, outputs and efficiency on display. This discussion allowed the public to see the progress made on the Business Plan goals. KCStat has been such a success that it's now being replicated in cities across the United States.

Additionally, efficiency is sought through our annual Citizen Satisfaction Surveys that are mailed out at random four times a year. I even received one in 2018, my first ever.

For the period covering August 2017 to April 2018, 9,000 Citizen Satisfaction Surveys were mailed out to households across the city. The response rate was just over 48 percent. The respondents listed the category "Streets, Sidewalks, and Infrastructure" as their area of highest importance, followed by was the category "Police Services."

The respondents also selected the categories for which they had the highest rate of satisfaction. Number one was "Fire/Ambulance Services," with "Parks and Recreation" finishing second. The category that had the worst satisfaction rate was "Streets, Sidewalks, and Infrastructure."

This data very clearly showed us that our streets sidewalks, and infrastructure were on the minds of our citizens and had to be addressed promptly. And by knowing what really matters and what problems were of the highest importance, we created a much greater level of efficiency as city government.

As mayor I constantly used data to make decisions. Across the board, for all of the 4-Es–Education, Employment, Efficiency, and Enforcement–it provided the baseline for what we did. Data takes the suppositions and the subjectivity out of decision-making. And data provides clear justification for the decisions made. It's all there; just take a look.

From data collection we advanced to predictive analytics. So instead of waiting for a water main to blow, we have a very good idea of which water mains will blow. We then dig them out and make the repairs in a controlled fashion, alleviating the crisis of a huge hole in the street. It's textbook proactive vs reactive thinking.

Additionally, during my time in office we created the Mayor's Challenge Cabinet, in which young women and men from across Kansas City were invited to apply for designated project teams and task forces. We wanted to build diverse groups, each consisting of five qualified individuals, to better Kansas City.

The Challenge Cabinet was an opportunity for thought leadership, in that it created a system where innovative and creative ideas could be brought to my attention. I wanted to hear from the people, and this provided another avenue of communication.

The Mayor's Challenge Cabinet was comprised of the Innovation Policy Task Force, the Open Data Project Team, the Technology Roadmap Task Force, the Community Engagement Project Team, and the Ideas Fair Project Team. We drew upon a diverse cross section of our citizens, who brought forth numerous great ideas and plans of action. And from this flowed even more efficiency in our city.

Far too often, when people think about government–be it city, state, or federal–they think of waste. And I don't blame them, because there can be a huge amount of waste in government– redundancy, reckless spending, unnecessary projects, and inefficiency to be sure.

As mayor, I made it a priority to eliminate waste and streamline our city government so that it was as efficient as possible. Simple things, like listening to the people and getting the various departments to communicate, went a very long way in this mission.

Chapter 29

Brazoria County, Texas

I took the phone call in my office at Kenner & James, not knowing exactly what to expect. On the line was the mother of a young black man who had been imprisoned in Missouri, but had been transferred along with 414 other inmates in the state to a private prison located in Brazoria County, Texas. She told me about the tales of mistreatment her son conveyed to her in his letters, starting with a school bus ride from Missouri to Texas with a bucket for a toilet and bologna sandwiches for meals. He told her that he'd been repeatedly abused by the guards since he had arrived at the private prison.

I'd done enough prison litigation by this point to know that what her son had claimed was probably right. But I also knew from experience that winning this type of case was like pulling a camel through the eye of a needle. So I told this woman that unless there was some type of concrete evidence, it would be her son's word against the word of the prison officials, and there was virtually no doubt how this would go with a jury and judge.

But there was concrete evidence, in the form of a videotape that had been anonymously leaked to the media by a prison worker. This videotape showed prison security camera footage of inmates, mostly black, being kicked and screamed at by the corrections officers, as well being made to crawl on the floor naked while guard dogs snarled, lunged, and even attacked . When I saw this, I thought, *Holy shit! I can actually show that these claims of abuse and mistreatment are true.*

So I took this case, and we were soon after inundated with requests from other prisoners who were reporting similar cases of abuse and seeking representation. We had so many requests in such a short period of time that we had to set up a new filing system and buy extra file cabinets for all the paperwork. We grew from one to more than 50 clients in less than 60 days, and by the time we filed suit in the U.S. District Court we had even more.

As I dove in, I discovered that there was a legion of other lawyers who were handling nearly identical cases. I realized that we all had to get together, and this was much bigger than any of us had initially thought. In total, this covered more than 700 Missouri prisoners who had all been shipped out of state. All of these inmates had been convicted in Missouri of committing state crimes, yet due to overcrowding in the Missouri penal system were now being housed in a private prison facility in Brazoria County, Texas, owned and run by Capital Correctional Resources (CCRI). The Missouri Department of Corrections (MDOC), CCRI, and Dove Development Company were named defendants.

What we uncovered during discovery was truly shocking. The abuses far exceeded what was revealed on video. Prisoners were routinely beaten, maced, pepper-sprayed, tear-gassed, and stun-gunned. Body cavity searches were conducted seemingly on a whim, black inmates were routinely called "nigger," there was inadequate medical care, and they failed to separate prisoners based on their tendencies toward violence. Although numerous inmates lodged repeated complaints with the MDOC, nothing was ever done.

The man in charge of the operations at this private prison was Wilton David Wallace, who was caught on the leaked security camera footage with his foot on an inmate's neck. Before taking his job with Capital Correctional Resources, Wallace had been a major in the Texas Prison System. That job ended when Wallace pleaded guilty to beating a prisoner with his nightstick, for which he received a five-month sentence. But being a convicted felon with a history of on-the-job violence hadn't dissuaded Capital Correctional Resources from giving Wallace a high- profile job.

One of Wallace's sergeants at the Brazoria County prison had previously been a manager at a Kentucky Fried Chicken, before going to work for Capital Correctional Resources as a prison guard supervisor. During his deposition, we asked him if he'd received more job training at Kentucky Fried Chicken or Capital Correctional Resources.

He answered, "Easy. At Kentucky Fried Chicken, without a doubt."

What became clear is that private prison companies only make money by housing as many prisoners as possible, and by keeping expenses as low as possible. And that is exactly what was happening with Capital Correctional Resources' prison in Brazoria County, Texas. The guards that were hired were poorly educated, poorly paid, poorly trained, and many of them had absolutely no business working in a prison at all.

The federal judge on this case, Nanette Laughrey, appointed me along with six of the other attorneys as "class counsel." In essence, we were responsible for directing the litigation for settlement purposes. The settlement class ultimately consisted of every Missouri inmate who had been shipped—make that bussed—to Texas between January 1, 1995 and December 31, 1997. As class counsel we then filed an amended complaint, which consolidated all of the individual cases and defendants and brought the total to 2,100 class members.

We alleged civil rights violations and sought equitable relief to stop Missouri from sending any more prisoners to Texas, and to prevent Texas from receiving them. We also wanted Missouri to investigate the numerous complaints filed by multiple prisoners.

And we prayed for a monetary award to cover damages, legal fees, and expenses.

Rather than going to trial, all parties agreed to mediation to determine damages. Rich Ralston, a former federal magistrate, was named mediator, and after five days the case settled. The settlement agreement contained all of the equitable relief that we sought, plus $2.22 million to be paid into the settlement fund. A total of $900,000 of this sum was allocated for attorney fees, to be divided among more than 20 lawyers (myself of course included); with an additional $300,000 allocated for class administration costs and expenses. This left $1.02 million to be divided among the class members. It stood as the largest settlement against a private prison company in the history of the United States.

About eight percent of the 2,100 class members objected to the settlement—a figure of about 170 individuals. John Kurtz represented the objectors at a "fairness hearing" on December 3, 1999. Mediator Rich Ralston testified that in his experience with prisoner cases the juries usually found for the defendants or awarded only nominal damages. My fellow class counsel Craig Heidemann and I testified as to the difficulty of dealing with the Missouri and the Texas defendants, and to the fact that each class counsel would lose approximately $97,000 in time and expenses even with the current allocation for fees. Frank Carlson, another class counsel, testified that the number of prisoners with physical injuries was about 57.

Taking all of the testimony and evidence into account, including the financial condition of the defendants, Judge Laughery found that the settlement was "fair, reasonable, and adequate." She then approved a reduced fee of $800,000 for total attorney fees, and $300,000 in costs and administrative fees. Judge Laughrey then set up a matrix to determine how much each individual inmate would receive.

This wasn't the end of things, however, as the state of Missouri immediately moved to seize every prisoner's settlement amount.

Under Missouri law, if a prisoner wins the lottery or receives an inheritance, the state can claim the money and apply it toward the cost of their incarceration.

After all of this work, there was no way that I, or any of the other lawyers involved, was going to allow Missouri to take this money from the prisoners, who had all suffered really inhumane abuse. Happily we were granted injunctive relief, so that our clients received all of their money due.

But I will tell you, despite this being a record award, the money was nowhere near enough. Of course these people were all convicted criminals, violent criminals in some cases, but they were still human beings. And they were American citizens with Constitutional rights. The Eight Amendment prohibits cruel and unusual punishment. This surely includes being forced to crawl naked on the floor while a guard dog bites your upper leg.

We determined that our costs exceeded our legal fees by about $97,000. We were all out-of-pocket for some of our travel expenses. Nor would we ever be made whole financially for the countless hours put into this class action.

But this absolutely did not matter to me. This was truly meaningful litigation. It was never about the money. Had it been, I never would have taken the case in the first place.

The larger issue, beyond the abuse of inmates, was that they had been shipped out of Missouri to Texas, and incarcerated in a private prison run by a for-profit corporation. The vast majority of people convicted of felonies don't come from wealthy families. So trips, or even one trip, hundreds of miles away for a prison visit by family become a huge hardship. And often it means that the visits become financially impossible.

I would imagine that for prisoners a visit from family members, be it spouses, children, parents, siblings, grandparents, and the rest, serves as one of the lone bright spots in their life. And now that is taken away because you're essentially sold by the state of Missouri to a private prison in another state. I couldn't abide by this at all, regardless of the crimes that these people had committed.

Combine the isolation with the abuse, and this was a wrong that had to be made right. Had it not been for the security footage leaked by an anonymous whistle-blower who worked for Capital Correctional Resources, there never would have been a case at all.

This case was ultimately one of the most rewarding of my legal career. Like the Michael Keith Samuels and Sam Dowdy cases before it, this class action was exactly the reason why I went to law school.

In all three instances I knew that I was firmly on the right side, and I gave these cases, and my clients, absolutely everything that I had, financial gain be damned.

Chapter
30

Enforcement

The final "E" in my 4-E Agenda was Enforcement. This is essentially the law and the police dealing with gun crimes and violent crimes across our city. There is no doubt that we struggled with the inability to bring these rates down. But one of the main factors without question was that we had no control over the main instrument of death—guns. Missouri state law preempted and prohibited us from doing anything in this area. As a municipality we weren't able to regulate guns or bullets. In the state of Missouri, if you're 19 years old you can legally own a gun. You don't need a permit; just go out a buy one. Your gun can be on you or in your car or in your home. It doesn't matter. And there is nothing legally that we can do as the city.

So our police roll up late at night on a car with four young men who all have guns, and the officers can't do anything. Why would these kids all need guns while driving around after midnight? They're not out deer hunting. They're not defending themselves, because there's no immediate activity that requires defense. So what are they doing with these guns? Are they like pieces of jewelry, worn to look cool or gain respect? Or are the guns for something criminal, and possibly deadly?

The proliferation of guns is just like the proliferation of anything else. For instance, there are going to be more auto accidents when one million cars are on the streets than when there are 50. That's just common sense, and it's just that simple. Yet it's more difficult to get a driver's license than to get a semi-automatic weapon

These guns are often in the hands of kids and young adults who never had a quality education, starting with pre-K. They never learned conflict resolution, how to get along with others, and appropriate behavior. All of these things that should have been taught at an early age need to be taught to these gun owners who are 18, 19, and 20 years old. And often by then, it's far too late.

Instead of knowing that it's better to walk away or talk something out, these arguments, disagreements, and slights often turn deadly. Someone disrespects your girlfriend on Facebook, so you go and shoot them to death. And with a legally possessed and owned gun.

In February 2019 State Representative Andrew McDaniel of Deering, Missouri actively proposed a bill which would require every Missouri citizen over the age of 21 to purchase a handgun. If this isn't bad enough, he also proposed a 75 percent tax credit, so as to make the purchase easier. Rep. McDaniel has to be joking, right? Further, he compounded this folly with a companion bill that would have required all Missouri residents between the ages of 18 and 34 to buy a semi-automatic weapon, such as an AR-15. These transactions would have been offset with tax credits as well.

Although the bills didn't pass in the Legislature, such extreme positions illustrate Missouri's approach to guns in the state. Missouri has never really been what one would call measured and balanced on this issue, but at least until recently residents had to acquire a permit from the local sheriff's office to conceal and carry a weapon. And they then were to go through mandatory firearms training. But in 2017 the Missouri legislature, in a profoundly ill-advised move, decided to eliminate even these basic safeguards. Gone were the laws put in place so that the wrong people didn't acquire guns and the right people learned how to use guns responsibly.

Perhaps you'd think that in a state with some of the weakest gun laws in the U.S., and simultaneously with one of the highest rates of gun-related violence and deaths nationally, even these legislators might finally see a correlation. And perhaps they would then stop what they were doing.

But if you thought this, you'd be completely wrong. Instead, these elected officials decided to resurrect a bill that had previously passed, only to be vetoed by Democratic Governor Jay Nixon, which literally banned the enforcement of all federal gun laws in the State of Missouri.

In 2019 Missouri State Senator Eric Burlison and Representatives Jered Taylor and Jeff Pogue introduced versions of the Second Amendment Protection Act (SAPA).

SB 367 and HB 786 state in part:
All federal acts, laws, executive orders, court orders,
rules, and regulations, whether past, present, or future,
which infringe on the people's right to keep and
bear arms as guaranteed by the Second Amendment
to the United States Constitution, and section 23 of the Missouri
Constitution, shall be invalid in this state, shall
not be recognized by this state, shall be specifically
rejected by this state, and shall be considered
null and void and of no effect in this state.

The law then goes so far as to allow local jurisdictions, at their discretion, to prosecute federal agents who might attempt to enforce federal laws in those jurisdictions. An interesting conveyance of power and local control to those same jurisdictions denied the right to locally control the access to and use of weapons within their locales. The legislature tried this with Democratic Governor Jay Nixon and failed. The fact that Republican Mike Parson (a decent man with whom I disagree on issues such as this) is now the governor of Missouri has given them reasonable hope that this time the bill will not face a veto.

The sad thing is, I know from spending time with Governor Parson, alongside St. Louis Mayor Lyda Krewson, that he has seen up close the evidence of unbridled gun possession and use. Sadder still is the political reality that the Republican Party is so extreme on this issue, that Governor Parson puts his political future in jeopardy if he even hints at a more reasonable and moderate view on guns.

As a former sheriff in mid-Missouri, Governor Parson has law enforcement experience, and as such I know that he is truly concerned about the safety of law enforcement officers in the state. But the ultra-extreme SB 367 and HB 786, as well as the mandatory ownership and state tax credit bills of Representative McDaniel, cannot possibly make law enforcement for the officers and residents of Missouri safer.

On top of our city being completely beholden to state gun laws, Kansas City, Missouri is an anomaly as the only major American city that does not control its own police department, and it's been this way since 1939. So, rather than the traditional structure followed by the rest of the country, where the city council, mayor and/or city manager control the department and hire and fire the police chief, the KCPD is controlled by a five-member board consisting of four gubernatorial appointees and the mayor.

In 1939 the notorious political boss Tom Pendergast and his political machine wrestled control of the police department from the state. After seven corrupt years under Pendergast, however, the State Legislature regained control and continues to hold it in regards to the KCPD.

In 2013 St. Louis used a statewide initiative petition to regain local control of its police department. For Kansas City the Missouri Legislature has, through statutes: codified the makeup, qualifications, and appointment of the members of the Board of Police Commissioners; established the qualifications of police officers; set policies regarding salaries, vacation, pension, and overtime; and determined what the city is obligated to pay for the department.

Section 84.730 RSMo states:

Except that in no event shall the governing body of
the cities be required to appropriate for the

use of the police board in any fiscal year an amount in
excess of one-fifth of the general revenue fund of such year.

In all of my eight years in office, as well as for many years before, the budget of the police department has easily exceeded the one-fifth of the general fund mandated by the statute. In each successive year, the budget has been increased. When you add in the cost of fire and ambulance, the total amount for public safety literally dwarfs all other departments dependent on general fund dollars to do their jobs in our city.

Despite the year-over-year budget increases, there is pressure from the public, often fueled by the Fraternal Order of Police, for more money, more officers, and more salary raises. Yet the separation of the department from the city has created some inefficiencies due to duplication of some of the administrative functions. And yet despite these issues, the relationship between the city and the department has been relatively cooperative during the eight years of my tenure as mayor.

The same cannot be said regarding the city's relationship with the state legislature, especially regarding gun laws.

With all of this in mind, I believe that citizens have a huge role in law enforcement, because there are going to be far more people in a neighborhood who see things than police officers on the street. But unfortunately it's often the case that people don't come forward. It could be fear of retaliation or being labeled a snitch, or perhaps they are covering for a family member or friend. And then there are the numerous cases of vigilantism, where the citizens enact justice in their own neighborhoods by committing retaliatory killings. These people won't talk to the police, as they choose instead to go out and murder the murderer, or at least who they believe to be the murderer.

One of our big moves through the Enforcement agenda is KC NoVA (Kansas City No Violence Alliance), which is focused on group-related violent crimes. We've elected to use the word "group" instead of "gang," because these are really groups with members constantly coming and going, and nothing more. People think of gangs in terms of the Bloods, the Crips, MS-13, and the like. But what we're talking about here are loosely-affiliated groups of people, usually based in neighborhoods or specific parts of the city.

The Board for KC NoVA is comprised of the local agents in charge of the FBI and ATF offices, the chief of police, representatives from the offices of Probation and Parole, the U.S. Attorney, the Jackson County Attorney, and the mayor.

There are regular meetings and constant contact. Plus, we'll refer cases to the FBI and ATF if our local prosecutor can't pursue them. The impact has been extremely positive, as it has furthered our relationship with federal law enforcement, and these group-related violent crimes have gone down. Unfortunately, though, the level of non-group-related crimes remains unacceptably high.

Another aspect of KC NoVA is the quarterly "call-in," by which we contact some of the people on probation who we suspect are back running with the wrong crowd. The probationers are offered a choice. The KC NoVA Board members attend and tell them that we all truly care about them, and illustrate this with offers to assist in areas such as finding a place to live, getting a job, and securing a GED. But they must agree to work with us, and they must stay out of trouble. That's the carrot.

The stick is that we show them photos of attendees from previous call-ins who declined the offer of help, and have since been arrested and jailed. Perhaps the most important part of the call-ins occurs when Roslyn Temple and her "Mothers In Charge" talk about how they have all lost a child to violence. They speak emotionally about how these deaths have affected their lives, and the lives of their families. Roslyn and her group relay stories of going to the scene of every homicide in the city, so that they can give support and comfort to the families and loved ones of the victims. I've seen some of the most hardened attendees cry when they hear these first-person accounts. Happily, KC NoVA now has well over one hundred call-in participants receiving social services in this vital program.

Within the framework of KC NoVA, we created a program called Teens in Transition (TNT), where good kids who are at high risk of moving toward criminal behavior are brought into a nine-week summer work program. They're paid a wage, given set hours, and truly work to better themselves. This involves courses in life skills, conflict resolution, job training, and art.

The transition in these teenagers is remarkable. In the beginning they have closed body language, don't make eye contact, give one-word answers, and are generally far from receptive. In the middle of the program, it's clear that they're opening up and letting their guards down. By the end of the nine weeks, you see smiles, hugs, laughter, and full-on interaction.

Of the kids who complete Teens in Transition, 68 percent don't get into trouble with the police afterward. It's been so successful that we actually opened a second location in the city for the program. In total, the TNT program cost $180,000 annually, and it's been money extremely well spent. So much of enforcement for me is being proactive rather than reactive.

There is clearly a need for our city's police officers to be outside of their squad cars more, and actually talking with people face to face. People naturally trust the police more when they know the person behind the badge. And a way to accomplish this is through positive interaction between the police and the people. It's really a throwback to the old neighborhood cop who knows everyone on his beat by name.

Statistics show that people tend to commit crimes largely in their own neighborhoods. And in largely poor neighborhoods, regardless of the racial makeup, there is more unemployment and there are more low-wage earners. When people have fewer options in life, they naturally have more stress. Add guns into this mix, and there are more problems. A city's most violent areas aren't populated by PhDs and corporate executives. Instead, they're filled with high school dropouts who barely have enough money to survive. Often people in these circumstances are angry about their plight in life. They've lost hope. So they resort to the lowest level of means, which is criminal behavior.

Our current Chief of Police Richard Smith recognizes this issue, and he's trying a novel approach. Chief Smith hired social workers using a combination of public funds and grants from the Hall Foundation, and embedded them in the police stations that are located in the highest crime areas. The social workers have the opportunity to meet the neighborhood residents and work with them to solve problems before they reach critical mass.

So often politicians are only looking to perform those short-term acts which will get them reelected for another term. I completely reject this way of thinking, as my goal as mayor was always to take on the long-term and politically difficult issues. My reasoning is that this was the right thing to do. Period.

As a society we seem to spend most of our time looking at the end of the disease, rather than the germs that started it. And we don't do a very good job of treating the disease. Plus, there's never any talk of disease prevention.

The political discussions about alleviating poverty, increasing educational opportunities, decreasing segregation, and creating employment all seem to be absent. It's all about adding police officers and getting tough on crime. But these things address the problem, and not the solution.

As mayor, I chose to spend money on kids, because if we don't then eventually we're going to spend money on prisons. There have certainly been uphill battles, because it can and usually is a tough sell when it comes to preventive programs. Many people fail to see the long-term implications and benefits. It's a lot easier to say that you're tough on crime and go after the criminals. As mayor I chose to go after the kids, starting with pre-K education, so that they would never know the inside of a police car, criminal courtroom, or cell.

Chapter 31

Running for Mayor

Even though my legal career was thriving, I slowly began to feel burned out as a working lawyer by the end of the 1990s. My law partner Nancy Kenner and I continued to practice together until 2002, when I formed my own firm and began devoting more time to mediations and civic engagement. We remained great friends, and still shared work on occasion. I stayed close as well with her husband David, who was my long-time lawyer.

During this period, my thoughts were drifting more and more to politics. I seriously considered challenging incumbent Kansas City Mayor Kay Barnes as she sought re-election in 2003. But I was now the father of four, as Licia and I together had son Kyle and daughter Aja, and the time commitment that it would take to run just felt too daunting. Plus, I knew and liked Kay, and I probably would have lost.

Licia was just starting work on her master's degree, and Aja was set to enter high school. No way was I going to sacrifice this valuable family time, when I knew that I needed to be fully present and available to my wife and kids.

Kay wound up being elected to a second term as mayor, and she appointed me to the Land Clearance for Redevelopment Authority and the Economic Development Corporation. I was already on the Jackson County Ethics Commission, and politics was becoming an increasingly bigger part of my life.

I continued to think about running for mayor, but again decided against it in the 2007 election, after Mayor Barnes served her second term and was unable to run again due to term limits.

Mark Funkhouser was elected as the new mayor of Kansas City, and very quickly I could see the way that things were going: in the wrong direction. Running for mayor was now an easy decision for me to make.

I saw the other people who had run for mayor and I felt confident that I could as well. And I truly felt as though I had nothing to lose. Anything short of election and I'd still have my law practice. And besides, a person who never took a chance never had a chance.

There was no doubt in my mind that if elected mayor I could genuinely affect change. I was not happy at all with how things were being run, and how our city was being perceived, under Mayor Funkhouser. In fact, it was an embarrassment.

Funkhouser's wife, Gloria Squitiro, had started a self-written newsletter called "Notes from the Double Wide," in which she would talk about subjects such as the mayor's proctology exam or her arguments with airport employees. She was the quintessential *Do You Know Who I Am?* type of person.

Beyond this, there was no advancement of the city at all. Funkhouser didn't like development, and everything had come to a standstill. The final straw for me was the failure to land the new stadium for our Major League Soccer club Sporting Kansas City (at the time known as the Kansas City Wizards). The ownership ultimately built their $200-million state-of-the-art venue in Kansas City, Kansas, and the organization has had phenomenal success.

The story that I heard, and that made the rounds, was that Funkhouser invited executives of the club over to his house to discuss a problem with the stadium project. Immediately, I found it weird that he would have this meeting at his home, rather than at City Hall. Stranger still, Gloria apparently started rubbing her husband's shoulders during the meeting, and then was asked by Funkhouser what she thought he should do. Supposedly she said no to a stadium deal, and that was that.

I thought, *How could you lose this?*, and *Why did you lose this?* I now had the final push that I needed to challenge Funkhouser when he sought election to a second term in 2011.

Now deciding to run for office and actually running for office are two very different things. You declare your candidacy, and then what? Even though I had received my political appointment to the various boards and commissions, I'd never before sought political office in my life. This was a completely foreign process to me.

I decided as my first step I needed to hire a campaign manager. In Kansas City there is a list of the usual suspects whose job it is to guide political campaigns. So I decided to meet with all of them. A number of them didn't like my chances and thus didn't want to take me on. Some were downright shady, and thus not even an option. One person actually told me, "You can't possibly win." Another wanted to remake me completely, which as you're no doubt fully aware by now, wasn't going to happen.

Finally I met with Larry Jacob, and the connection was instantaneous. I told Larry, "I'm not going to run as a politician, I'm going to run as me. I don't like being handled and I don't want to be handled. Now, I'll listen when you tell me to say something a different way. But it always has to be in keeping with my vision and my beliefs."

Larry was fine with all of this and agreed to run my mayoral campaign. Invaluable to me as an unofficial adviser was my good friend and law partner Nancy Kenner, who tirelessly worked with me on fundraising. We then hired Global Strategy Group to do our polling and strategist Martin Hamburger for commercials, and our team was complete.

During my time on the trial team I'd handled several cases for a security company owned by Steve Kander. Steve had a son, Jason, who at the time of my run for mayor was serving in the Missouri House of Representatives. I'd gotten to know Jason through his father while I was handling Steve's cases.

Jason and his wife, Diana, who was a successful entrepreneur, became friends and early supporters. They introduced me to Margaret Hansbrough, a young woman who had worked on Jason's campaigns. Margaret and I hit it off. She was the second person I hired to work on my campaign and ultimately worked on policy in my office after I was elected.

I also hired Brian Noland, a great guy with tons of brown curly hair and a cherubic face, whom I quickly nicknamed "The Adult Gerber Baby." Brian was my organizer for the campaign, and he and Margaret were a better team than I could have hoped for. I don't know that I could have won the election without them. Jason Kander's bold endorsement, my first from an elected official, helped a lot as well.

Leading up to the Primary Election of February 2011, I spent a full year just going around and talking to people across the city. I asked them what they liked, what mattered most to them, what they thought the major issues were. From this, the "4-E Agenda" of Education, Employment, Efficiency, and Enforcement was born. It's the thread that ultimately ran through everything that I did as mayor, and of which I'm extremely proud. I'm also extremely proud of the fact that as a private citizen, as a candidate, and as mayor, I always have said what I think. This of course often doesn't sit well with some people, but it's who I am.

One of my constant critics the *Star's* Dave Helling will tell you that I'm prickly and thin-skinned. I'd retort that this isn't the case at all; I just didn't like the way that every question he asked me sounded more like an accusation than a question. As you know well by now, we did not get along or like each other much.

I quickly learned that running for political office is done in phases. The initial phase was all about making contacts and getting the word out that I was actually seeking the office of mayor. Larry Jacob was clear in that you can't assume people know what you are doing; you have to tell them. I'd meet business owners, members of the Chamber of Commerce, school officials, law enforcement personnel, prominent citizens, everyday citizens, and anyone else who would see me. We'd have a meal, a cup of coffee, or perhaps just a brief conversation. Doing this for well over a year really adds up.

As a past president of the Kansas City Metropolitan Bar Association, I felt that I could, and should, corner the attorney market. I was one of their own, and it was very important that every lawyer in the city knew that I was running. Their support was key.

The next phase was fundraising, which I hated. To my surprise I was decent at fundraising, but it never sat well with me. It's not a fun experience to call people you know, and who in many cases are longtime friends, and ask them for money. It's awkward for them, and it's awkward for you. We raised more than $1 million for this campaign, which we needed, and which we put to great use through tactics such as television commercials and mass mailers. But the process was awful.

From there I moved to the debate stage, literally and figuratively. In these numerous debates held across the city, I was with Mayor Funkhouser and five other challengers, in addition to myself. About halfway through the series of debates I noticed that I was being asked more questions than most of the other candidates, which I took as a really good sign. And I had long since noticed that Mayor Funkhouser was not being well-received.

The structure of the mayoral election in Kansas City is completely nonpartisan. Every declared candidate, including the incumbent, runs in the Primary, with the top two finishers advancing to the General Election. I didn't have to win in the Primary, just finish in the top two. And with every debate I grew more and more confident that this was a completely attainable goal.

Despite his incumbent status, Funkhouser didn't seem like a worthy adversary during the debate phase, but others certainly did. Deb Herman struck me as a really smart woman, yet she didn't seem to gain much traction. Jim Rowland was a former City Council member, and highly accomplished. He and I got along and often talked about coaching our kids in baseball, but he had a reputation for being irascible.

Then there was Henry Klein, who was a really nice guy, but he seemed to only want to talk about ridesharing and carpooling programs. He dropped out before election night, as did Charles Wheeler, who had been mayor of Kansas City from 1971 to 1979 but at age 84 didn't mount a very enthusiastic campaign.

Confident, but not cocky, I felt really good about my chances of finishing in the top two in the Primary Election. Aside from what I had witnessed in person, the polling was strongly in our favor. As we drew closer to the Primary Election day of February 22nd, I could see that the post-debate crowds were gravitating around Mike Burke and me. I wound up in first place with 27 percent of the vote, one percentage point higher than second-place Mike Burke.

Mayor Funkhouser had basically been reduced to a non-entity and a non-factor. To his humiliation, he finished third in the Primary with 21 percent and didn't advance to the General Election. With that, Funkhouser became the first incumbent mayor of Kansas City to fail at this stage of the electoral process since the 1920s. Jim Rowland placed fourth with 13 percent, and Deb Herman fifth with 11 percent.

So the voters would now choose between Mike Burke and me to become the next mayor. The turnaround was extremely quick, as the General Election was set for exactly one month ahead on March 22nd.

I had known Mike for quite some time, and knew that he was the political insider. A fellow attorney, Mike was very influential and accomplished in real estate development law, and he knew his way around City Hall. He had always struck me as a smart and honorable guy, and I considered him a friend.

I said to him, "Mike, let's not get stupid. Let's stay on point and remain friendly." He agreed, which I really respected. We also agreed that regardless of who won, the winner would involve the other in governance wherever possible.

Just before the General Election someone ran a negative piece on me. My campaign team thought the ad had come from Mike's camp. I called Mike and told him that we had agreed not to do this type of thing. My team was telling me that we had to respond, and I told them that I didn't want to go in that direction. But I understood that if he didn't relent, then I had to answer. I made all of this clear to Mike during the call. He told me that he didn't want to do anything that would be perceived as mudslinging and that he would pull the ad immediately, which he did. And there was no more negativity or attacks the rest of the way.

Mike and I had a lot of similarities. Aside from both being lawyers, he was big on development and the arts, just as I was. We actually joked that we could switch each other's political messages and no one would ever know the difference.

My memory of the night of the General Election remains an absolute blur. I knew that Mike was a worthy candidate, and the polling showed that it was going to be really tight. Gone was my easy confidence from the eve of the Primary Election just a month prior.

All of my kids were at the house and we were watching the election returns on the local news. My sons Malik and Kyle moved to watch together on an upstairs TV, and were suddenly crushed by the idea that I was going to lose.

"Dad, you only have 38 percent north of the river. You're going to lose," Malik called out dejectedly.

"No, I responded. That's great news. 38 percent north of the river means that I'm going to win!"

The part of Kansas City located north of the Missouri River was unquestionably Mike Burke's stronghold. I was never going to win it. What Larry Jacob and my campaign team had told me repeatedly was that I only needed 33 percent of the vote there, because the rest of the city belonged to me. What my sons thought was ruinous news turned out to be the information that I needed to finally relax, and let the reality sink in that I was about to become the next mayor of my city.

In the end it wasn't terribly close. I defeated Mike by a margin of 54 percent to 46 percent. But I was thankful for the polling that indicated a much tighter race, as it compelled me to campaign as hard as I could all the way to the end. The old axiom is true: you either run scared or you run unopposed. I ran scared.

For their part my political team, featuring Global Strategy Group for polling and Martin Hamburger for media and commercials, won a national industry award for the best local campaign. They had been outstanding, and led by Larry Jacob they had believed in a man who had never before run for political office, and who proudly saw himself as the outspoken anti-politician.

Late that night we all arrived at our victory party, held at the Negro Leagues Baseball Museum in the city's historic 18th and Vine District. I was surrounded by Licia, my mother Melva, my kids, family members, friends, colleagues, supporters, and my great campaign team. The news media was there in full force, and the reporters and journalists kept asking me the same question, "How does it feel to be the new mayor of Kansas City?" And every time I kept giving the same answer, "It feels like I need to get to work."

Chapter 32

The Vote for Universal Pre-K Education

During my first term as mayor, the Kansas City Missouri Public Schools (KCPS) leadership convened a group of experts to look at the possible expansion of their pre-kindergarten educational programs. They had a lot of solid ideas, but funding remained the one problem that they could not solve. Their initial funding plan was a property tax levy increase for those located within the KCPS footprint. I was never fully on board with this, however, as it would only serve the kids in their district, rather than every kid in Kansas City, Missouri. But at least it was better than nothing.

In order for this funding scenario to proceed, the various charter schools located in the KCPS district had to come on board, which they ultimately didn't. So without the charter schools' agreement and support, there was no chance of getting this through the legislature.

In response, a new working group was formed, and this one included my education adviser, Dr. Julie Holland. The approach now was to look at the pre-K plans of other major cities. Of the largest 40 cities in the United States, which includes Kansas City, 20 of them were funding pre-K education. This list of 20 included Boston, Denver, Seattle, San Antonio, and Cleveland–all of which were studied by the KCPS-created working group.

The group reviewed the 43 U.S. states that provide some level of funding for pre-K. Of those states, Missouri ranks number 42 at $17 million. By comparison, Kansas is $38 million, and Illinois is $308 million. The $17 million for the entire state of Missouri, which of course includes Kansas City and St. Louis, is, quite frankly, woefully insufficient.

Through the on-site visits of numerous major cities with thriving pre-K programs, the working group determined that Denver was a good model to follow. That city's program began in 2006 with a 0.1 percent sales tax, which generated $23 million annually for pre-K. While their main school district was involved as a partner, the district did not control the program or the money.

So, Denver became the primary model as the plan for Kansas City was put together. Dr. Holland eventually let me know when their working group felt that everything was in place and ready to be put forward. A group of petitioners then gathered the requisite minimum 1,700 signatures to place the plan on the ballot. This plan involved a 3/8-cent citywide sales tax as the funding mechanism, to be voted on in a November 2018 referendum. Once word got out, KCPS and all of the other 14 school districts located fully or partly within the city limits of Kansas City, Missouri started protesting that they hadn't been involved in the process, and that they had no idea what was going on. This was interesting in that this working group had flowed directly out of the original KCPS-created committee, and some of the early childhood staffs from several of the city's school districts had participated in the working group.

And of course the *Kansas City Star* jumped on the bandwagon of dissent, making the pre-K plan their latest anti-progress cause celebre.

After listening to the complaints of the school districts and consulting with the Greater Kansas City Chamber of Commerce, who had adopted kindergarten readiness as one of its "Big 5 Initiatives," I agreed to move the issue from the November 2018 ballot to the April 2019 ballot. This was my earnest attempt to come to consensus.

Clearly this was a complex issue, as the full pre-K plan was contained in a 77-page report generated by the working group. This plan was designed to address the two main barriers for parents seeking a high quality pre-K program for their children: accessibility and affordability.

Accessibility was targeted, because we discovered to our shock that a full 40 percent of our city's zip codes contained no quality pre-K programs. And this wasn't just limited to the inner city and low-income areas. This problem existed in the more affluent northern and southern sections of Kansas City, Missouri as well. It was absolutely a citywide issue. We fully understood that it was impractical to create a new system where more kids are invited in, and yet there is no place for them to go. Further, we knew that it was imperative for pre-K facilities to be located close to either the parents' homes or jobs. If someone has to get on a bus to travel across town for their kid's pre-K every day, the burden will most likely become too great. The kids will stop going, because the parents will stop taking them. Transportation is always an issue when it comes to education, no matter the level of schooling.

We projected that $30 million for pre-K education would be raised annually through the 3/8 cent economic development sales tax. The authorizing economic development statute required that 20 percent, or $6 million, would be allocated every year for bricks and mortar. Simply put, existing facilities could apply for funds to expand or improve their building and play areas. Additional funds could then be contributed as part of the capital stack for new construction.

Our plan also provided funding for quality improvement in all of the participating pre-K programs. This could help provide additional education or training for the staff, business training for the facility owners, on-site visits from pre-K experts, and new teaching materials.

The second component of the pre-K plan was affordability. We considered pre-K to be high-quality when, amongst other criteria, it's full-day and year-round. The modern reality, of course, is that in single-parent and two-parent households the adults are working one or more full-time jobs. And child care is hugely expensive.

The working group determined that the average cost of a quality full-day, year-round pre-K school in the city was approximately $12,000 per child, per year. For minimum-wage and lower-wage earners, this sum is completely unrealistic. Pre-K becomes about as attainable as buying a yacht or an airplane.

Through the $30 million raised annually, parents would receive a tuition discount based on their income and family size. A full chart was created, providing a sliding scale based on the income of the family who sends their child to the highest-quality pre-K. For example, a person earning $35,000 or less would receive a $12,000 tuition discount toward their child's tuition at the highest-rated pre-K facility. The city would pay the pre-K facility directly. The pre-K providers would be incentivized to increase the quality of education, as their high rating would make them eligible to receive a larger tuition discount.

So under this system, parents would be incentivized to seek out the highest rated pre-K schools, and the schools would be incentivized to obtain the highest quality rating. A classic win-win.

By statute, a five-person tax board would be appointed to account for all of the money. They would be the gatekeepers of the $30 million which would be generated for the citywide pre-K program. There would be oversight and transparency; every single dollar would be accounted for and documented. A governing board of 17 was contemplated for the purpose of operating the program, hiring experts and consultants, and implementing the plan.

With our plan in place, we arranged meetings with a representative group of four school superintendents and Dr. Gayden Carruth, the executive director of the Cooperating School Districts of Greater Kansas City. It became clear that what we were really dealing with were 15 different kingdoms, each headed by their own king. They took the position that the reason they didn't like the plan was that only they and their elected school boards were qualified to operate the pre-K systems in the city. And each of them had their own pre-K systems.

My first sign that we were not on the same page occurred when they rejected a media request to attend the meetings. I had no problem with the media being present, because we had nothing to hide. We were extremely proud of our pre-K plan, and wanted it to be widely known and fully understood. Interestingly, though, the *Kansas City Star* never raised the issue of a lack of transparency in this context.

Allan Katz, Distinguished Professor of Public Affairs and Political Science at the University of Missouri-Kansas City and the U.S. Ambassador to Portugal under President Obama, was brought on to serve as the facilitator. Allan is an expert in civil discourse, and his skills were certainly needed.

It took an extremely long time to get them to even meet with us. Delay, upon delay, upon delay. When we were finally all together, the school superintendents immediately argued that the proposed 3/8-cent sales tax for pre-K was unconstitutional. Their stance was that money should simply be allocated to them, and that they would know best how to spend it within their own districts. They hated the idea of any control moving past them and their respective school boards.

Although the school districts argued that pre-K should be left to their sole discretion, the fact was that most eligible four-year-olds were not in their systems. Of the estimated 6,800 eligible four-year-olds in Kansas City, Missouri, only approximately 35 percent were in a quality pre-K program. And the school districts didn't even educate all of this 35 percent, proving once more that access to quality pre-K was a huge problem.

For example, Head Start had only 1,000 seats for 2,400 qualifying children. Most of the pre-K in our city, quality and otherwise, is provided by community-based facilities and programs such as Emmanuel Family Care Center, St. Mark's, Kiddie Depot, Laugh and Learn, Clay/Platte County Center, and other private and commercial providers. All of them had a waiting list of parents who wanted their children to attend and unfortunately had nowhere else to go, while they hopefully and often anxiously waited for a spot to open.

The school superintendents ignored all of this, and they also incorrectly claimed that what we were proposing was a voucher system. Now a voucher system essentially means that you're taking money out of their system and giving it to someone else. We were going to give them money from an outside source.

One superintendent pulled out his phone and read to me the definition of *voucher*. He then announced self-assuredly, "It's public money going to private entities."

I responded to him, "That's a very broad definition. You pay private bus companies to transport your students, correct?"

"Yeah, but it's not a voucher if we do it," he replied.

I shot back, "That's nonsense. So it's not a voucher if you do it, but it is a voucher if we do? Got it. You realize that we are going to give you money, right? We're not taking your money."

We listened earnestly to what the superintendents had to say, and tried to respond to their concerns. I told them that we were willing to deal with their grievances point–by–point. But there were two things that were absolutely non-negotiable. First, this has to be a uniform quality pre-K system. Second, the pre-K educational needs of every single child in Kansas City, Missouri have to be addressed, not just of those who live in your school district.

We acquiesced to 85 percent of their very long list of demands, but on these two crucial points we were simply not going to budge.

An issue that the school superintendents could not get past was the idea that some of the pre-K money would be going to schools that were housed in churches. As many parents who have put their kids through pre-K know, it is not unusual for the school to be

THE VOTE FOR UNIVERSAL PRE-K EDUCATION

located within the confines of a church, even though there is no direct affiliation with that particular religious institution. This was the case with my two younger kids when they were in pre-K. It's often just a practical matter of space, as churches often have a lot of extra room. These are very often secular, 501(c)(3) state-approved pre-K facilities that have absolutely nothing to do with religion. If there was a religious curriculum or religious artifacts in a pre-K, then it would not be eligible for our program.

Yet the school superintendents kept claiming that we were going to be giving money to churches. And they said that this violated the Missouri State Constitution.

I let it be known that it wasn't in fact unconstitutional, and that we possessed a legal opinion from our lawyers stating as such. Their response was that their lawyer disagreed.

I then relayed to them a 2017 United States Supreme Court case where a Missouri preschool located in a church had been denied a grant by the state government. This secular preschool had sought the grant so that they could purchase crushed rubber for their playground, to increase the safety for their special-needs students. The U.S. Supreme Court ruled that just because the preschool was housed in a church didn't mean that it was a religious institution. Public money therefore could not be denied simply based on their location inside a church.

During oral arguments, one of the Supreme Court Justices asked the lawyer who was defending the state of Missouri if it was unconstitutional for the fire department to put out a fire at a church.

The lawyer responded that of course this wasn't an unconstitutional act.

The Justice then very cleverly pointed out that this was a clear example of public money going toward a private religious institution. Nonetheless, the school superintendents never modified their position.

The long and short of it was that they felt that we should just give them the money, and then get out of their way. These superintendents all believed that they had systems already in place to do things better than we ever could, and that they would expand their own pre-K programs and pick up more kids, and thus more revenue.

It certainly would have been a great system for them: take the money and expand your own insular systems, while leaving the other kids on their own. Status quo.

The system isn't working. And yet the school districts never articulated a plan which would reach beyond their own separate jurisdictions.

What added to all of this contention, and created a new level of confusion, is the fact that of the 15 Kansas City, Missouri school districts only three are wholly located within the city limits. The other 12 exist in part in neighboring municipalities. Claims were made that only the kids who actually lived in Kansas City, Missouri would benefit for the pre-K initiative; the others would be left out. We immediately let it be known that this was completely untrue, as money would be put into their systems, and could then be repurposed to benefit all of their students.

Mark Bedell, superintendent of KCPS, kept telling me that he was against our pre-K plan because the tax created for it was "regressive." Now keep in mind that Bedell was the fourth KCPS superintendent during my eight years in office as mayor. But to his point, I countered that what is actually regressive is poverty. Oh, and crime is also regressive. Having kids who are lost because they never received quality pre-K, or any pre-K education at all—well, this is regressive too. I really believe that Bedell got it, and I believe that had the tax passed we could have worked together to help him expand his pre-K system. However, partly because of the superintendents' united stance, it was not to be.

Amazingly, the NAACP decided to come out against us as well. Why they chose to do so remains a mystery to me. This would have made a huge positive impact in our city's black community.

What I am clear on is that if black people aren't willing to make an investment in black kids, then it's then very difficult for me to convince white people that they should do this.

As part of the campaign I participated in numerous forums and meetings, in a continual effort to gain support. I was continually amazed by the misrepresentations and misunderstandings of the plan. The opposition often claimed to be open to expanding pre-K; however, they never said what their plans were in regard to accomplishing this. What the opposing superintendents did say, though, was that they hoped the state of Missouri would contribute more money to pre-K education, and perhaps raise the property tax levy.

Let's be clear, hope is hope, and a plan is a plan. Just because they are both words containing four letters doesn't mean that *plan* and *hope* are synonymous. Hope is not a plan.

If anyone really thinks that the state of Missouri, which ranks second to last nationally in money allocated for pre-K, is going to save the day, well, I have bad news for them. This is a state government with budget problems that keep them from fixing infrastructure, roads, and bridges.

But the school district superintendents never came around to our side, and all 15 of them stood united against us in their opposition. This no doubt hurt us on Election Day. So did a *Kansas City Star* editorial condemning our pre-K plan that ran the week before the vote.

As we moved toward the end of the campaign, I felt that it would be close. Unfortunately, it really wasn't. The voters rejected our pre-K plan by a margin of 66 percent to 34 percent. Despite our plan being extremely viable, supported by data from similarly-modeled and highly successful pre-K programs in cities such as Denver and San Antonio, we could never gain the momentum needed.

My emotions upon defeat were a raw mix of sadness and anger. I was sad primarily because this "No" vote directly hurts the kids of our city. A lot of people worked their asses off with no other agenda than to do what was right. And I was angry because although the school districts quickly and repeatedly acknowledged the value of pre-K, they never once offered a viable alternative to our plan. And they certainly never offered a solution to the problem at hand: the lack of accessible and affordable quality pre-K across our city.

A great example of how the school districts and school superintendents viewed our pre-K plan came from the KCPS' own website, which they used to promote their cause. On it they wrote: *Passing of the sales tax means that families will have more choices. We will have to fight for our seats. We must demonstrate accessibility and quality.*

Looking back, I realize that this was always an uphill climb for us. People hate new taxes, no matter what they will be used for. And to the voters who didn't really dig deep into the real issues at hand, the lack of support from all 15 school districts and their superintendents was probably enough to sway them to a vote of "No."

But despite the defeat I'm immensely proud of what we attempted to do, which was create accessible and affordable pre-K education for every single child in Kansas City, Missouri. We raised the profile on this issue so much that after the fact the *Kansas City Star* wrote an article opining that there should be a renewed effort to expand pre-K, albeit through a different plan. I'm interested to see if the *Star* remembers this a year from now.

Even though I'm no longer in office, it's a fight that I will continue to wage. Until we succeed, more and more kids will be denied the valuable opportunity to be ready to learn on the day that they enter kindergarten.

Chapter 33

President Obama and Me

The morning after my election as mayor I attended the Chamber of Commerce's Unity Breakfast. This is where all factions get together and basically sing "Kum ba yah," in an effort to mend fences, heal wounds, and generally get everyone on the same page in optimistic anticipation of the new administration. This was March 23rd, and I wasn't set to be sworn in and officially take office until the first day of May. So for me, after a very long campaign, I was there to eat my cold eggs and make pleasant small talk. After the breakfast, my agenda consisted of deciding what I would now do with my law firm and getting my team in order for City Hall.

But as the event was coming to conclusion I was asked if I could stay late, as there was a pressing issue. The city was in the process of finishing their negotiations with Google, and Mayor Funkhouser was no longer taking part. I was told that he had "checked out" since his defeat in the Primary Election the month before, and that Google was growing impatient and frustrated. This was a massive deal to bring the tech giant to Kansas City with their state-of-the-art fiber, and it was now in jeopardy because of a void in civic leadership.

I told everyone that I was happy to help, but reminded them that I hadn't even been sworn in yet. It had been less than 12 hours since I was declared winner of the General Election. They then let me know that, in addition to the looming Google crisis, AMC was ready to depart Kansas City, Missouri for the metro area's Kansas-side suburbs, and this issue desperately needed attention as well.

So, I literally started my work as mayor that day. There was never any transition period. There's no office space given to the mayor-elect, so I had to work out of my law firm and from home until my official swearing-in. I wasn't yet the mayor; I was just acting like one.

During this period Funkhouser refused to meet with me. It's of course customary for the ingoing and outgoing leaders to meet, not to discuss politics, but rather to aid in the transition of one administration to the next. It's absolutely needed, and it's the right thing to do. But I repeatedly asked him for time so that we could get together, and he repeatedly said no, or more often ignored my request entirely. When Funkhouser finally did grant me a meeting on what was his final day as mayor, he was absolutely no help at all.

"These bluebloods are going to eat your lunch" was one of his many choice statements to me. He also told me, "You're not going to get anything done."

I asked him if he had any fun while in office. "None," he replied sternly. I didn't say it, but I certainly thought, *Well, then why did you run for a second term with this attitude?*

From the day that I did officially take office on May 1, 2011, my staff and I were inundated with meeting requests. I quickly learned that Funkhouser had been labeled a "hermit mayor." Apparently he had been given a mandate, make that an order, from his wife Gloria Squitiro that he was home every day by 5 p.m. These timelines are completely incompatible with the job of a big city mayor. So it turned out that Funkhouser had relatively infrequent meetings with people who wanted to do business with the city.

When I was elected the Associated Press wrote that I'd be inheriting a city budget "in turmoil" and on the verge of losing "an estimated $200 million" in 2012. I also inherited a mayor's office that had become a laughingstock as a result of Funkhouser's inaction and his wife's actions.

Although she had no official duties, responsibilities, or title, Squitiro began keeping an office at City Hall early in her husband's administration. In response to the immediate criticism, Funkhouser told the press, "I know what I need. And I choose to have my wife beside me. And I don't give a flat damn who cares."

A workplace harassment suit, claiming Squitiro continually engaged in overtly sexual and racist discussions, was eventually filed against her. She allegedly had even called a city worker "Mammie." It became so bad that the City Council ultimately voted 12-1 to ban relatives from working on a frequent basis in city offices, which was unquestionably designed with her direct removal in mind. The only dissenting vote—Mark Funkhouser, who then vetoed the ordinance only to have it overridden.

Squitiro had become such an issue during the 2011 Primary Election that the most common question asked to me was, "If elected mayor, will your wife be at City Hall with you?" I'd always laugh and tell the questioner that my wife wasn't even in attendance on this occasion, and she sure as hell wasn't going to be sitting beside me in the mayor's office. Licia never wanted anything to do with politics, or government, or running the city. Fortunately for all involved, she has always had her own interests and her own life. Mark Funkhouser very well may have failed in his re-election bid even without the constant presence of his wife, but Gloria Squitiro certainly didn't help his cause.

My first year in office was a whirlwind, it was hugely satisfying, and it was brutal. We counted more than 550 appearances outside of the office that I made across those initial 365 days. As part of my reading program, I was determined to personally read to as many elementary students as possible across the city. I wound up visiting 140 schools.

This was important work–all of it. I felt a true sense of obligation as mayor to work late into the night seven days a week, and accept every invitation to meet, speak, and appear in a show of support. After two years I discovered that this was an unsustainable pace, but in the beginning it was exhilarating.

My first month as mayor involved getting snapped into the job, straightening out our agenda, lining up the duties of my staff, getting to know the City Council members, meeting with numerous business and civic leaders, and going out to visit with the public.

Month number two featured my first U.S. Conference of Mayors meeting, which took place in Baltimore, and this was a watershed event for me. I was introduced to Ralph Smith from the Annie E. Casey Foundation, who spoke to me about the critical importance of third grade reading proficiency. It was in this initial conversation with Smith that he told me, "Up to third grade, you're learning to read. From third grade on, you're reading to learn."

Smith also gave me truly eye-opening information and data about third grade reading skills, such as the direct link to education levels, juvenile crime, substance abuse, career earnings, and even life expectancy. According to Smith, 75 percent of kids who aren't proficient in reading by the third grade never catch up, and 84 percent of kids who lack this proficiency in third grade fail to graduate from high school.

This encounter with Smith directly led me to launching Turn the Page KC, and gave a new focus to my education agenda. I was shocked to discover that at that time only 33.8 percent of third graders citywide were reading proficiently for this age. Working with numerous public and private partners as an umbrella organization in a collective impact model, we've attacked this problem head-on by focusing on the pillars of school attendance, summer learning, kindergarten readiness, and volunteer adult readers for these kids. And it's absolutely working.

Also at my first U.S. Conference of Mayors, I was invited by Antonio Villaraigosa, the mayor of Los Angeles at that time, to join his group in visiting the White House. I immediately accepted and was able to meet President Barack Obama, alongside Villaraigosa and 12 other mayors, including Detroit's Dave Bing, Sacramento's Kevin Johnson, Oklahoma City's Mick Cornett, Philadelphia's Michael Nutter, and New Orleans' Mitch Landrieu.

They walked us to the Eisenhower Room, where we were first greeted by Senior Presidential Advisor Valerie Jarrett, who was extremely welcoming. Next up was Chief of Staff Bill Daley, followed by Vice President Joe Biden. Living up to his billing, Biden exhibited his big- time personality and warmth. "Hey, great to meet you. How's everybody doing?" There was no artifice about him at all.

Finally, President Obama entered, and everyone fell quiet. Jarrett, Daley, and Vice President Biden took their seats beside him, and we fell in around the huge conference table. The President asked questions and was fully engaged in the group discussion. As I had only taken office the month prior, I sat there in silence. After about an hour, a previously hidden side door opened and a presidential aide walked through. He politely approached the President and whispered in his ear. This was our indication that the meeting was about to conclude. To my complete surprise, President Obama then looked at me and said, "Well Sly, it looks like you get the last word."

I had no idea what to say, so I just started to talk about Kansas City. A White House photographer captured the moment, which shows my face in profile, with the President and my fellow mayors looking right at me. This is the coolest damn photo in the world. It hangs proudly and prominently in my office.

President Obama warmly thanked all of us and graciously exited the Eisenhower Room. After he departed I spoke with David Agnew, who was Director of Intergovernmental Affairs. In our conversation I mentioned that as an added bonus to meeting the President, I got to do so on June 22nd–my wife's birthday. Agnew laughingly asked if she had actually given me permission to be away from home. I told him that we didn't have that type of relationship, and that by now she was used to me being gone on her birthday; it was just the life that I had led, and was continuing to lead.

About two months later a card arrived in the mail postmarked from Washington, D.C. It read:

Dear Licia.

Thanks for allowing Sly to come visit us at the White House on your birthday.

The card was personally signed by President Obama.

After my first U.S. Confrence of Mayors I became a regular attendee. Genuine friendships developed, including with Philadelphia Mayor Nutter, Louisville Mayor Greg Fischer, and of course Charlotte Mayor Anthony Foxx. As I mentioned earlier, it was Foxx who told me about the positive impact that streetcars had on his city, and the success of his program let me know that this was absolutely the right thing to do. And he was instrumental in guiding us through the process of receiving the Tiger Grant for our program when he was Secretary of Transportation.

After those eventful first two months I firmly settled into office.

Although I've never thought of myself as a politician, the job of mayor absolutely suited me. Of course there were frustrations and challenges, but I loved it; I absolutely loved it. As I wrote previously in this book, I had pretty much burnt out as a lawyer. The business of law had all but lost its appeal for me, and I needed something new. And serving as the elected head of my hometown was exactly what I needed.

During my first four-year term as mayor of Kansas City we ran 14 elections, of which we won 13. While my pace with respect to public outings slowed down in years three and four of this term, my workload and enthusiasm for the job did not. As the elections of 2015 approached, there was never even the briefest hesitation about seeking re-election.

We were having success, things were going well, and what I wanted to get done was getting done. Beyond this, the City Council was working well together and there were no real problems or conflicts. As I mentioned earlier, you either run scared or you run unopposed. While I definitely would have preferred to run unopposed, this was not to be the case.

Chapter 34

The General, Chastain, and My Second Term

When I first ran for mayor of Kansas City in 2011, I had a number of worthy opponents, including Deb Herman and Mike Burke. I liked and respected them both so much that as mayor I appointed Deb to chair the PIAC (Public Improvements Advisory Committee) and Mike to chair a bi-state team about how to implement Google's One Gig To The Home program and an arts task force. I wasn't going to waste talent just because they had run against me.

But as I sought re-election in 2015, it was a far different story. My only two opponents in the Primary were Clay Chastain and Vincent Lee.

Chastain considered himself a professional activist, who was notorious in Kansas City for creating petitions for tax increases to fund a light rail system. An electrical engineer by trade, Chastain was actually not living in Kansas City, but instead residing full-time in Virginia when he launched his campaign to challenge me.

Lee, who continually referred to himself as "The General" (for reasons that have never been made clear), was a high school dropout with no known occupation. He told the media at various times that he was a "consultant" and a "businessman." He also once told the press that he grew up with "two brothers and four or five sisters," as the specifics seemed to escape him.

I was extremely reluctant to debate either of these guys, as it seemed like a colossal waste of time. But my campaign team told me that I had to acquiesce, so I reluctantly agreed.

As we walked onto the debate stage Chastain said to me "I'm here to kick your ass. I'm coming after you." I had been continually instructed not to react, which is exactly what I did in this instance, and for the most part throughout the night. But it was hard–very hard. During the debate I couldn't help myself a few times, such as when I said to him, "That would be a great answer, if only it was true." I also let loose with, "If you don't care anything about facts, then what you just said makes sense."

But compared to The General, Chastain almost seemed to have a clue. This guy was a hoot, not to be taken seriously. He was dressed in a flashy suit, complete with gold chains, expensive cuff links, and jeweled buttons. When asked about the possibility of renovating our city's airport, The General responded that the airport needed to be relocated to Missouri, so that we could create more jobs for our city. I quickly reminded The General, or perhaps I was letting him know, that the airport, which opened in 1972, is located in Missouri. It's in Kansas City, Missouri, to be precise.

It was painfully obvious throughout this debate that neither Chastain nor The General had any idea what they were talking about. I thought many times that night, *Why am I up here with one guy who doesn't live in this city, and another guy who thinks our airport is in Kansas?*

Chastain stayed on the attack throughout, and grew meaner and meaner as the debate progressed. I just wanted this to be over and to go home. After one particularly hateful personal attack, which caused the crowd to groan, The General leaned over to me and said, "I'll tell you what Sly. If I don't win this election, me and you are going to have to gang up on this motherfucker."

The General actually made it through the Primary Election, as Chastain finished in third and last place. My tally was 85 percent of the vote, with Lee getting nine percent and Chastain claiming six percent. In response Chastain filed suits against me multiple times, all of which were thrown out. When his pursuit of legal action failed he began showing up in the lobby of my 29th floor office at City Hall, with a photographer alongside, shouting at me to come out and that I was a coward. Never once did I think about confronting him. People like Clay Chastain hate to be ignored more than absolutely anything else. There was no reason to feed him. He wanted to be confronted, engaged, debated, and acknowledged. And I'll be damned if I was going to give him the satisfaction. My course of action was always to take a back staircase down one flight, and then catch the elevator to the ground level. He never did figure this out.

The General Election was held June 23, 2015, and my percentage of votes went up two points from the Primary. I defeated the General with 87 percent of the vote. While I was elated and thankful to be reelected, I couldn't help but think, *What in the hell happened to that other 13 percent?*

By far the biggest change for me at the start of my second term was the new City Council. Their attitude was summed up perfectly by the comments of a newly-elected councilperson, who said to me, "We're here to fix all of the mistakes of the last City Council." I responded, "That's great, but you don't even know where the bathroom is yet. And you're going to fix all of the mistakes?"

That was their pattern throughout my second term in office. They were great at finding fault with everything. We got off to a poor start, and the relationship never fully recovered.

The first encounter that I had with the new City Council as a whole came in the form of a retreat held at the Southeast Community Center, located in Swope Park. Twenty-four hours prior to the retreat I received a call from our Housing Department informing me that the Department of Housing and Urban Development (HUD) would be in Kansas City the next day, and that I needed to meet with the federal agency to discuss a $30 million opportunity grant. My presence was needed to welcome the HUD officials to our city and discuss the potential grant. Even though I was supposed to be at the retreat with the City Council members, the meeting was scheduled early enough for me to attend and still make the retreat. I realized that this was far more important. I wasn't going to blow the chance for the city to receive $30 million. And anyway, I'd be at the retreat right after the HUD meeting. They didn't need me to be there when it started.

The next day the HUD officials arrived later than expected. Nonetheless, we had a great meeting. They told me that this was the first time that a city mayor had ever come to meet with them. And I had gone a step further by serving them coffee and donuts in a warm and relaxed atmosphere. I responded that this was how we did things in Kansas City. They were here to discuss helping us, so my attendance at the meeting was the right thing to do.

On my way over to the retreat, my staff called to let me know that one council member was stirring up the rest of the group because of my late arrival. I was being labeled rude and disrespectful because I wasn't there from the start.

When I walked in to the retreat, quietly and without fanfare, I announced, "It's my understanding that there's a problem. So, what's the problem?"

The council member responded, "Well you should have been here when we arrived. If you didn't have to be here early, then neither should we." The other new council members then followed suit.

I then told the group that, as they already knew, I was meeting with HUD about a $30 million grant for our city. And I stated that if it's between millions of dollars for Kansas City and being on time for this retreat, well, the money for our citizens was going to win every time.

"This is the way I work," I continued. "This is the way it's going to be. My job is to do what's in the best interest of the city."

As I scanned the room I realized that not all members of the City Council were there anyway, which I quickly noted out loud. So much for a friendly retreat in Swope Park. That was how we started, and it was pretty much like that for the remainder of my second term as mayor.

I heard that there was a contingent of people who didn't like some of what I was doing as mayor. So they began to recruit individuals to run against me when I sought re-election. But no one ever emerged as a viable candidate; thus my only challengers wound up being Chastain and The General. This contingent then turned their efforts to the City Council, with a plan to elect Council members who could stop what I was doing.

And so in my second term I had to work with people who were less active and more critical than the previous council. This City Council would frequently balk at contracts signed during prior administrations, simply because they weren't there when those deals were made.

As disagreeable as some of my opponents on the City Council were during my second term, at least they never rushed me on stage. The same, however, can't be said for a former candidate for the Missouri State House. My encounter with this man, Derron Black, made national and international news and actually landed me on CNN, where I was interviewed live by Wolf Blitzer.

During my 2013 State of the City speech at Kansas City's historic Gem Theater, Black ran onto the stage, knocked over one of the flag stands, grabbed the microphone away from me at the podium, and said, "This man has just got through talking about exactly what the fuck he ain't goddamned did." He was then tackled by Marlon Buie of my security team and wrestled to the ground. Black of course was arrested, and ultimately pled guilty to misdemeanors for resisting arrest and obstruction of government operations.

It's funny how things work, in that for all that I felt was accomplished in my eight years as mayor this odd and random incident seems to be one of the most memorable. I'm still asked about it, usually with the main question of how I stayed so calm. It's true that when Black moved beside me at the podium and started speaking into the microphone, I never flinched. Instead I just stared at him as he spoke. Immediately I saw that he had nothing in his hands, so I didn't consider him a threat. He was just really disgruntled.

I never had any animosity for Derron Black, and I never will. Until he rushed the stage I hadn't had any contact with him whatsoever. I'd hadn't even heard his name mentioned. Like my former client Michael Keith Samuels, who had threatened to kill President Reagan, Black clearly had mental health issues. I didn't press charges and I didn't want to see him harmed in any way. Rather, I only wanted him to get the help he needed. This was never the big deal to me that it was for so many others. I didn't feel that my life was ever in danger, or that Black intended on confronting me physically. So, it is easy to laugh it off now. Hell, it was easy to laugh it off then.

And I'll say this for Derron Black: unlike my other critics and detractors, City Council members most definitely included, he at least was willing to be direct in his confrontation. The others always preferred to go behind my back.

Chapter 35

What Fuels My Passion for Purpose

Although **I** held political office as mayor of Kansas City for eight years, I never considered myself a politician. And I never will.

For me, running for and then ultimately serving two terms as mayor was born from a passion: a passion for purpose to leave the city better off than I found it. And I've done that .

Never once was I afraid to take on the big issues, be it the $6 billion lag in infrastructure maintenance, the new airport single-terminal project, the streetcar, the new Downtown convention hotel, the Linwood shopping center and supermarket, the problems with kids massing on the Plaza, or the issues of pre-K education and third grade reading proficiency. The way I always looked at things: if you're not going to tackle the big issues, then why are you there?

Not once was I driven to make a decision because of party politics. I was elected as a nonpartisan, and I remained defiantly nonpartisan as mayor—beholden only to the citizens, and not a political party and its doctrine.

The big issues, and the little issues attendant to them, are the things that you use to build the city for future generations. We're not building the city for us. Instead, we're building it for our children and grandchildren and beyond.

We were able to get a lot of big things done, because we weren't afraid to take on the big things. It's just that simple. When I was first running for the office, my constant refrain was "Go big, or go home." And once elected I always went big when I felt that something mattered, consequences be damned.

I made friends, and I made enemies. But I always put the city first. If I offended a few politicians, business leaders, school superintendents, and reporters along the way, so be it. I worked for the people of Kansas City, not for a political party or special-interest group.

Joni Wickham, my great chief of staff whom I love dearly, reminded me that while I was in office there were 18 elections. Of those, she reminded me as well, we won 16. Now I don't remember what all of those 16 were. I don't even remember all of those 16 victories. But I certainly will not forget the two that we lost: pre-K and streetcar expansion to the east side of the city.

I really don't like losing. Of course nobody does. But beyond that, I'm haunted by these missed opportunities, which I felt would have hugely benefited the people of our city, and thus benefited our city as a whole. Political philosophy and the party line never played into these two issues, nor did they play into the 16 issues that we won. I was adamantly for all 18 because I knew in my head and in my heart that they were what was right for Kansas City, and they would all create long-term benefits.

When I took office in 2011, downtown Kansas City was not what it is today. I look at a city's downtown as its heart, and our heart wasn't pumping blood to the extremities. And because of this, the extremities were struggling.

Now that our heart is stronger, more and more things are getting pumped to the extremities. It's just that simple. Strong heart, strong limbs. But there is still a lot more work to be done.

And there is much, much more work to do in the areas of education, affordable housing, job training, public transportation, and crime.

My time as mayor was term-limited, but I'll always be a citizen of Kansas City. It's my home, and the home of my children and grandchildren, so I'll always remain fully invested in the city's success.

Until I ran for mayor, I'd never before sought political office. The mayor of Kansas City, Missouri was the first and only political office that I wanted. Having replaced Mayor Funkhouser, who had left the office nonproductive and the city stagnant, I knew that there was no time for me to slowly get up to speed. I wasn't afforded the luxury of a learning curve as the head of city government. As I wrote earlier in this book, the meetings started the day after I was elected, and continued nonstop until and after I was sworn into office.

But I truly believe that having been a political outsider helped me, in that I didn't have any preconceived notions of how politics work. I came in with the same work ethic and dogged determination that I had possessed as an attorney, and really that I had possessed my entire life.

There is no doubt that my philosophy of not dealing with negative people, and not particularly caring what they have to say, really helped me in office. No matter what you do, someone is going to be mad at you for something. But if you start letting the reality of people being angry, or people not liking you, have an impact, then you'll eventually curl up in a fetal position in the corner of your office.

None of this negativity ever bothered me. It just wasn't a big deal.

During my first term, I was very fortunate to have a great City Council. They had served their first term under Funkhouser, and were so glad to be rid of him that working with them was a breeze. They just wanted to get things done, which had been impossible during the previous administration. No question that I was given the benefit of the doubt simply because I was someone, anyone, other than the previous mayor. But we really did work well together.

This isn't to say that we always agreed. Many times they would modify things that I had worked on, which would lead to a few contentious moments. But I really respected that this City Council was not shy about always trying to move the needle forward. I liked them as a body, and I liked them as individuals.

During my second term as mayor the City Council was a completely different story. My word for them would be populist. My summation of them is that they wanted to tear systems down, but never had adequate replacements. And I found them to be very racial. But a huge part of being a mayor is dealing with your city council, no matter who they are.

Having an outstanding chief of staff (as I did with my previous Chief-of-Staff John McGurl and Joni Wickham) is of paramount importance to be a successful mayor, and so too is having a great relationship with your city manager. Mayor Funkhouser absolutely hated his city manager, Wayne Cauthen, and got him fired. Funkhouser then moved this job out of the city budget, which predictably created a huge mess for his administration and for the municipal government.

City manager, Troy Schulte, was absolutely fabulous. I figured out very quickly that the city manager can either help you get things done as mayor, or keep you from getting things done. Troy liked to accomplish things, and more importantly he knew how to get things accomplished. Numerous times I turned to him for his expertise in budget, as he could always figure out how to finance a project that on its face seemed nearly impossible.

It cannot be overstated that the relationship between a mayor and a city manager is absolutely crucial. The relationship between a mayor and city council is definitely important, but not to this degree.

The City Council can of course be influenced by me, but they can also be influenced by the public. If I had the public with me, it was hard for the Council to say no. But if the public was against me, then it was very hard to get those things accomplished through the Council's vote.

I was blessed with very high ratings throughout my two terms and eight years as mayor. The reason that I mention this is not because of ego, but rather because of practicality. This popularity aided me in my ability to sway the City Council members toward giving me their support, and thus their votes on the issues that truly mattered.

Because of my consistently high job approval rating, combined with factors such as my landslide re-election, what was accomplished during my time in office, and the overall thriving nature of the city, I'm often asked if I would attempt to stay in the job, if not for term limits. My truthful answer is that I just don't know. Had I gone into office initially knowing that I could have served three terms instead of two, or that term limits didn't exist, perhaps I would have paced myself differently. Everything would have been more spread out. And then perhaps another four years would have made sense.

But because I knew from day one on the job that I would get a maximum of eight years in office, I spent my energy accordingly. And this was an all-out devotion to the job that I loved. I did this job full tilt. There was no half-stepping, and no coasting. And in the process, I gave up my law practice and requisite financial benefits that came with having your own firm. Plus, of course, I spent countless hours away from my family, because that is what the job of mayor demanded. I couldn't have, and wouldn't have done it any other way.

So because I knew that there was a fixed expiration date on my tenure as mayor, I paced myself accordingly. And as such, I was ready to depart.

As you well know by now, I'm not about legacy; I'm about results. I'm extremely proud of the results from my eight years in office.

Beyond this, I'm extremely proud that I was never once influenced by party politics, or lobbying, or special interests. I worked for the people of Kansas City, Missouri. More correctly, I worked for the children of my city, and their children, and theirs. Every single program, policy, and project that I supported and fought for, be it pre-K, the streetcar, or the new airport, I did so because I felt that it was the right thing to do. Win or lose, I fully believed that I was correct; these things were in the best short-term and long-term interests of Kansas City.

My father raised me with the idea that I could do whatever I wanted to do. The fact that I was neither white nor wealthy just meant that I might have to work harder. He passed away long before I was first elected mayor, but I don't think that he would have been surprised that his oldest son had reached this height.

Sylvester James Sr. instilled in me a philosophy for life to look at myself as an individual, with regard to what I could and couldn't do. He also taught me that you can never go wrong by doing right. With all of this, I knew that I could become a man who actually made a difference.

Acknowledgments

I **want to** personally acknowledge and thank all of the people and organizations who have so kindly and lovingly contributed to my vision, work, and life. Nothing I have done in my life has been the work of a solo artist, but rather every success has been the product of personal collaborations. I accept personal responsibility for my every frailty and failing.

A grateful and belated thank you to my late father, Sylvester Sr., whom I miss, and who I especially wish could have been here these last 10 years. I know that he would have enjoyed the ride. To my stepmother, Melva, who became my mother, as she stood with my father and instilled in my brothers and me a work ethic and understanding of the importance of education.

To my brothers LaFrance (deceased), LaVance, Jeff, Melvin, and sister Arrella; and my aunt Pat, all of whom occupy their own individual places in my heart and mind.

To my beautiful, diverse, and acclaimed family who continue to stand by me and support me in all things: my wife since 1981, Licia Ellen Clifton-James, Ph.D.; and my children, Eric (deceased) with whom I left too much unsaid; Malik, a lawyer and jokester with whom I share an additional bond as a Marine; my delightfully imaginative son and entrepreneur, Kyle; and the amazing and strong Aja, the fitness queen, model, and fledgling author.

To my in-laws who have enriched my life as well as the lives of my wife and children: my mother-in-law Florene, who accepted and loved me from day one; my daughters-in-law, Jessica, the accomplished chef, business woman, and nurturing mother of the bright and brilliant Race; and the loveable little monster, beautiful and expressive Grey.

To Kyle's wife Stephanie, the most recent beautiful addition to our family. To "Memaw" and "Boompa" for all that they did for me when I needed them most. With love and confusion for Annie, who started a chain of events that brought Jane and Ama into my life. And to Audra, Jason, Cruz, and Mena, who are constant reminders of the love of the Lund family.

To my lifelong friends who have brought me nothing but joy and memories of a lifetime: Chipp, whom I have known since our days together at Immaculate Heart of Mary grade school and rhythm guitarist in the Amelia Earhart Memorial Flying Band (a/k/a Manchester Trafficway); our leader Chris Immele; and our drummer, Robert 'Bucky' Kort. The three of you have always been there for me. To Jim Cassidy, brother of the band's founder, Tom (deceased) who played a huge role as the band's manager.

To my college friend, Johnny "Disaster" McMaster, a guy so loyal that he would literally give you the shirt off his back; and Nancy Kenner, my law partner, who took a huge chance with me and then led us to success. "Best friends" hardly describes the roles you have played in my life.

To my most recent Chief-of-Staff and business partner, Joni Wickham, the "hat and shoes girl from North Carolina," whose thoughtful leadership of our staff and insistence on providing avenues for their personal and professional growth was simply extraordinary. To my first Chief-of-Staff, John McGurk, who established the framework for my administration, and got me hooked on bow ties.

To the wonderful members of my staff over the years, who accepted responsibility for the day-to-day grind of the office, our policies, and projects. You took too many arrows for me and received too little reward. Without all of you, none of what we accomplished would have been possible. I am proud to have worked with you.

To Troy Schulte, the City Manager, and tremendous partner responsible for the administrative side of the city. You're a man who often worked in the background, but always found a way to do those things necessary to make our city great.

To the city department heads and their staffs, who were constantly called upon to do more with less. Yet you always answered every bell. I was constantly amazed by the expertise of our department heads who could have easily made more in the private sector, but chose to serve our city.

To the city workers who chased the dogs, trimmed the trees, patched the roads, delivered the water, took care of the parks, accounted for the revenues and budgets, cleaned the environment, put out the fires, enforced and practiced the law, and every single one of the hundreds of other things necessary to keep this tremendously complex city operating. Much respect and appreciation for all your efforts.

To all of the KCPD officers on my security team who protected me, laughed with me, and took such great care of me. Much love and respect.

To the City Council, especially Mayor Pro Tem Cindy Circo, Jan Marcason, Melba Curls, John Sharp, Scott Taylor, Tim Glover, Jermaine Reed, Scott Wagner, Ed Ford, Russ Johnson, and Dick Davis; most of whom served in the controversial Funkhouser administration. Thank you for guiding the city during that period, and then moving aggressively and collaboratively to make sure our city was open for business thereafter. It was an honor and privilege to work with you all. To members of the second term Council, thank you for your service to our city.

To the Chambers of Commerce throughout the city, the Civic Council, the Economic Development Council, the Kansas City Area Development Council, and Visit KC, for all that you do to promote the city, and create jobs and economic development. "That's how we do Kansas City!'

To my publisher at Ascend Books, Bob Snodgrass, for raising the idea of this book; my co-author Sean Wheelock for collaborating with me so that we could breathe life into this project; and my editor Mark Fitzpatrick for ironing out word wrinkles and unsplicing sentences. None of this would have been possible without the three of you. Thanks for your guidance and patience.

Finally, to all the citizens of this great city, named and unnamed, who so graciously allowed me serve as your mayor for eight years. I am humbled by the faith you showed in me. I am grateful for your willingness to collaborate in order to create the world-class city in which we live, work, and play. A special thanks to all the citizens who so freely and frequently volunteer your time to serve on the hundred-plus city boards and commissions that do so much of the work to enact city policy and processes. I am humbled and proud to have been of service to the citizens of our city.

About the Authors

Sly James

Sylvester "Sly" James was sworn in as the 56th Mayor of Kansas City, Missouri in 2011, and was reelected for a second term in 2015. A native Kansas Citian, James served as a military police officer in the Marine Corps during the Vietnam War era. Prior to his entry into politics, James was a highly successful attorney.

As mayor, James created the "4-E Agenda," which focused on Education, Employment, Efficiency, and Enforcement. He worked extensively to raise Kansas City's statewide and national profile, and was an advocate for common-sense gun control laws, a minimum wage increase, and the addition of more high-quality seats in classrooms. James has also been active in leadership positions in several national mayoral organizations.

Sean Wheelock

Sean Wheelock has authored two other books. He's also written numerous articles for various websites and publications. He is also one of the best known and most experienced television commentators in combat sports, having commentated for numerous major fight promotions globally. Wheelock also serves as a Commissioner of the Kansas Athletic Commission, and as Chairman of the ABC's Mixed Martial Arts Rules and Regulations Committee.